Just Trading

Just Trading

On the Ethics and Economics of International Trade

Daniel Rush Finn

Abingdon Press
Nashville
in cooperation with
THE CHURCHES' CENTER FOR THEOLOGY
AND PUBLIC POLICY
Washington, D.C.

JUST TRADING: ON THE ETHICS AND ECONOMICS OF INTERNATIONAL TRADE

Copyright © 1996 by Abingdon Press

This book is printed on acid-free, recycled paper.

Library of Congress Cataloging-in-Publication Data

Finn, Daniel Rush, 1947–
    Just trading: on the ethics and economics of international trade
/Daniel Rush Finn.
        p.   cm.
    Includes bibliographical references and index.
    ISBN 0-687-05209-2 (pbk.: alk. paper)
    1. International trade—Moral and ethical aspects.   2. Economics—
Religious aspects—Christianity.   3. Economic development—
Environmental aspects.   4. United States—Commercial policy.
    5. Canada—Commercial policy.   I. Churches' Center for Theology and
Public Policy (Washington, D.C.)   II. Title.
HF1379.F563   1996
382—dc20   96-25172
                                                                              CIP

Scripture quotations, unless otherwise indicated, are from the New Revised Standard Version Bible, copyright © 1989, by the Division of Christian Education of the National Council of the Churches of Christ in the United States of America.

Portions of the text and some graphs were originally published in "International Trade and Sustainable Community: Religious Values and Economic Arguments in Moral Debates," *Journal of Religious Ethics* 22, no. 2 (Fall 1994): 213-73. Copyright © 1994 by the Journal of Religious Ethics, Inc. Used by permission of the publisher.

96 97 98 99 00 01 02 03 04 05—10 9 8 7 6 5 4 3 2 1

MANUFACTURED IN THE UNITED STATES OF AMERICA

To Nita Jo Rush

CONTENTS

Contents

PREFACE

Each January I attend the annual meeting of the American Economic Association and, shortly afterward, the annual meeting of the Society of Christian Ethics. The first includes several thousand economists from the academy, government, and business in the United States, while the second gathers approximately five hundred Christian ethicists from colleges, universities, and seminaries in the United States and Canada. It is no surprise that these two groups differ in important ways, but in January of 1993 I was particularly struck by the clash of views expressed at panel presentations on international trade at each conference. The first meeting was in California and the second in Georgia, so geographically the panels were a long way apart; conceptually, the gap was even greater.

Participating on the panel at the economics meetings were several of the best-known international economists in the United States. The views presented were typical for such a setting: increased international trade was agreed to be a good thing. Conversation focused on recent developments in international trade agreements, celebrating the accomplishments and lamenting the failures of efforts to reduce trade barriers around the world. Collaborating on the panel at the ethics meeting were three Canadian ethicists who were highly critical of increased international trade, particularly that which had been encouraged since the implementation of the Canada-U.S. Free Trade Agreement four years earlier. Increased trade between the U.S. and Canada had had nothing but bad effects in Canada, as evidenced by the worsening condition of the Canadian economy in the early 1990s.

The chasm between these two perspectives was striking. The people on both panels were intelligent, highly educated, and morally concerned for the economic well-being of ordinary people. Yet each panel either ignored the perspectives of the other or, at best, articulated the other group's arguments in caricature. It seemed quite likely that neither group had read the other group's books and essays, even though both appealed to economic facts and moral values in arguing for their position. Is there any hope for bridging the gulf?

This volume has grown out of an attempt to sort through the arguments—both economic and moral—about the effects of international trade. If it is successful, it will help the reader better understand a number of issues concerning trade. As a particular case study, it may also contribute to a wider conversation about the appropriate interplay of economics and ethics in public policy. Of course, like the economists and ethicists on those panels, I too make assumptions and am no doubt uncritically oblivious of some of them. I look forward to help on that from readers gracious enough to assist me.

I am indebted to many people and to St. John's Abbey and University for help in this project. These include Carol Inderrieden, Maggie Schindler, Chad Leither, Sean Singwald, Matthew Brown, Timothy Ward, David Hollenbach, Joseph Friedrich, William Cahoy, Charles Rambeck, Nita Jo Rush, William Everett, Dale Launderville, and many others. I am especially grateful to John B. Cobb, Jr., and Herman E. Daly for dialogue on these topics in recent years. I remain deeply indebted to Alvin Pitcher and Gibson Winter for their formative help in undertaking a morally and intellectually responsible dialogue between Christian ethics and economics. I am grateful to the *Journal of Religious Ethics* and its able editor, Diane Yeager, for permission to use portions of an earlier article on this topic (vol. 22, no. 2, Fall 1994), and to the

World Bank and the MIT Press for permission to use figures 7.6 and 9.1.

I also owe a debt to countless others throughout history who have labored to understand economic and moral life. The debt is an obvious one, but naming it helps to rekindle the sense of responsibility that accompanies the gift.

CHAPTER 1

TRADE TALK: A CACOPHONY OF VOICES

The daily news is filled with reports of large and complicated problems facing people in the modern world. Of these, few are so large or so complicated as international trade: the buying and selling of goods and services across international boundaries. Christians and others wanting to make a moral judgment about trade—Should we trade? how much? with what restrictions?—are often overwhelmed by the complexities and confused by contradictory opinions concerning trade.

SOME BASIC FACTS ABOUT TRADE

It is a challenge simply to grasp the scope of international trade today. As figure 1.1 indicates, there has been immense growth in the volume of goods traded internationally in the past century.

Considering only those goods moved by oceangoing ships, more than four billion metric tons of merchandise is transported between nations each year. Even though this figure ignores the goods transported by truck, train, or pipeline between adjacent countries (as in much of Europe or between the United States and Canada) this mass of goods is almost unthinkably large. To get some picture of world maritime trade we might begin by thinking of the Great Pyramid at

15

Giza, tomb of the Pharaoh Khufu in ancient Egypt. The Great Pyramid is about one-sixth of a mile on each side and stands over forty stories tall. Estimates are that it is made up of about two million large blocks of stone, each weighing two and one-half tons. Thus we might ask: How does this massive structure compare with the weight of goods traded by ship each year? We get a clearer picture of the scale of international trade when we note that world oceangoing trade by ship is itself equivalent to the transportation of the complete Great Pyramid at Giza every twelve hours.

World Merchandise Trade

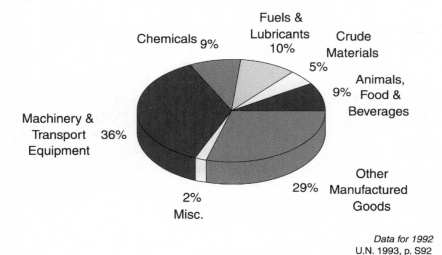

Data for 1992
U.N. 1993, p. S92

Figure 1.1

Recognizing the immense scale of trade we might then ask: What *kinds* of goods are traded each year across international borders? All kinds. Figure 1.2 gives a rough breakdown of all world merchandise trade (not simply that transported by ships) based on the standard classifications that the United Nations and its member governments have adopted for the accounting of international trade.[1]

More than half of all international trade in merchandise consists in the exchange of manufactured goods (machinery, cars, and trucks). Food and crude materials (such as mineral ores and timber) are significant but small slices of the overall activity in trade.

16

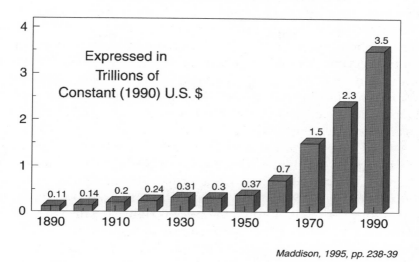

Total World Trade in Merchandise

Expressed in Trillions of Constant (1990) U.S. $

Maddison, 1995, pp. 238-39

Figure 1.2

International trade in services—travel, transportation, insurance, banking, construction, advertising, and so forth—is also sizable, averaging about one-quarter the value of international trade in goods. However, because most of the controversy surrounding international commerce concerns the trade in goods, this volume will focus attention there.[2]

For the world as a whole, whatever is exported from one nation must be imported by another. Individual nations, however, specialize, exporting products that are either more abundant or more cheaply produced there and importing products more abundant or more cheaply produced elsewhere. Thus, the United States and Canada, the focus of this volume, export and import products in each classification. Each nation both imports and exports wheat, automobiles, mineral ores, dairy products, computers, and most other things. This is often something of a surprise to people when they first hear it, but the fact is quite an ordinary one for three reasons.

The first is that each category is quite broad and includes quite diverse sorts of products: For example, a nation may export some kinds of chemicals while importing others. The second is transpor-

17

tation costs. Within any one nation some products are produced in one geographic area and consumed in another. Should there be a foreign source of this product closer to the point of consumption than are the domestic producers, international trade may occur in that product even though the nation itself also produces it. Thus, the production of oil and natural gas in Alberta makes Canada an exporter of these products, which enter the midwestern United States by pipeline, even though immense amounts of oil and natural gas are produced within the U.S. as well.

A third reason for a nation to export and import the same or similar products might be called the happenstance of economic differences. Just as a manufacturing firm in Toronto might purchase products from a supplier in Windsor rather than a (geographically closer) supplier in Hamilton if the price is right, so a firm in Buffalo may choose to purchase parts from a firm in Hamilton even though other Buffalo-based companies produce the same items.

The United States has roughly ten times the number of people found in Canada and has an economy roughly ten times larger as a result. Nonetheless, as figure 1.3 illustrates, the two nations are remarkably similar in the pattern of their exports and imports.

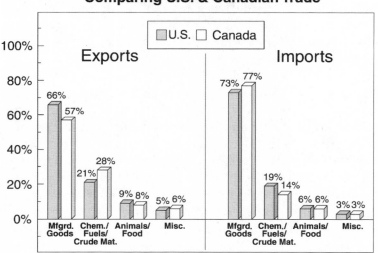

U.N. Internat. Trade Statistics Yearbook 1992, 1993, p. S92

Figure 1.3

The primary difference between the two is the need of the United States to import far more fuel than Canada and the ability of Canada, given its natural resource base, to export fuel and other "crude" materials, such as minerals and timber.

For all of the importance of international trade for most products, only a small portion of the world's total production is actually traded internationally. Figure 1.4 indicates the proportions for a number of key primary products.

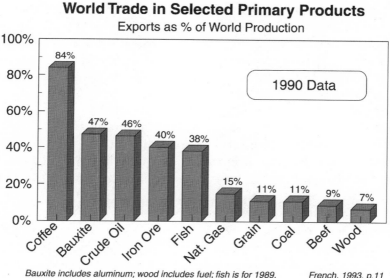

Figure 1.4

Clearly those products which can be produced in only a few places on the globe but which are consumed nearly everywhere will be heavily represented in trade figures. Most products—those providing nourishment, clothing, shelter, and other daily needs—are produced almost everywhere and tend to be consumed closer to home. Of all the world's production that is sold in markets, approximately 86 percent is consumed in the nation where it is produced.[3] Most of the controversy about the other 14 percent—the goods traded internationally—focuses on those goods that *could* be produced domestically but which are imported from abroad instead.

19

CACOPHONOUS VOICES

Public discussion about international trade is remarkably strident. In part this occurs because so much talk about trade surrounds concrete political choices facing national governments. Debates over the approval of the Canada-U.S. Free Trade Agreement (1987–88), the North American Free Trade Agreement (1992–93), and the "Uruguay round" of the General Agreement on Tariffs and Trade (1994–95) were the occasion for public controversy. When divisive issues are about to be resolved, the rhetoric becomes most shrill. Nonetheless, even when there are no immediate policies to be decided upon, the issues surrounding international trade still tend to be characterized by sharp divisions, sometimes involving differences in moral valuation but always entailing differences in empirical assessments about "how things work."

For example, both the left and the right have sharply criticized recent trade agreements for their mind-numbing complexity and their tendency to grant concessions to special-interest groups. (Trade documents run into the hundreds and even thousands of pages!) Thus Paul Hawken, a strong critic of increased trade, asserts that "not surprisingly, when the fine print is read on the GATT treaty, it turns out not to be as free as its proponents assert. It is full of loopholes, concessions to special-interest groups, variable tariffs, and out-right giveaways to industries that happened to be sufficiently wealthy and strongly represented in the negotiations."[4] Simultaneously, Llewellyn Rockwell, Jr., an adamant defender of "free trade," makes a remarkably similar criticism from the right: "As usual when D.C. is calling (and aiming) the shots, arcane regulations will redistribute billions of dollars to well-connected corporations, and even more power to the managerial state. This is not the free market."[5] Although Hawken and Rockwell agree in this critique, their solutions are radically different. Hawken proposes that we depend on much tighter regulation of trade as the only credible means to prevent the abuses to persons and environment which unrestricted trade causes. Rockwell rejects this view of the way the world works and instead calls for even fewer restrictions than currently exist on international trade as the road to greater prosperity and freedom. In these two general assessments of trade, we can see differences in both moral judgment and empirical assessment. Such discrepancies also typify the debates over narrower issues within trade.

Almost every industrialized nation in the world has used import restrictions and subsidies to assist its own farm sector. The number of farmers and farms has dropped precipitously in the United States and Canada in recent decades, and farmers in both nations are vividly aware of the effects of imports on their own sales. Durum wheat farmers in the United States have been hurt by the freer importation of wheat from Canada, while Canadian dairy and poultry farmers fear what would occur if historical restrictions on imports were lifted and American dairy and poultry products were allowed in. The trend in recent trade agreements to reduce the subsidies national governments grant their farmers is perceived as a threat to farmers generally and to the small "family farmer" in particular. As one critic of the Canada-U.S. Free Trade Agreement phrased it, "The U.S.-Canada deal, negotiated by right-wing governments in each country, shows that international agribusiness wins while family farmers, farm workers, food-industry workers, and consumers tend to lose."[6] At the same time, because both the United States and Canada are highly successful exporters of food products, freer agricultural trade will help many farmers. Many farmers' organizations in both the U.S. and Canada have argued for greater ease of export, including export subsidies for farm products. From a moral point of view, many observers of these arguments see an objectionably selfish motive here: Farmers want to export their products to other nations but don't want foreign farmers to be able to sell their products here. Confusion is added to the complexity when observers must sort through apparent inconsistencies in the position of even individual experts. For example, Mark Ritchie, Director of the Institute of Agriculture and Trade Policy, asserts that farm subsidies to farmers who must sell their crops below the cost of production are actually subsidies to the agribusinesses that buy them.[7] At the same time he asserts elsewhere that grain traders see farm price support programs as "impediments" to their ability to maximize profits.[8]

A similar diversity of opinion involves the effects of international trade on the environment. Critics of increased trade point to the flagrant pollution by "maquiladoras" along the United States–Mexican border.[9] In addition, they argue that the inclination of industries to move to areas of the world with low pollution-control costs causes all national governments to be hesitant to increase or even enforce current regulations. As Paul Hawken put it, increased trade means that "international economic advantage would go to the companies that were best able to externalize environmental and social costs; companies that internalized those costs and took full responsibility for their environmental impact would be placed at a disadvantage."[10] At the same time, advocates of increased trade argue that it will lead to the faster transfer of "clean" technologies to the Third World, and would allow for greater efficiencies in the disposal of hazardous wastes if international trade in wastes became less regulated.

Perhaps the most controversial issue related to international trade is employment. Shortly after the Canada-U.S. Free Trade Agreement began in 1989, one Christian ethicist argued that the agreement would cause "massive unemployment" (in the range of 500,000 to 800,000 jobs).[11] Canadian critics of trade were particularly concerned about a likely loss of jobs as capital flowed out of Canada into the United States due to the lower cost of the social guarantees for workers there. At the same time, other critics of trade argue that inflows of capital to purchase domestic companies are themselves destructive: "One thing that's sucking wealth out of Canada is that so many Canadian companies are being sold to foreign companies since free trade went through. When that happens, all the profits that used to stay in Canada go to the U.S. or to France or wherever. There is no guarantee that any of those profits will be reinvested in Canada."[12] Even one not schooled in economics can see that there are conceptual difficulties when people on the same side of the trade debate argue that capital flowing out of the nation is harmful but that capital flowing into the nation is also bad.

Some of the most vigorous rhetoric for and against trade occurred during the debate over the North American Free Trade Agreement (NAFTA). In the United States, Ross Perot and many other critics of increased trade argued that the lower wages in Mexico would "suck" jobs out of the United States, seriously harming the welfare of U.S. workers. At the same time, proponents of the agreement argued that the increased exports the U.S. would enjoy would create a million jobs more than would be lost by the admission of imports from Mexico. Quite clearly the average citizen has a difficult time sorting through such charges and countercharges.

Even in the relatively staid realm of academe, discussions on international trade are acerbic; they exhibit not just differences of opinion but at times mutual accusations of incompetence. Paul Krugman, one of the leading young economists in the English-speaking world, has been engaged in at least two lively interchanges with economists, historians, and others, accusing them of being unaware of even elementary principles of international trade. They have responded with charges that he epitomizes the abstract, out-of-touch analysis that has given *laissez-faire* economics its bad name.[13] Irony is added to controversy when we note that Krugman himself has been one of the creators of the "new international trade theory" that has caused more economists today to doubt simple "free trade" proposals than at any time in the last century and a half. If the experts are in such disarray, what hope is there that the average citizen can form a carefully considered opinion about the morality of international trade?

THE PLAN FOR THIS BOOK

In order to sort through the challenges for Christians in assessing international trade, this volume will review current arguments about trade, will consider relevant theological and ethical resources available in the Christian tradition, and will examine more closely three concrete issues most fundamental to contemporary arguments about trade.

Chapter 2 will outline the arguments for and against increased trade, including both economic and moral assessments on each side. Chapter 3 will examine the biblical and theological themes that are relevant to the debate over international trade. Chapter 4 will review a series of more focused ethical concerns that can assist us in our assessment of the concrete elements of trade itself. Chapter 5 will identify a number of "background convictions" that stand behind but greatly influence narrower debates about trade. For some, particular commitments in *other* areas of life—the environment, social justice, the role of government, and so on—are so strong that they seem to determine that person's position on trade, in spite of any arguments about trade itself. Chapters 6, 7, and 8 focus on the three problems central to continuing trade controversies: agriculture, environment, and employment. These three areas of economic life appear again and again in everyday debates about the alleged positive or negative effects of trade. Chapter 9 will attend briefly to the possibilities for improving the rules of trade to bring them more in accord with the fundamental values endorsed within Christian ethics.

As will become clear in chapter 5 on background commitments, the ultimate moral sense of the debate over international trade really must be rooted in understandings of more pervasive issues. These include the character of faith, one's view of the human person and human community, and one's perspective on appropriate economic development, the role and limits of government, and the biospheric situation within which human life occurs. Whatever we may learn about trade will remain of only relative importance for a responsible life of faith in the modern world in comparison to the backdrop of far more important and fundamental issues. Although this book will make reference to these broader issues, it will not and cannot investigate them directly, in spite of their importance. Nonetheless, because many of the disputes about trade rest on differences and misunderstandings of a narrower sort, a volume such as this may indeed prove helpful.

CHAPTER 2

THE ARGUMENTS FOR AND AGAINST TRADE

The first step in our attempt to sort through the cacophony of voices addressing international trade is to attend more systematically to the arguments on each side of the debate. Speaking of simply two opposing positions oversimplifies a complicated set of issues, but it will assist in sorting through the claims that are made about trade.

The first section of this chapter examines the "economic" arguments in favor of trade. For simplicity, the terms "economist" and "economics" are used here to refer to the mainstream position represented by the vast majority of United States and Canadian economists. There are, of course, many other significant "schools" of economic analysis—Institutionalism, social economics, Marxism, feminist economics, Austrian economics, and so forth—which provide both a critique of the mainstream view and alternative analytic structures. Restricting the term "economics" to the mainstream position oversimplifies, but it implies no derogation of such "heterodox" economists. Their critique of the mainstream view is badly needed. Heterodox economists, however, are more apt to agree with the mainstream view on trade than on many other issues.

Because of the diversity of perspectives among those critical of increased international trade, a concise and comprehensive summary is not easy. The very helpful work by Herman E. Daly and John B. Cobb, Jr., in their *For the Common Good,* here provides the organizing principles for reviewing such arguments. Although Daly and Cobb make no claim to represent other groups, they provide an articulate critique of trade's effects and include in their purview nearly all of the issues voiced by others critical of trade.

It is helpful to note at the start that the phrase "free trade" will not be used in this volume. Talk about "free trade" is inaccurate and misleading. It is inaccurate because there is no such thing as "free trade" or a "free market" in any literal sense. Every endorsement of economic freedom implicitly presumes many communal restrictions such as laws against murder of one's competitors, violation of contracts, insider trading, and, to varying degrees, against a multitude of other abuses which a free interchange of self-interest in truly unregulated markets would otherwise inevitably cause. It is misleading because it polarizes the discussion and subverts the effort to introduce important distinctions having to do with the degree and focus of regulative law. When the issue is named "free trade," its opponents are tempted to support almost any government restrictions that will reduce trade, and its supporters are tempted to resist even appropriate restrictions on trade designed to eliminate self-interested abuses. It is both more accurate and more conducive to real dialogue to focus instead on proposals for and against increased trade.

THE ECONOMIC ARGUMENTS FOR INTERNATIONAL TRADE

To understand the traditional endorsement of international trade within economics, it is helpful to review several foundational presumptions of mainstream economic science as well as the more explicit benefits from trade which the discipline has recognized. Although the standard economic defense of trade often sounds abstract and sometimes even sterile, there are in fact morally more important commitments implicit there.

Welfare, Specialization, and the Extent of the Market

The first and most important step in the argument for international trade has nothing to do with trade at all. The argument for trade begins, rather, with a usually unspoken moral judgment about the merits of economic welfare: Increases in economic welfare are good for people. Mainstream economics considers itself incapable of defending or even analyzing this moral judgment, but the judgment nonetheless drives the moral conviction which others can easily hear in the voices of most economists defending international trade.

This self-imposed inability to assess moral judgments renders mainstream economics ignorant of many crucial elements in the arguments of its critics. Neoclassical economics considers intractable within the discipline several critically important issues, such as justice in the distribution of economic goods to rich and poor, the potential for excessive consumption by the affluent, and even the difference between wants and needs. Still, economists are correct in their fundamental perception of the moral importance of economic welfare for humans everywhere. In fact, nearly all proponents and critics of increased international trade agree that food, clothing, shelter, and a substantial list of other economic goods are conducive to the overall well-being of humans. Economists hold to a more general assertion: Economic goods are good for people, particularly the poor.[1]

In addition, such emphasis on economic welfare stresses the effect on consumers, a much larger group than producers. As we shall see, the trade-off of benefits between consumers and workers is an important one in debates on international trade.

The second step in the argument for international trade is, like the first, one that remains within national boundaries. If we ask why some nations have generally low levels of economic welfare and others much higher levels, we have asked the question behind Adam Smith's best-known work, *An Inquiry into the Nature and Causes of the Wealth of Nations* (1776). Smith's answer was a simple one, and it remains the answer provided by mainstream economics today: Individuals, groups, and nations experience greater economic welfare when productivity rises; they will not experience growing prosperity if it does not. Smith was arguing against the Mercantilists, who

27

identified economic welfare with the interests of the commercial class and with exporting more goods than were imported as a way to increase a nation's wealth. He asserted that a nation's wealth is to be measured neither by the precious metals held within its borders nor by its balance of trade, but by the goods produced and consumed by that nation's populace during the year, a measure akin to today's gross domestic product.[2]

Smith's analysis begins with persons involved in production and consumption. Although this bias toward the individual economic actor carries with it dangers when applied simplistically to government policy, it is essential here. Smith argued that most of the increase in economic welfare enjoyed by prosperous nations is directly attributable to increases in what he called "the division of labor." Economic prosperity is brought about by specialization in production. As he put it,

> What is the work of one man in a rude state of society, [is] generally that of several in an improved one. In every improved society, the farmer is generally nothing but a farmer; the manufacturer nothing but a manufacturer.[3]

Simply put, if a single farm family in the United States or Canada today had to produce all the goods it was to consume during a year, its level of economic welfare would necessarily be quite low. If individuals specialize in the production of one good, they not only tend to become more proficient at what they do, but, as Smith observed, they are far more likely to devise helpful inventions or improvements in the process than are those who spend only a small portion of the workweek at this task.

Such increases in skill and technology improve the hourly productivity of each worker. Because workers' output per hour rises, their wages rise as well; workers and their families then have more money to spend on other goods. Just as important, however, is the effect all this has on the economic welfare of others in the community. Because the cost of production falls, the price of those goods falls, increasing the economic welfare of all consumers of those goods. The increased productivity from specialization increases the prosperity of both workers and consumers, and this in turn increases

28

the demand for a wide range of other goods, permitting further specialization in their production as well.

The third step in the argument for international trade can also be traced to Smith and his conviction that "the division of labor is limited by the extent of the market."[4] Basically, this is an assertion about the physical transportation of economic goods. As technological improvements in transportation lower the costs of transporting goods longer distances, producers may now be able to specialize (and become more productive) in a particular commodity even while still located in the same geographic area, heretofore unable to sustain such specialization. Put simply, those U.S. and Canadian farmers on the Great Plains prior to the building of the railroads produced by themselves nearly everything they consumed. They not only grew their own food, but made their own clothing, churned their own butter, and produced their own soap. The primary advantage of the railroad was that the farmers could now specialize in farming: They could sell their produce to others across the nation and could then buy the panoply of goods from soap to clothing which they had previously produced themselves. Looking back, we have great admiration for the skill, perseverance, and self-sufficiency of these pioneering families. Nevertheless, when given the choice, they themselves chose, as people today continue to choose, to give up literal self-sufficiency in return for greater productivity and a higher standard of economic welfare.

Of course some producers are hurt in this process. Consumers in large cities may no longer buy food that is produced ten miles away but now buy it from a hundred miles away, or perhaps even from abroad, because it is available at a lower price. If so, the local farmers must now find other work. Because economists tend to assume that both workers and owners of capital put their assets to work in the most productive opportunity available, this change in agricultural markets means that the displaced farmers will most likely end up in alternative employment where they are less productive and have lower annual incomes. They have "lost their jobs," but that does not mean that there are no jobs for them, though their search elsewhere does tend slightly to lower the wage for all workers in industries to which they might turn for employment. Understandably, when the lower-priced goods are available for import from other nations, firms and workers currently producing those goods domestically often turn to government to protect their interests, which earns them the label "protectionist." Yet the losses these few face will be outweighed by the advantages of trade for a large number of others in the economy. As Smith put it,

> In every country it always is and must be the interest of the great body of the people to buy whatever they want of those who sell it cheapest. The proposition is so very manifest, that it seems ridiculous to take any pains to prove it; nor could it ever have been called in question, had not the interested sophistry of merchants and manufacturers confounded the common sense of mankind.[5]

Not only will protectionism mean higher prices, but other nations inevitably retaliate, trying to protect their own workers from imports, causing unanticipated unemployment among our domestic workers currently producing goods for export.

Whether we consider the building of railroads in the United States and Canada during the nineteenth century, the digging of canals in England during the eighteenth century, or the improvements in transportation brought about by air travel, electronics, and computers in the twentieth century, the argument is the same. The mainstream economic view is that when improved transportation allows people to make economic exchanges with others at greater distances—whether across the nation or across the world—there will be more specialization in production, higher productivity, and higher levels of economic welfare. From the economist's perspective, then, the debate about international trade is about taking advantage of markets that have been extended by technological capacity but restricted by legal intervention.

The Benefits of International Trade: Static and Dynamic Gains

Current economic discourse about international trade divides the benefits of trade into two categories: static and dynamic. Static gains occur without any change in the techniques of production. Dynamic gains are those brought about when greater trade induces producers to employ better techniques. The theoretical analysis of static gains has not changed much in the 170 years since David Ricardo published

The Theory of Political Economy and Taxation. "Dynamic" benefits have long been acknowledged within economics but have only in the last two decades or so been carefully modeled and examined. These relatively recent developments have engendered the "new" international trade theory that has led some mainstream economists to question what has historically been an almost unanimous endorsement of "free trade" within the discipline.

Static Gains from Trade

The most obvious form of static gain occurs when another nation is, for some reason, able to produce a good more efficiently than we can at home. In this situation the other nation enjoys what economists describe as an "absolute advantage." If a better climate, a history of greater skill in production, or some other factor enables our trading partner to produce a particular good more efficiently than we can, then our nation will be better off if we buy that good from abroad and employ elsewhere the resources formerly used to produce it at home.

Consider a timely example: sugar in the United States. Currently about 40 percent of the sugar consumed in the United States is produced from sugar beets, mostly on rich farmland of the upper Great Plains. It is no surprise that sugar can be produced more efficiently in regions closer to the equator where longer growing seasons and more direct sunshine enable the sugarcane plant to yield sucrose in greater abundance than does the sugar beet in Minnesota. Beyond a small quota of duty-free imports, current U.S. law prevents the importation of sugar by means of a prohibitively high tariff. Smith's advice would be to allow U.S. citizens to import as much sugar as they wish from lower-priced producers abroad. Both sugar and products made with sugar would then be cheaper, and, most important from the point of view of economic welfare, consumers of these items would have income left over to purchase other goods they are currently unable to afford. The economic welfare of a very large group of consumers would rise.

Static gain from "comparative advantage" is more complicated and less obvious. In fact, the very subtlety of comparative advantage and the ignorance of most noneconomists about it seem to have

31

contributed significantly to economists' tenacity in endorsing increased trade.[6]

The classic argument was made by David Ricardo, who asserted counterintuitively that it makes sense for one nation to trade with another not only when the latter nation is more efficient in producing a good, but also when that other nation produces goods less efficiently.[7] Ricardo's famous example compares England and Portugal, where Portugal produces both cloth and wine more efficiently than England (nine workers instead of ten to make a bolt of cloth and eight workers instead of twelve to produce a barrel of wine). Thus it might seem that international trade could not be in Portugal's interest. It might seem that Portugal could only lose if it imported from England products that "cost" more to produce there than in Portugal.

Ricardo's insight, however, is based on the comparison of the trade-offs *within* each country. Since a bolt of cloth "costs" the time of nine workers and a barrel of wine that of eight, the cost in Portugal of a bolt of cloth measured in barrels of wine is 9/8, or approximately 1.1 barrels of wine. This is in a sense the "price" of a bolt of cloth within Portugal; domestically, the Portuguese can only "buy" (that is, produce) an extra bolt of cloth by giving up 1.1 barrels of wine. Thus, if the Portuguese were able to make a deal with the English to exchange one barrel of wine for one bolt of cloth, the Portuguese would be willing to make the trade, since that would be a cheaper way of getting cloth than producing it themselves. To understand whether trade would occur we must also consider the possibilities from the English perspective.

In England, where the production of a barrel of wine requires twelve workers while a bolt of cloth requires ten, the "price" of a barrel of wine is 12/10 or 1.2 bolts of cloth. The British, then, would be interested in trading cloth for wine if they could do so at a lower "price," such as one bolt of cloth for one barrel of wine. Thus, both nations find themselves interested in exchanging cloth and wine even though Portugal is more efficient in the production of each.[8]

Later economists coined the phrase "comparative advantage" to describe the relative position of England in the production of cloth. Although Portugal has an absolute advantage in the production of both commodities, both nations will gain if Portugal shifts workers and capital from cloth to wine and England shifts workers and capital from wine to cloth. In effect, a resource which is "relatively" scarce in one nation (that is, scarce compared with other resources in that nation) is supplemented, through trade, by the relative abundance of that resource in the other nation.

Ricardo explained why this relatively inefficient production of cloth in England would continue. International trade is in one important way different from trade within a nation: Although *goods* move across international borders relatively easily, Ricardo observed that neither workers nor capital does. Consider what would happen if two areas *within* England exhibited the differences in productivity assumed to exist between England and Portugal. Ricardo's presumption, an accurate one, is that both investment capital and workers from a "less efficient" region would move to a more efficient region in the same nation because both profits and wages would be higher there. This movement of resources would tend to lower the rates of profit and wages in the more productive area and tend to raise them in the less productive, moving the nation toward an equilibrium. The critical difference in international trade is the immobility of factors of production. There is an almost complete immobility of labor, due to both culture and immigration laws, and, at least in Ricardo's scenario, a general immobility of capital,[9] an assumption we shall see challenged by critics of international trade today.

Dynamic Gains from Trade

In addition to the static gains from international trade, economics identifies "dynamic" benefits of trade that arise from three main causes: economies of scale, positive externalities, and intensified producer rivalries.[10] Although economists have long been aware of these effects, it has only been in the last quarter century that more precise theoretical models of them have been devised and tested.

The first of these dynamic benefits comes from the Smithian fact that, in many industries, increasing the scale of production allows for greater efficiency through innovations that are economically feasible only at higher levels of output made possible by expanded (domestic or foreign) markets. A classic example can again be the production of wheat in the Great Plains of Canada and the United States. If farmers produce only enough wheat for themselves and for the residents of local towns, the quantity produced is quite small and the technology for producing it quite basic. It is only when there is a predictably large demand for grain that a farmer in the nineteenth century would even consider a machine (the "combine") that would both cut the wheat and separate the grain from the chaff. As exports increase, industry scale and innovation increase.

The second dynamic benefit of trade is the presence of positive externalities in production. Externalities are effects of any process borne by others outside that process, with pollution being the classic *negative* externality. A *positive* externality of production is an increase in welfare outside the firms engaged in that production process. A timely example is the many positive externalities generated by a large high-tech electronics industry in one's nation. In addition to the usual advantages of high-paying jobs and earnings from exports, there are other pervasive effects on the nation: demand for more higher education (a larger and better school and university system, helpful to many other industries as well), the cross-fertilization of ideas among industries, and a kind of cultural self-confidence that seems to accompany high-tech industries. There is also the generation of "spin-off" technologies, which not only make other production processes more efficient, but which, because they are generated in one's own nation, give fellow citizens a leg up in developing and marketing them worldwide. Even industries that export nothing can generate positive externalities, but industries with large export potential generate strong positive externalities. Expanding such exports enlarges those industries and increases the external benefits.

The third dynamic benefit of trade comes from intensified rivalries among producers. Put most simply, the availability over the past quarter century of imported Japanese and European automobiles in the United States and Canada has played a strong role in the continuing reconstruction of North American automobile manufacturers. The millions who have purchased Japanese or German cars are not the only ones to benefit from the international rivalry. The purchasers of domestic cars now manufactured with greater quality control benefit indirectly, but benefit nonetheless. Increased trade generates not just the static benefit of lower prices but also the dynamic benefit of higher-quality domestic production.

34

The first two of these dynamic benefits examined by the new international trade theory since the late 1970s have led to something of an in-house revolution within mainstream economics. Traditional analysis, based on the static gains from comparative advantage, says that any nation which constructs protectionist barriers to imports actually hurts its own economic welfare, even if other nations do not retaliate. Substantial gains for each of a small group of "protected" producers are outweighed by smaller losses for each of an immensely large group of consumers. The "new" international trade theory, developed by economists such as Paul Krugman and Avinash Dixit, acknowledges this net "static" loss but argues that in some circumstances careful intervention in markets by national governments can give advantages to domestic firms in international competition and can, if done properly, lead to higher national standards of living due to the advantages garnered (at the expense of other nations, of course). After years of such research, however, most leaders in this movement have come to the conclusion that, empirically, these theories about "strategic trade policy" have not much to offer.

Krugman himself cites two primary reasons for this. The first is that even if the national government makes a perfect decision the gains are not massive. Focusing on the most plausible argument against free trade, external economies, he phrases the following question.

> Suppose that the United States were to carry out a clever, completely antisocial attempt to corner the world market in high externality industries, and that the rest of the world were to remain entirely passive as it did so. How much would this raise real income in the United States?[11]

Krugman's answer is "less than 1%." Of course, other nations are not apt to sit back and allow the United States to capture this advantage, so the resulting advantage would be in fact much less. However, even were the gain to reach 1 percent, it would easily be dwarfed by more important factors affecting long-term national income, such as productivity growth.

The second reason to downplay the significance of the new trade theory is that governments are rarely able to make perfect decisions.

We hear far more about the successes of Japan's Ministry of International Trade and Industry (MITI) than its failures. It is exceedingly difficult to choose the "right" industries to subsidize, and other "wrong" industries will also demand subsidies, which often eat up the gains made from the wise decisions. And even if wise decisions subsidize the right industries temporarily, it is politically almost impossible to end the subsidies after they become economically inappropriate.

Krugman himself, for both political and economic reasons, has proposed a limited strategic U.S. industrial policy to support industrial research and development consortia.[12] The new international trade theory is taken up by opponents of increased trade to endorse proposals for far more substantial expenditures, subsidies, and import restrictions. The authors of these theories now face the irony of seeing their own work quoted in protectionist arguments they themselves reject.

THE ARGUMENTS AGAINST
INTERNATIONAL TRADE

As is always the case with groups defined by their opposition to something, the opponents of increased international trade appeal to a number of quite distinct arguments and proclaim loyalties to a variety of different social, political, and economic groupings. Some groups opposed to increased trade maintain historical alliances, while other groups find themselves cooperating with traditional opponents. In order to simplify the task, the focus here will be on a single perspective: that proposed by Herman Daly and John Cobb in *For the Common Good*. Because the authors endorse the ideal of bioregional self-sufficiency and because they articulate an ethical vision founded on the importance of community, their position might best be referred to as "bioregional communitarianism." Although Daly and Cobb do not speak for all opponents of increased international trade, they present a responsible and comprehensive argument about economic life today and include in their opposition to increased trade nearly all the leading arguments employed by various groups who also stand in opposition.

Daly and Cobb begin their analysis of economic life with a critique of economics as a discipline. Like other disciplines, economics has been characterized by a narrowed focus and increased abstraction. Most important, economists tend to *presume* that their theories correspond to the real world, a mistake Alfred North Whitehead called "the fallacy of misplaced concreteness."[13] Economists, they assert, begin with an admittedly artificial model of human decision, *Homo economicus*, and then proceed to presume that all people really act as rational maximizers. Similarly, Daly and Cobb argue that land has disappeared from modern economic analysis much to the detriment of a real insight into agriculture and resource depletion. In resource economics, such oversights, combined with misplaced concreteness, amount to a denial of the second law of thermodynamics. It is no wonder, they argue, that economists who can ignore basic physics can also overlook the moral claims of future generations, of other species, and of the biosphere. They direct one of their most thorough critiques at the notion of gross national product. GNP is a measure of economic *activity*, but it is regularly used as a measure for economic *welfare*, even though this use is deeply flawed. It measures many costs as if they were benefits, including necessary but unfortunate "defensive expenditures" (for example, the increased expense for personal safety and for commuting to work) required by deteriorating social conditions brought on at least in part by economic growth itself.[14] To endorse increased trade on the grounds that it promotes economic growth as measured by GNP is circular and morally objectionable.

Because Daly and Cobb aim for broad appeal, most of their arguments do not presuppose Christian belief on the part of their readers. Nonetheless, they make clear their own views as theists and argue that Christian commitments concerning the human person, community, and the natural world call for a communitarian, bioregional economic system, one where international trade is strictly curtailed. They present four principal arguments against trade. In each case, they argue, misplaced concreteness within the discipline of economics leads economists to undervalue the damage caused by trade. The first argument highlights the effects of trade on domestic employment.

Losses in Employment and Social Welfare

Concerns within the United States about loss of employment through international trade were highlighted during the 1992 presidential campaign when Ross Perot associated the North American Free Trade Agreement (NAFTA) with "a great sucking sound" of jobs being siphoned from the United States to Mexico. Many Canadians expressed similar concerns. The argument is that with cheap labor available in developing countries, there will be a movement of jobs away from industrialized nations such as the United States and Canada, causing downward pressure on the number of jobs, on the wages of those jobs that still exist, and on expenditures for social programs such as unemployment insurance, worker's compensation insurance, and health insurance. In much the same way as individual cities within Canada and the U.S. have often competed with one another to offer tax incentives and a positive "business climate" for firms planning to build a new factory, so the same sort of competition will force the United States, Canada, and other industrial nations to lower wages and benefits in the private sector and lower levels of government-financed social welfare.

Daly and Cobb analyze the economic forces more closely. Relying on economist John Culbertson, they point to an astigmatism demonstrated by most mainstream economists in the discussion of comparative advantage and international trade. Central to Ricardo's argument, but kept out of focus in most mainstream discussions, are two presumptions—about the agents of trade and about the immobility of capital—which diverge from the facts of the real world.

Who are the agents of international trade? Ricardo's explanations of trade, as well as the foundational examples presented in most international trade textbooks today, begin with the notion of two nations trading with each other and end with the judgment that "both nations will be better off" if international trade occurs than if it does not. Daly and Cobb argue that this represents another instance of the economists' misplaced concreteness, presuming that the real world corresponds to their simplified model. It is not nations who are the agents of trade but rather individuals or, more likely, corporations.[15] The simple model tells us that both parties to the exchange are better off than before, but in the real world there are a multitude of "third parties" who are affected by the exchange and whose welfare may worsen considerably. Not only does the model ignore these many others, but it apparently lures economists into an unwarranted moral judgment that the nation as a whole is better off because of the exchange. The same discipline which eschews moral judgments and resists "interpersonal comparisons of utility" finds itself here making a methodologically unsubstantiated public policy recommendation.

Concerning the second assumption, Daly and Cobb ask: "Is capital truly immobile?" Ricardo himself noted that if it were not for the immobility of capital and labor in his simple example, English capital and workers would move to Portugal in the same way they currently move from Yorkshire to London in response to the differences in the rates of profit and wages. However, Ricardo observes, the "fancied or real insecurity of capital" invested in a foreign country and the "natural disinclination which every man has to quit himself of his country of birth and connections" leads to a nearly complete immobility of capital.[16] He reports that he would be sorry to see these feelings of capitalists weakened, since, although capital mobility would be advantageous for the capitalists of England (higher profits) and for the consumers of both countries (lower prices), the loss (of jobs) in England would be a huge cost. Daly and Cobb argue that in the time between Ricardo's era and our own there has been a dramatic change: "In today's world, national boundaries do not inhibit the flow of capital investment."[17] Those who are making decisions about capital movements are no longer "very British" capitalists but are rather "cosmopolitan money managers and transnational corporations" that have no such nation-based hesitations.[18] Tremendous increases in the efficiency of transport, communications, and networks of control within widespread corporations have greatly reduced the "fancied or real insecurity of capital." As travelers to the developing world today know well, even the rare Ricardian corporate manager who *is* disinclined "to quit himself of his country of birth and connections" will hardly know he has done so when he checks into the local Hilton hotel.

The inevitable effect of this, say Daly and Cobb, is that capital, represented primarily by the investments of multinational corporations, will flow out of high-wage nations to low-wage nations leaving behind large numbers of unemployed workers, who will then, in competition with currently employed workers, depress the wages in remaining industries. At the same time, pressure will mount on regional and national governments to reduce "expensive" social guarantees (such as worker safety laws, aid to the poor and unemployed, legal support for trade unions) in an effort to convince transnational corporations *not* to move jobs elsewhere. As usual, it is those with the fewest options (the least "mobility") who are hurt most: workers. The distribution of income becomes more and more skewed in favor of the wealthy, a morally unacceptable result.

The authors argue that, unlike Ricardo's example of a barter economy where the physical efficiency of one nation is compared with that of another, the real world today bases decisions on the monetary cost of hourly labor, not on the physical productiveness of such an hour. Thus, the drastic differences in wage rates between industrialized and developing nations means that "a country's absolute advantage may now depend simply on low wages (low standard of living) rather than on more efficient use of labor."[19] In effect, owners of capital in the United States are

> telling U.S. laborers . . . to compete in the world market against the poor masses in the overpopulated Third World. . . . No longer will U.S. labor have the advantage of superior technology or management, because those attributes move with capital. . . . Equalization of wages means that U.S. and European and Japanese wages fall to the Third World level, and the Third World level rises hardly at all.[20]

Anticipating such a tragedy, critics of trade would restrict imports to preserve domestic jobs. Some necessary trade with other nations would be allowed, but only by a national decision concerning national interests. Individuals or firms would not be free to trade any way they wished, although once the nation decided that trade in certain products would be to its national advantage, then such trade would indeed be taken up by individuals and firms.

To their credit, Daly and Cobb recognize that consistency requires restrictions not simply on the inflow of imports but also on the outflow of capital from the nation: "Balanced trade and capital immobility imply each other."[21] Even if import restrictions eliminated the sale of Third World products in the high-priced markets of the United States and Canada, North American capital resources would still move into Third World nations to manufacture products there for sale to other nations. This loss of investment would cause job loss at home. As a result, this view calls for a literally balanced trade between countries and almost no transfer of private capital.

Damage to the Environment

Many proponents of increased trade share a fundamental conceptual shortcoming concerning resource depletion that actually originates within the character of mainstream economics: It is both abstract and highly anthropocentric. It focuses on individuals making choices. While this has a number of advantages in understanding such interactions, it is also a moral liability when approaching environmental issues. It eclipses the physical biosphere within which such social interactions take place. Thus, nearly every introductory economics textbook begins with a "circular flow" diagram. This is a picture of the overall economy depicting how firms pay out money in return for access to resources (labor, buildings, land, etc.) and then produce goods and services, which they sell in return for money from consumers. The picture, then, is one of real resources flowing from consumers to firms and real goods flowing from firms to consumers, with a stream of money flowing in the "opposite" direction: each a circular flow.

Herman Daly has argued persuasively that this image of the economy is all too partial and is literally out-of-touch with the real world. The alternative picture Daly proposes shows the economy embedded in the biosphere, using up valuable resources in order to produce goods and services desired by people, leaving behind wastes, which are left within the biosphere at the end of the process.[22] The standard circular flow picture of the economy ignores completely the natural world as a source of assets and sink for wastes.

Of course, mainstream economists respond that the circular flow diagram is not designed to deal with environmental issues, which instead are treated under the topic "externalities." Daly replies that this reduces the economist's attention to environmental damage, leaving it to be treated as a sort of appendage to the "truly" important analysis of market decisions. An ethically adequate approach to

41

economic life will need to integrate biophysical as well as social analyses of our problems and prospects.

One result of this mainstream tendency to treat environmental problems as secondary, critics argue, is that economists tend to overlook the fact that weak environmental standards in developing nations act as cost-lowering inducements, particularly attractive to firms that generate significant amounts of pollution.

Most industrialized nations have taken substantial steps to implement the "producer pays principle." They have tried to "internalize" the negative externalities of pollution in the production process. On this both environmentalists and economists agree: Pollution will be curbed when the social costs of pollution are internalized within firms producing the pollution (with costs necessarily passed on to consumers). This can occur through governmental regulation of various sorts. Critics of increased trade point out that developing nations that are heavily dependent on export earnings (to cover the cost of debt service and imported goods) have strong incentives to minimize environmental regulation and thereby keep production costs low, in order to lure multinational enterprises to operate there.

Daly and Cobb here identify a critically important divergence between environmentalists and mainstream economists. From the economists' point of view, a nation's policies about environmental standards are a social choice, not a moral obligation. Economists argue that the individual assessments of citizens—concerning moral obligations, tastes, current severity of pollution, the local environment's absorptive capacity, and other factors—vary greatly and heavily influence any nation's policy. There is within mainstream economics no grounds for any underlying presumption that pollution in the developing world should be reduced. In fact, a memo attributed to economist Lawrence Summers raised the hackles of many both within and outside the environmental movement for its judgment that the developing world is in general "underpolluted," and that economic efficiency and world prosperity might be sensibly increased by the movement of heavily polluting industries to developing countries.[23] Critics of international trade substantiate suspicions here with vivid images of maquiladoras along the Mexico–United States border, where ditches flow with chemical wastes and the incidence of pollution-related health problems is high.[24]

An additional environmental deficit caused by more international trade is increased reliance on long-range transport and concomitant increased energy use. One of the most attractive elements of bioregional self-sufficiency is the simplicity of producing more products closer to the point of consumption with the consequent decreased reliance on petroleum-based fuels inevitably used in transport, whether by sea, land, or air.

A more general and fundamental way of summarizing these concerns is Daly's description of a sustainable scale for the economy:

> The input of raw materials and energy must be within the regenerative capacity, and the output of waste materials and energy must be within the absorptive capacity, of the ecosystem.[25]

As trade increases, production and the environmental damage it causes will predictably be farther and farther separated from the consumers who reap its benefits. Such trade allows the importing nation to exceed its own domestic limits for regeneration of resources and absorption of pollutants, but only by exporting the problems to another part of the globe. The world is nearly "full" with humans and their furniture.[26] Although the increased specialization which trade brings about does tend to increase the efficiency with which some resources are used, Daly observes, the negative side effects more than outweigh these advantages.

Loss of Democratic Control

The third argument against international trade focuses on its political effects. Industrialized nations have for more than a century relied upon the communal decisions of national governments to enforce environmental, health, safety, and a variety of other standards. They now face a loss of national autonomy when international competitive pressures make it more difficult to sustain those same levels of security. Transnational corporations operate above the level of nations, or as Daly and Cobb phrase it, "between communities," and thus are not sufficiently subject to communal restrictions within the nations where they operate.

It is exceedingly difficult, they argue, for the democratic structures of industrialized nations to control their own multinational firms, and it is even more difficult for developing nations to do so. Third World elites have much to gain from cooperating with trans-national firms, and, as a result, democratic movements are often thwarted. The effects on the local autonomy of indigenous peoples are severe. As multinational agricultural operations expand in northern Mexico, for example, much of the land that would other-wise be available for subsistence agriculture is bought up, and its current peasant owners become farm employees or, worse, are forced to move to the cities in search of work.

This loss of democratic control is exacerbated by international trade agreements themselves, not just by their tendency to increase the power of multinationals. Multilateral agreements, like the World Trade Organization (WTO) and its predecessor, the General Agree-ment on Tariffs and Trade (the GATT), and regional agreements, like the Canada-U.S. Free Trade Agreement and NAFTA, usually in-clude a dispute-resolution process where a small committee, ap-pointed by the member governments, hears challenges to member activities and "hands down" a ruling that is binding on the nations involved.[27] The board is unelected, its deliberations are often secret, and it usually ignores many goals, like environmental quality or equity, that member nations actually hold but which were not writ-ten into the trade agreement. As Herman Daly has argued elsewhere, the GATT allows member nations to erect trade barriers to protect their citizens from products made elsewhere by foreign prison labor, but it has no analogous exceptions when imported products are cheap because of child labor, subsistence wage labor, or uninsured risky labor.[28] Increased trade erodes democratic control over the conditions of daily economic life.

Loss of Community

Closely related to the loss of democratic control, and still more important, is the threat to community that increased international trade presents. Daly and Cobb offer a view of the human person based on Whitehead's process philosophy, one that recognizes hu-mans as constituted by their relationships. They point out that mainstream economists *believe* their models and view persons only as "individuals," self-constituted persons who choose to relate to others to accomplish their goals—another example of the misplaced concreteness of economic science.[29]

Because human well-being is founded in healthy and supportive communal life, community is essential. In addition to all the market's productivity and its ability to provide things people need, market relationships tend toward depersonalization and the instrumental use of others. Markets break down community. This is obvious in many impersonal urban "neighborhoods" as well as in the gradual disappearance of formerly robust rural towns.

Critics of trade attach less value to trade-induced lower prices and more value to the communities that sustain the people who buy the product. Daly and Cobb advocate a reduction of trade in agricultural products, for example, in large part because it would render sustainable the community life of small towns in rural areas. More local production in agriculture and industry would not only be more benign for the environment but it would also provide more jobs for workers locally, sustaining community. They point out that when Smith and Ricardo presumed that English owners of capital would *not* shift their capital to more profitable foreign investments, they were understanding these capitalists as having internalized community-based values.[30] It is in fact the loss of community over the years which leaves individual investors and firms today to think only of "the bottom line." International trade undermines local community.

A LOOK FORWARD

A Christian ethical assessment of international trade must include sorting through the conflicting claims of supporters and opponents of increased international trade. Most of this volume attends to such claims in the three areas of agriculture, environment, and employment. Before turning to these, however, it is important to attend first to the religious foundations of any Christian economic ethic.

CHAPTER 3

BIBLICAL AND THEOLOGICAL THEMES RELEVANT TO THE DEBATE

C hristian faith is rooted in the experience of God. That experience occurs today, but Christians recognize the foundational authority of the revelation of God experienced by our biblical "ancestors." The meaning of the scriptural record of that experience—and of later theological reflection on that record—is no simple matter. Nonetheless, most Christians can recognize in the scriptures and in subsequent theology several fundamental themes constitutive of a life of faith generally and helpful for a more specific set of policy issues surrounding international economic trade today.

It will help to recall briefly three clusters of biblical and theological themes and to review the limited, though helpful, accounts of international trade itself within the Bible.

THE MATERIAL WORLD: CREATION, OWNERSHIP, AND STEWARDSHIP

The Bible begins with a creation narrative and focuses throughout on the creative and saving power of God. Even though redemption in Christ is the most fundamental lens of faith through which we view the world, Christians must rely extensively on the doctrine of creation in their approach to economic life. So much of what we know about the economic world around us is embodied in that doctrine.

As Genesis 1:2 puts it, "The earth was a formless void and darkness covered the face of the deep." God created the world out of chaos, or in later theological reflection, out of nothing. By either interpretation, the earth and its inhabitants take on critically important characteristics because they are God's work. The world is a gift. It is not a conquest, not a vacant land that some cosmic travelers happened upon and decided to colonize. Even Christians who reject "creationism" still recognize God's creative hand in the evolutionary process and know that life itself is a gift, not a prize in some meaningless cosmic lottery of stochastic biochemical evolution. Rather, as the Hebrew Scriptures and later Christian theology came to understand it, God made a free and loving gift of the material world to its inhabitants. This giftedness of creation entails important consequences.

The first is that the material world is good. The creation story reports that "God saw that it was good" after each day of creation. Thus Christianity rejects the notion that growth in the life of faith requires an escape from the material world or a retreat to a more important or more "real" realm of spiritual life. Although the material world bears dangers, Christianity is not an "other-worldly" religion; it affirms both this world and the hope of an ultimate eternal existence with God. As a result, the productive work of the average person is religiously significant; the daily work of "making a living" bears meaning in the plan of God.

This insight has been understood more vividly at some points in Christian history than in others. To recapture the religious significance of the life of the ordinary Christian was a critical part of the Protestant Reformers' goals. Here they were responding to an overemphasis in medieval Catholicism on the clergy and on the "evangelical counsels" of poverty, chastity, and obedience embodied in the life of religious communities of men or women. In doing so, the Reformers were calling Christianity back to a truer and more fundamentally correct view of the importance of routine, daily work. In fact, in their best forms, even secluded religious communities were

48

not so spiritualized and removed from the realities of work as many Reformers themselves sometimes thought. Many early monastic communities arose in response to the watering down of Christian life that occurred when the conversion of Constantine made Christian faith socially advantageous: They were themselves a reform movement. In the *Rule of Benedict*, the charter document for Benedictine monasteries since the fifth century, the twofold focus on "prayer and work," the care for ordinary objects such as shovels, pots, and pans, and the place at Sunday prayer of those assigned to kitchen duties for the week indicated that even these secluded communities did not intend a diminution of the religious importance of daily work.[1]

Alongside this respect for even the ordinary routines of daily life is the awareness of the Creator's original plan that humans live in consort with God and enjoy the material goods of the garden. The biblical witness points to the dangers of the material world after the fall, but it does not denigrate the world's goodness for humans. Yahweh promises to Israel a land flowing with milk and honey (Exod. 3:8). As Deuteronomy describes the Lord's promise:

> He will love you, bless you, and multiply you; he will bless the fruit of your womb and the fruit of your ground, your grain and your wine and your oil, the increase of your cattle and the issue of your flock, in the land that he swore to your ancestors to give you. (Deut. 7:13)

This same basic endorsement of the goodness of creation appears in the New Testament as well. Jesus warns of the dangers of wealth as bringing about a hardness of heart and standing as a barrier to the disciples' relationship with God and the poor. Nonetheless, Jesus' frequent participation in the feasts of his time seems clearly to indicate that the Christian's primary concern is to remain in loving relation with God and neighbor and that in such a context the good things of the earth are to be rightfully enjoyed.

A second critical implication of the doctrine of creation is that the giftedness of the world implies a relation of intentionality between God and the earth's inhabitants. The people of Israel had a continuing relationship with Yahweh, and they understood that the world around them was theirs only tentatively: Yahweh remained ultimately in possession of the world. As the Psalmist put it,

49

> The earth is the LORD's and all that is in it,
> the world, and those who live in it;
> for he has founded it on the seas,
> and established it on the rivers. (Ps. 24:1-2)

As a result, humans are not given license to do anything they wish with this gift; they need to respect the purposes of the Giver. Ancient Israel embodied this requirement in the Torah, which included a compendium of regulations for worship, food preparation, familial relations, and, most important for our purposes, economic life. Examples of the latter include the requirement that any sheaves of grain left behind in the field during the harvest not be later retrieved but be left for the widow, the orphan, the stranger. Similarly in harvesting grapes, the harvesters were forbidden to make a second pass through the vineyard to retrieve fruit left earlier; this was to be left for the needy of the nation (Deut. 24:19-21). The owner could harvest the field, but was obliged to leave its corners unharvested, "for the poor and the alien" (Lev. 19:9-10). Just ownership entailed obligations to the dispossessed.

The New Testament record gives ample evidence of Jesus' admonition to his followers to live in response to God's loving care. Jesus' own interpretation of such a response included the appropriate enjoyment of the good things of the earth at weddings and banquets along with the admonition to end anxious worries about having still more material goods. Similarly, Paul preached Jesus' victory over death and entreated his listeners to live according to God's plan from the founding of the world as revealed in Jesus the Christ.

Not only did this gift-character of the world entail requirements for the treatment of the dispossessed of society, but Christian ethics has come to see in the notion of human dominion over the world (Gen. 1:28) an additional requirement in humanity's relation with the natural environment. The biblical notion of "dominion" arising from the creation story has been criticized by many for legitimating the destruction of the environment brought about by industrial society in the last two centuries.[2] Recent theological retrieval of a more adequately ecological theology, however, has come to a different conclusion. The problem of ecological destruction is a result not of the necessity of subduing a hostile environment but rather, as James Nash argues, of "imperialistic overextension—abusing what is divinely intended for use, subduing far beyond the point of necessity, imagining despotism rather than dominion, and failing to nurture benevolently and justly nature's potential hospitality."[3] Although not absent from the tradition, a widespread theological retrieval of a Bible-based respect for creation is a relatively recent development. Nonetheless, it is a natural extension of biblical stewardship to recognize our common responsibility for the environment, including the atmosphere, the seas, rivers, and lakes, that are held in common, unowned by any person or group. Although much theological and ethical work still remains to be done in this relatively new area, there is a growing awareness that the Christian doctrine of creation entails ecological responsibility and respect for the natural order.

The doctrine of creation, then, provides two fundamental insights which form the basis of a Christian approach to economic life: The world is good and the world is a gift, to be used carefully, in the presence of the Giver. Participation in the world forms an essential part of the believer's relationship with God, whose vision of goodness and justice holds out the promise of a full and fulfilling life for all.

HUMANKIND: PERSON, COVENANT, AND CREATION IN GOD'S IMAGE

The Christian understanding of the human person has been deeply shaped by its roots in Judaism. Most fundamental is the understanding in accord with Genesis 1:27 that humans have been made "in the image of God." This should be understood not as a result of the arrogance of humans in setting themselves above the rest of the natural world but as a part of God's plan for creation itself. Jesus' own teaching consistently stressed God's personal interest in each individual. As a result, the tradition has seen each human being as an individual with a personal dignity which all other humans have an obligation to respect.

Sometimes lost, however, to the twentieth-century Christian is the rooting of the individual—and of the very meaning of personhood—within a communal structure for life. In the Hebrew Scriptures, it is clear that there is no meaning to being a Jewish person apart from the covenant between Yahweh and the people of Israel. Theirs was no "me and God" religion. While God deals with individuals in numerous Bible stories, none of those interactions makes sense without the context of the Covenant, the agreement between Yahweh and the people founded on Yahweh's saving action in the Exodus from Egypt. A true son or daughter of Israel is one who willingly lives in accord with the requirements of the Covenant, requirements willingly accepted by a people grateful for that rescue.

The Christian scriptures continue this understanding of both a communal and an individual relationship with God in the awareness of a new covenant established in Jesus the Christ. Any true disciple of Christ will live out Jesus' teaching in service to others in vibrant community life. Paul employs the Greek notion of *koinonia* to capture the sense of communal interdependence and flourishing because it entails not simply a sort of spiritual sharing of faith but a sharing also based in material goods. Paul makes this point clearly when urging his communities to contribute to the collection for the faithful in Jerusalem (e.g., Rom. 15:26-27).

There has, of course, been a continuing development in the meaning of this God-given dignity of humans. For example, earlier in the tradition certain forms of slavery were accepted as morally justifiable, but in more recent centuries all slavery has come to be understood as a violation of the God-given dignity of the person. An additional example is the endorsement of democratic political structures by Christian churches. Although earlier understandings endorsed a religious legitimation of emperors, kings, or other rulers, the Christian tradition later came to uphold the political rights of ordinary people in self-determination. Claims to political freedom for individuals within the Christian tradition are ultimately based in this notion of creation "in the image of God."

This same understanding of the human person as both an individual and social being created in God's image stands at the base of a Christian understanding of economic life. As a member of God's people, each person bears responsibilities rooted in God's plans for material creation and in the explicit economic requirements of the covenant. At the same time, however, the individuality of each person and the freedom and creativity implicit in being created in the image of God render individual economic actors able to shape their world to improve their economic well-being.

The scriptures do not speak frequently of business acumen, but the condemnation of the wealthy by the Hebrew prophets and Jesus himself was a condemnation of immoral treatment of the poor, not a judgment on business enterprise itself. In addition to other themes, the story of Jacob makes clear that his prosperity while in voluntary exile after winning his inheritance from his brother Esau came because of his business skills as a herdsman and breeder, even in the face of trickery of others (Gen. 30:32-43). Similarly, Joseph's rise in Egypt from slavery to political and economic influence under the Pharaoh was due not only to Yahweh's assistance in interpreting dreams. Joseph also is given considerable credit for his own administrative abilities and their effectiveness in anticipating times of great economic scarcity.

The economic life of Palestine in Jesus' day was not much different from what it had been a thousand years earlier. Although dried fish, olives, and dates were exported to other parts of the Roman Empire, the vast majority of people lived in the poverty typical of ancient times. Jesus himself made clear both the dangers and the obligations of ownership of wealth, but in spite of the use of economic images in his parables, he said very little about how daily economic life should be conducted. The apostle Paul said not much more in his writings. He himself seems to have remained gainfully employed to prevent his being a burden on others. Still he reports receiving economic assistance for his work of spreading the gospel, and it comes from wealthy individuals, at least some of whom are still apparently active entrepreneurs (Acts 16:14; 17:4, 12).

These biblical attitudes toward business acumen and gainful employment were apparently so uncontroversial that they seem not to have needed any theological defense. Nonetheless we know that the biblical understanding of humans as created in the image of God animates and undergirds any adequate Christian economic ethic. It encompasses the grounds for individual economic creativity and success as well as a covenanted responsibility for the poor and marginalized.

THE REIGN OF GOD: SIN, GRACE, AND REDEMPTION

That same creation story that holds out the promise of a harmonious use of the world in accord with God's wishes also outlines the paradigmatic case for the violation of God's purposes: the appearance of sin in Adam and Eve. In essence, their sin consisted in a rebellion against God, willfully violating God's stated intentions for their use of the garden, destroying the harmony between humanity and God for subsequent ages. Christian theological interpretation of this first sin came to understand it as marking a fall in the nature of humanity, initiating the history of the world as one where human sinfulness is ever ingrained in both personal and communal life.

Both the Jewish and the Christian traditions have recognized that in the face of such inveterate human sinfulness, the only real hope is the saving hand of God. Ancient Israel celebrated the story of the Exodus, Yahweh's people-defining deliverance of Israel from slavery in Egypt. Such deliverance did not remove sin against Yahweh from their midst, but, in a manner constitutive of a later Christian view of redemption, left a people with the knowledge that their ever-present inclination to sin and rebel occurred against the backdrop of an ancient and yet continuing rescue.

Christian communities have recognized preeminently this saving hand of God in the life, death, and rising of Jesus Christ. This redemptive intervention of God in the life of humanity was completely gracious, undeserved by humans, freely given. In addition, the bodily resurrection of Jesus made clear in an ultimate sense God's valuing of the material world in which humans are ever engaged. Like the ancient Israelites, Christians, both in the early church and today, recognize that even persons already experiencing this redemption live nonetheless in human sinfulness and have to depend on the grace of God in their efforts to overcome their own inclination toward sin. Thus it is that the Christian moral life remains a life of response to the invitation of God. Salvation itself is not a prize earned through good works, but a life of faith is one committed to living lovingly and virtuously in accord with God's plan.

Although humanity will never bring about the reign of God on this earth, human striving to live in accord with God's gracious plan for life can make significant improvements in both individual and communal existence. It is in this context that Christian reflection on economic life has attempted to overcome the sinfulness that so often characterizes the lives of individuals and all societies. The drive to improve the lot of the poor can be helpfully understood in this context.

The requirement that the rich help the poor has been preached in each era and is a fundamental response to human sinfulness in the light of God's grace. Of course, this leaves the Christian with a dilemma in a world laced with inequality. On the one hand, God's plan for humanity is for a fullness of life including, though not limited to, economic prosperity. On the other hand, the character of God as one who demands justice for the poor, outcasts, and the weak requires that Christians struggle to assist those less favored in attaining the good life God envisions for all. It is clear that the theological endorsement of economic welfare ought not be allowed to justify a self-satisfied prosperity for the wealthy peoples of the world while multitudes of their fellow human beings live in squalor and deprivation.

At several points in the tradition, a radical redistribution of goods has been held out as the ideal. In ancient Israel, the Jubilee Year was to occur every fiftieth year, during which all property was to be restored to its original owners (Lev. 25:8-17). There is no evidence that the Jubilee Year was ever implemented, but it stands as a principle limiting the ever-increasing claims of property owners. The church in Jerusalem in the first century clearly practiced a radical redistribution of property, as Luke reports (Acts 2:44-45; 4:32-35). Yet this instance of communal property seems to have been unique in the early church. Though Paul, who received endorsement for his ministry from the leaders in Jerusalem, exhorted his new Christian communities around the Mediterranean to contribute to the "collection" in supporting the needy in Jerusalem (e.g. Gal. 2:9-10), he did not himself urge converts to hold their property in common and was eager to support himself economically so as not to be a burden for those to whom he preached. In Constantinople in the early fourth century, John Chrysostom proposed that the Christians of that city emulate the Jerusalem community and hold their goods in common, though that seems to have been more a rhetorical challenge than one he felt had any real possibility of success.[4]

While these examples of advocacy of a radical redistribution of economic goods represent a theologically important challenge to individualistic notions of ownership, they nonetheless stand outside the mainstream of the tradition. A complete explanation of this fact would take far more space than is available here, but the mainstream position might be summarized by saying that in every era—representing significantly different social, political, and intellectual contexts—the mainstream of the Jewish and Christian traditions has always been aware of human frailty and sinfulness. That is, sinfulness not only tempts the wealthy and powerful to exploitation; it also tempts all of us to shirk our rightful responsibilities if we were given a guarantee that we could share equally in the prosperity which the hard work and effort of others has brought about. Thus, for example, while Paul taught that the love Jesus preached required the wealthy to help the poor, he also cautioned that "anyone unwilling to work should not eat" (2 Thess. 3:10). This by no means eliminates obligations on the wealthy, but it requires better solutions to the problem of poverty than simple redistribution alone can provide.

INTERNATIONAL TRADE AND THE BIBLE

It would be a serious mistake to expect to find in the biblical sources a neatly transferable ethic of international trade for Christians today. At the same time, however, we would be mistaken to presume that international trade is a purely modern phenomenon. Ancient Israel's geographic location guaranteed the importance of international trade in its own history and, just as critically, ensured the importance of Israel for the trade of stronger nations both near its borders and far distant. The history of biblical Israel makes sense only when we understand the realities of international economic trade.

Long before the growth of identifiably Israelite settlements within Canaan in the twelfth century B.C.E., the territory was crossed by two main north-south trade routes. The first, now known as the "Via

Maris," extended from Egypt northward along the seacoast of the Mediterranean to what is now Lebanon and Turkey. The second, termed the "King's Highway," ran northward from the Arabian peninsula east of both the Gulf of Aqaba and the Jordan River into what is now Syria and beyond. Several east-west highways crossed Palestine, connecting these two. Any nation that controlled a substantial portion of the two main trade routes benefited not only from easier access to products but also from the duties customarily charged traders moving along them. Such control over movement on these highways is acknowledged early in Israel's story when Moses sought but was denied permission by the kings of Edom and the Amorites for the people of Israel simply to pass along the King's Highway (Num. 20:17; 21:22).

Through much of its history, Israel was a minor presence in the region, controlling relatively little territory, not on the major trade routes themselves. International trade undoubtedly occurred between Israel and its neighbors even then, but it is only with the fully developed monarchy that the biblical sources provide much information about these international economic relationships. The descriptions of economic prosperity under King Solomon allow us to view the economic forces at work.

With the collapse of the Hittite Empire at the end of the twelfth century B.C.E. and the division of Egypt into north and south kingdoms at about the same time, political and economic instability returned to Palestine. Scholars note the attendant loss of benefits that had been provided by secure markets and predictable patterns of trade, but they also cite the opening these changes brought about, allowing the emergence of a cultural, religious, and eventually a national identity for Israel.[5]

With the eleventh-century conquests of Saul in the Transjordan and his struggle to remove Philistine influence from the central hill country, the political boundaries for an eventual nation-state of Israel were drawn. Saul, David, and eventually Solomon, were able to isolate the Philistines in a small portion of the Mediterranean coast (roughly from what is now Gaza to Tel Aviv) and thus came to control the Via Maris, opening up a very profitable economic relationship with the sea-trading Phoenicians farther north, in what is Lebanon today. For example, Solomon set out to construct a temple of the Lord (as well as a royal palace) by importing cedar and cypress timber shipped down along the Mediterranean coast from Tyre, part of a broader agreement with Hiram of Tyre, a principal Phoenician leader (1 Kings 9:10-11). Control of the territories in the Transjordan similarly gave Israel control of a large portion of the King's Highway.[6] Solomon is described as building a fleet of ships in the port of Ezion-geber, at the northernmost point of the Gulf of Aqaba (1 Kings 9:26-28).

The vast wealth which the Scriptures describe as typifying Solomon's life arises from a number of sources. There was clearly the availability of slave labor brought about by the conquest of neighboring peoples. And, as the Scriptures reveal, substantial tax revenues were available to the king "from the business of the merchants, and from all the kings of Arabia and the governors of the land" (1 Kings 10:14-15).

The Scriptures leave us with many unanswered questions about trade, but it is clear that substantial portions of it were administered directly by the king and his household. Solomon "pays" for the cedar and cypress timber by giving to Hiram twenty cities in northern Galilee (1 Kings 9:10-11). Solomon imports horses and chariots from Egypt and becomes an arms trader himself by exporting some of these to the kings of the Hittites and of Aram (1 Kings 10:28-29). The famous visit by the Queen of Sheba to Solomon demonstrates the importance of Israel to the international trade of Arabia and indicates the diversity of products traded across national borders, not a small portion of which were for the luxury consumption of Solomon himself: spices, gold, and precious stones (1 Kings 10:1-13).

The chroniclers clearly identify God as the source of this prosperity. In another reminder of the morally positive status of material well-being in ancient Israel, the text reports that even the visiting queen recognized the God-given wisdom Solomon enjoyed. Solomon later becomes a tragic figure punished by God, but this is never attributed to his material wealth or abilities as an international economic and political actor. Rather, Solomon's heart was not true to the Lord in his willingness to follow other gods and to take wives and concubines from other nations contrary to the Lord's command (1 Kings 11:1-10).

While the account of prosperity under Solomon is clearly exaggerated for religious and political purposes, we can nonetheless see that the alliance with the sea-trading Phoenicians was remarkably productive for Israel. Scholars presume that it was Phoenician technology that allowed the landlocked Israelites to build a fleet of ships for sea trade at the Gulf of 'Aqaba.[7] The biblical texts report that Solomon's ships (no doubt sailed by Phoenician sailors) went to Ophir and brought back gold, silver, almug trees, precious stones, ivories, and even exotic animals such as apes and baboons (1 Kings 9:26-28; 10:11, 22). The exact location of Ophir is unknown, perhaps being in India or Africa, and the frequency of trade is uncertain, though the text reports that the fleet of ships traveled once every three years (1 Kings 10:22). Still, it is clear that the prosperity of Solomon and of Israel at this time was directly attributable to the alliance with Phoenician traders and the trade itself with far distant lands in addition to the more ordinary Middle East trade along the caravan routes.

Following the death of Solomon and the division of his kingdom, the Egyptians, under Pharaoh Shoshenq ("Shishak" in the biblical text), invaded Palestine, routing all armies there, destroyed the port city near Megiddo, and apparently exacted as tribute most of the treasures of Solomon as the price for sparing Jerusalem (1 Kings 14:25-26).[8] In character, the chronicler views Rehoboam's humiliation before these Egyptians as a punishment from the Lord for having abandoned the law. Nonetheless, it is also clear that the Egyptian incursion broke the trade monopoly Jerusalem and Tyre had built and from which they had benefited so richly.

The scale of international commerce is difficult to assess from this distance, but we have some clues. One of the fundamentals of trade in the era was frankincense, due to its religious importance in nearly all Mideast cultures. Made of resins tapped from trees in Arabia, frankincense was shipped in large quantities over long distances. Scholars report that in a single temple in the sacred Egyptian city of Thebes more than 30,000 bushels of incense were burned each year. Chaldean records indicate that as much as 250 tons of incense was burned annually in front of the altar of Baal.[9] In this commodity alone, the volume of trade (and the value of customs duties) was immense. Estimates of quantities in the ancient world are rare, but both biblical and other sources identify the variety of products. Solomon traded wheat and oil, and probably wine, with the Phoenicians (1 Kings 5:11).[10] In the midst of Ezekiel's lamentation over Tyre, we see vivid awareness, both of the extent of the multinational trade in which that Phoenician city was engaged and of Israel's own exports, including wheat, millet, honey, oil, and balm (Ezek. 27:17; 2 Chron. 2:7-10). There was even what we today would call international trade in services, as Solomon arranged for stonecutters, masons, and other construction workers to move between Tyre and Jerusalem for the construction of the Temple (Ezra 3:7; 1 Kings 5:13-18).

During New Testament times, of course, Palestine's relations with the outside world occurred under Roman rule. Both the archaeological and literary records indicate substantial international trade in the region. Fragments of marble, luxury goods, small ointment bottles, and other wares give evidence of such trade throughout intertestamental and New Testament times. Literary texts alone indicate that various towns in Galilee imported such diverse products as "Babylonian beer, Egyptian barley beer, smoked fish and lentils from Egypt, cheese from Bithynia, mackerel from Spain, imported wines, asses from Lydia, purple dye from Tyre, jewelry from Egypt, as well as parchment and papyrus."[11] Exports from the region of Galilee included vegetables, grain, olive oil, balsam, salted fish (from the fishing industry around the Sea of Galilee), and even some intermediate goods such as rushes for the making of rope.[12]

What are we then to make of this? The first response must be: Not too much. Biblical scholars have long cautioned against the simple transfer of social patterns from biblical times to our own. Still, we ought not to make light of it either. This is especially true for citizens of the United States born during the first half of the twentieth century, a time when the United States was less trade-dependent than any other industrialized nation on the earth. In a nation with little or no international trade, a "closed economy" in economic jargon, any prospect that prosperity or economic dislocation might be tied to international economic forces appears as an egregious loss of national self-determination. The biblical record and the experience of nearly all other nations ("open economies") of the modern world indicate that exposure to these influences is taken for granted and that the moral charge for the nation is not to eliminate such international relationships, but to structure life humanely within such forces.

Christian ethics, of course, recognizes the possibility for shaping our common life in ways not anticipated in the premodern world. This is, after all, the approach of Daly and Cobb in proposing a severely limited international trade. Because the biblical record alone cannot resolve such issues, we need more concrete ethical resources to correlate our questions about trade with the biblical and theological foundations of faith.

CHAPTER 4

ETHICAL RESOURCES RELEVANT TO THE DEBATE

A brief overview of biblical and theological themes offers little assistance in assessing international trade. The remedy is to draw from those themes ethical guidelines that are more concrete and that can be related to particular questions.

Even here, however, our guidelines will not provide neat answers to difficult problems. The history of Christian ethics has demonstrated quite well that differences among well-meaning Christians can exist side-by-side for centuries. It was only recently that Christianity as a whole condemned slavery and affirmed political democracy. It would be unrealistic to presume that Christian ethics can provide an unambiguous answer to moral questions about international trade.

Nonetheless, Christians can employ the following five guidelines to assist in the analysis of trade.

1. THE PRIORITY OF GOD'S REIGN OVER ALL INSTITUTIONAL FORMS AND INDIVIDUAL DECISIONS

Christian life is rooted in faith in God. Humanity stands in need of salvation, which only God can provide and which none of us can ever deserve. Thus if Christians are to be saved, it will be through the gracious act of God that this occurs. At the same time, however, Christian faith recognizes in Jesus, the Christ, that the saving hand of God reached out to humanity. Similarly, it recognizes in God's creation of the world a prevenient intention both for a proper order and for prosperity for humanity. As a result, Jesus' appeal to the reign of God is an apt metaphor for the historical presumption Christians make concerning both their individual and their collective lives. God's justice stands in judgment of all human life.

Christian ethics over the centuries has been far more attentive to the implications of God's reign for individual decisions than for the institutional forms within which individuals live. In fact some erroneously think of Christian ethics as focusing almost entirely on decisions that individuals make in their own lives. In the modern world, however, ordinary people—both Christians and others—have come to realize something not understood in earlier centuries: The forms of social organization within which people live are not only immensely influential but are also subject to change. How people organize their social, political, and economic lives in community has changed over the centuries within each culture and has developed differently in different cultures. Such patterns of communal life are not easy to alter, but their mutability opens the moral possibility of their improvement. As a result, Christian ethics understands God's reign over humanity to imply requirements not simply for our individual choices but for the way we organize our social life together.[1]

To gain perspective on the difficulty of assessing economic arrangements today, consider for a moment the attitude of Christians through the ages toward the possibility of political democracy and the end to autocratic rule by emperors, kings, and princes. For much of Christian history, democracy was nearly unthinkable. In the early church, simply surviving under the persecution of the empire was challenge enough. After a time of some optimism with the conversion of emperor Constantine, many Christians soon experienced the communal disabilities brought about when membership in the Christian church became socially advantageous. Rather than kindle hopes for a more humane political structure, this change instead brought about a reaction against the "watering down" of Christian life and faith. As a result we see both the establishment of monastic communities, where it was hoped Christian life could be lived more responsibly, and the rejection of the possibility of a Christian transformation of politics in Augustine's dichotomy of City of God and City of Man. Centuries later, Thomas Aquinas could consider democracy as an abstract possibility but exhibited a fundamental distrust of what "the people" could do, as illustrated in his rejection of tyrannicide as a moral option.[2] Martin Luther worked to reduce the power of ecclesiastical structures and stressed the ultimate importance of the relationship of the individual Christian to God's saving grace, and yet he condemned the rebellion of peasants against the political tyranny of the time. Even John Wesley, firmly committed to more modern notions of civil rights and liberties, lived throughout his life in support of the monarchy in England.[3]

These examples are not intended to discredit our theological predecessors. Each held up high moral standards for kings and other leaders of government. Such examples do illustrate, however, that even the most clearheaded and faith-committed of Christian thinkers did not envision something which most twentieth-century Christians now take nearly for granted: that political democracy is not only acceptable from the perspective of Christian ethics but—at least in the context of the modern world—is the optimal way for Christians and others to organize their political lives in accord with God's rule.

In an important way, the debate over international trade is a special case of the debate over the morality of markets and economic life, and more will be said about that debate later. Premodern ethical reflection on political life tended to focus attention on the moral requirements faced by individual political leaders. The move to an endorsement of democratic politics amounts to a recognition that the gospel mandate to love one's neighbor is better implemented politically through democratic procedures than through reliance on a king or prince. A similar question must then be asked concerning international trade. What does the reign of God require? There are lively differences among Christians as to whether trusting the market process will correspond to God's purposes for our common life or whether more particular rules and restrictions are required. In practice, of course, a combination of the two is inevitable. Thus, while all

65

Christians can endorse the principle of the priority of God's reign over both individual and group forms, its meaning is a tricky one. The meaning of this principle must be worked out in the analysis of policy.

Nonetheless, this general principle structures and grounds the Christian moral life—and each of the subsequent ethical guidelines in this chapter. In particular, it challenges all policy recommendations for simple procedural solutions, whether these are calls to "trust the market" or to "democratize all economic decisions." The outcomes of each policy option are to be judged according to the standards of God's reign.

2. LOVE OF NEIGHBOR AND A PREFERENTIAL OPTION FOR THE POOR

Christians place their faith in a God of love. Jesus, God's primary self-revelation to the world, consistently preached love of neighbor through parable and admonition and embodied this commitment most fundamentally in his own life and death. So central was this commitment to love of others that it was to be the distinguishing characteristic of his followers: "By this everyone will know that you are my disciples, if you have love for one another" (John 13:35).

Of course, love for others nearby was not a novelty; nearly all cultures promoted concern for friends, family, and members of one's own class. However, Jesus preached love of the poor, the outcast, those whom society rejected and demeaned. He admonished his followers not to seek the place of honor at table but instead to esteem those whom society dishonored, stressing a moral priority for the poor.

As we have seen, this commitment to the poor is deeply rooted within the biblical witness. The God revealed in the Hebrew Scriptures is a God who cares about the widow, the orphan, the stranger. This is a God who intends that creation meet the needs of all humanity, a God who knows that the powerful and prosperous can so easily forget the poor, whose needs are so often left unmet. In the late twentieth century, the traditional commitment to justice has

66

been identified with the phrase "option for the poor," borrowed from liberation theology.

The commitment of Christian ethics to this "option for the poor" is not only important for a responsible economic life but also illustrates some of the difficulties caused by developments in the understanding of moral obligations over the centuries. Although moral discourse today frequently employs the language of "rights"—including economic rights such as the right to food, clothing, and shelter—the Christian tradition prior to the modern period casts the argument somewhat differently: The focus there is on unmet needs. The fundamental reason for a response to the unmet needs of the poor is God's plan in creation and salvation and the commitment of the Christian to do what God asks. As a result, in focusing on needs rather than relative prosperity, the tradition does not call for an economic egalitarianism. Rather, it leaves the definite impression that if the economic welfare of the world's poor were secure, *differences* in income and wealth between rich and poor would not be morally problematic (even though wealth would still threaten to harden the hearts of the wealthy).

Christian ethical reflection, like all human thinking, is always embedded in culture. Biblical moral teaching, even from Jesus, was thoroughly Jewish. The early church slowly but steadily transformed itself from a Jewish mind-set to a Greek and Roman one. The best and most influential discourse about theology and morality in the Middle Ages as well as the Reformation lived up to the presumptions for responsible intellectual conversation recognized at the time. Thus when discourse about "human rights" becomes typical of moral arguments in the modern world, it is no surprise that Christian ethics should also recognize ancient moral claims as capable of being expressed in the language of rights as well. The mainline Christian churches have openly endorsed the notion of "economic rights" as adequately naming a claim of poor people, based on God's reign. Such rights must be implemented carefully to prevent the creation of dependency in the poor (itself a violation of their God-given dignity). But the Christian rejects the libertarian response—which denies the existence of both economic rights and our obligations to the poor.

It is helpful to note that the phrase "option for the poor" represents a stronger claim within liberation theology than within most European and North American theological perspectives. Many liberation theologians speak of this option as a type of *epistemological* privilege of the poor, arguing that the economic and political situation can only be understood when the Christian self-consciously takes the experience of the poor and oppressed as normative.[4] Doing so, of course, would helpfully disprove the false belief that the world is just—a view toward which the prosperous are perennially inclined. Nearly everyone involved in Christian ethics openly acknowledges that the experience and perspectives of the world's poor and oppressed are essential for moral discourse and are too often ignored. However, most outside liberation theology would argue that it is excessive, and in this case somewhat romantic, to assign a hermeneutically privileged position to the view of any one group.

3. COMMITMENT TO SUSTAINABILITY: STEWARDSHIP AND THE ENVIRONMENT

Because Christians understand that the world is God's creation, their relation to that world must respect the Creator's purposes for it. Discerning those purposes, of course, is a controverted process. And because we have only recently come to a general awareness of humanity's technological power to deform the biosphere, Christian theology and ethics are still working out an adequate analysis of environmental issues.

The conveniences of modern industrial society leave the well-to-do without much fear of the natural world except for occasionally destructive weather patterns. This, however, is a novelty. Humans—the vast majority today and throughout world history—have survived only out of a self-conscious wresting of the necessities of survival from a natural order that appears sometimes beneficent, sometimes maleficent, and most often simply indifferent to human survival. In times and places where hunting or subsistence agriculture characterizes the lot of most people, it is vividly clear that humans have much in common with the other animals inhabiting the planet: They must use, often forcibly take, other creatures that can provide food, clothing, and shelter.

In spite of such similarities, critical differences exist as well. Other animals do not possess human consciousness and thus do not share the requirements of morality. The hawk hunts the rabbit without moral deliberation and without need for moral argument. The biblical tradition has provided two fundamental moral warrants for humanity's use of the rest of nature. The first is the notion of God-given dominion: In the creation story God grants "dominion over the earth" to Adam and Eve and their descendants (Gen. 1:28). As we have seen, twentieth-century Christians have become vividly aware that this sense of dominion has in many ways been overextended, and recent theological attention has restricted this idea to a sense of stewardship, a standing in for the Creator in the household of creation. The second is the notion of creation of humans in "the image of God," endorsing a uniqueness of the human species on the planet and granting a kind of moral priority to humans while at the same time requiring them to respect a creation that lived in vital splendor before humans appeared and, except for humanity's threat, would carry on if humans vanished.

The modern, scientific awareness that creation existed long prior to the appearance of Homo sapiens has led many to recognize creation's intrinsic value, separate from any instrumental value it may have for human flourishing. The phrase "the integrity of creation" has come into frequent use in Christian ethics in an attempt to name that value, implicit in the biosphere, which humans have an obligation to respect. Some have preferred this language of integrity of creation over that of human stewardship for creation out of fear that the latter can feed into the well-proven arrogance humanity has shown in its relation with the rest of the natural world.[5] Nonetheless, because humans pose a real threat to the integrity of the biosphere and alone have the rationality capable of controlling that threat, the language of active stewardship in pursuit of sustainability seems equally appropriate.

In either case, however, the problem is to discern and implement a morally responsible presence of humans in the world recognizing that human flourishing requires the reorganization of the natural world in ways far more pervasive than we ordinarily think. Con-

69

sider, for example, a simple wooden table held together without steel brace or screw, surely one of the simplest of commodities in the modern world. This table, of course, requires only a tree. In addition, however, unless one calls for a return to a much simpler technological era, there is the chainsaw that cuts the tree, the truck that loads and transports it, the sawmill that transforms it into lumber, the woodworking shop that planes, rips, and joints the lumber and glues up and assembles the pieces, and the varnish and constituent chemicals that make up the table's final finish. Behind this process at almost every step are secondary industries, such as the capital goods producers who make the chainsaws, trucks, saw blades, jointer knives, and sandpaper, as well as the chemical industry making possible the glue for the tabletop, the chemicals for the varnish, the plastic in the workers' safety goggles, and the fuels that run the chainsaws, trucks, saws, and sanders. And, of course, behind these processes at almost every step are additional industries providing goods and services and requiring yet other industries in support. An item requiring "higher technology," such as the ordinary desktop telephone, has a more diverse list of inputs and sources, but the principle is the same. Each process begins when a natural resource is taken from its natural state and transformed by workers using tools which are themselves the result of such a process.

There are two critical dimensions of these processes that entail the responsibility of sustainability. The first is that natural resources are continually being "used up" in the production of goods deemed more useful to humanity than those resources in their natural state. The second is that these processes generate wastes whose presence in the biosphere almost always has unintended effects.

Of the two problems, discerning the requirements of sustainability in the consumption of resources is the more intractable and leads to the greatest conceptual disputes. Most attention here has been directed to the extinction of living species, with the crass commercial view valuing such losses at zero and "EarthFirst!" extremists on the other end of the spectrum condemning any human act that would result in such an extinction. The problem is complex, partly because species also disappear in nature without human influence. In addition, most species extinction today occurs not because of individually reprehensible acts but because of a pattern of use, usually the

70

destruction of habitat, where the loss of any one acre is immaterial but the accumulated transformation of wilderness into farms and suburbs has such effects. Nonetheless, a commitment to biodiversity is an essential piece of the broader commitment to sustainability.

Another cluster of issues concerns the consumption of a nonrenewable resource, such as petroleum. Although there are morally important dimensions of this problem, the worry about "using up" all of a resource represents a misconception because it looks upon natural resources on a par with flour in the pantry bin. The problem is that the flour could be completely used up to the last spoonful while exhaustible natural resources cannot, because there are extraction costs that vary with the location of the resource. Humanity first taps those sources for, say, petroleum, which are the least costly. As the resource becomes more scarce, sources that are more difficult to tap are used, raising the cost of production and the purchase price in the marketplace. The last barrel of oil on the planet will never be extracted because its cost of production would be far higher than its value in producing energy. In fact, the economics of exhaustible resources argues that vast reserves of oil, coal, bauxite, or any other mineral will never be completely harvested because of the role of pricing in the marketplace. As increasing scarcity hampers the extraction of one resource, another substitutable resource (a "backstop technology") begins to be used when the price of the original resource rises above the price of the alternate. Thus, the issue is not that of complete depletion but that of continued use, up to the point of substantially higher prices for those resources.

Although we will not literally "run out" of oil or coal or any mineral, there are two important moral problems related to this process. The first is the equity of a system when prices rise, rationing scarce resources to those interested and able to pay for them. On both a national and a world scale there is a critical responsibility of the wealthy to offset the harm done to the poor by such higher prices for life's necessities. The second, more closely related to sustainability, is the implicit presumption in the economic analysis that there *will* be a backstop technology that will eventually take over as prices rise.[6]

The second problem concerns the generation of wastes and their effects in the biosphere. Here we can helpfully distinguish between global and local processes.

Those issues of sustainability which concern inherently destructive global processes require both the most careful attention and the most thorough cooperation among nations. Global warming, brought about by the "greenhouse effect" of increasing proportions of carbon dioxide and other heat-trapping gases in the atmosphere, is a prime example. The depletion of ozone in the upper atmosphere caused by the emission of chlorofluorocarbons is another. The second process could ultimately threaten nearly all life on the planet through an overexposure to harmful solar radiation. The first threatens to induce significantly higher ambient temperatures (perhaps as much as 5°C during the coming century) that would raise sea levels, inundate coastal areas, and alter vegetation patterns and farming around the globe. Although there are important scientific debates about the urgency and character of such changes, a stewardly concern for the integrity of creation requires prevenient action to offset current trends.

Concerning local and regional problems of sustainability, there is a quite widespread agreement that such "external costs" ought to be paid by the producers of those costs, and perforce, by the consumers who buy and use their products. Frequently costs are "paid" through a governmental prohibition of certain acts, as when an industrial paint shop is required to "clean up" its emissions of toxic fumes. At other times, a "green tax" may be assessed, as European nations have done for decades with sizable taxes on gasoline, designating the revenues for programs, for example, to reduce air and water pollution in the nation.

Designing public policy that addresses each of these issues is a controverted process, involving differences in empirical, moral, and other presumptions about the world. Sustainability stands, however, as a moral requirement for economic life. Although creation is necessarily altered and "used" in human flourishing, it remains a gift, deserving of respectful treatment in the continuing presence of the Giver.

4. CONCERN FOR FELLOW CITIZENS AND FOREIGNERS: MORAL EQUALITY AND DIFFERENCE

Jesus' teaching concerning the two great commandments to love God and neighbor has pressed Christians over the centuries to strengthen the bonds of existing community and to stretch the boundaries of those communities to include ever more distant others. This can be seen as a continuing effort toward universalism, slowly restraining the provincialism, nationalism, and other forms of communal egoism to which the history of the world so readily attests. Including the stranger in Israel (along with the widow and the orphan) in the list of those for whom Yahweh has special concern was clearly an effort to offset the nationalistic moral norms that typified life in the ancient Near East. Jesus was asked, "Who is my neighbor?" and he responded with a story of virtue exhibited by a member of a hated foreign class. Paul's preaching of Jesus to the Gentiles argued that in Christ there is neither Jew nor Greek. This trend toward greater inclusiveness can be seen in a variety of theological and religious developments. In the relativizing of political claims accomplished by Augustine and Luther, in the universalizing of ethical standards by Thomas Aquinas, in the nineteenth-century social gospel movement, and elsewhere, Christian ethics moves toward transcending concrete communities and asserting the just equality of all human persons as children of God.

This commitment to love of neighbor, however, can also be understood as a deepening of communities that already exist. Christian ethics has traditionally recognized the importance of "special relations" and the concomitant obligations existing, for example, between spouses, parents and children, friends, and even fellow citizens.[7] The notion here, of course, is that we owe more to some people than to others. This does not require a judgment that these people are fundamentally superior or more deserving than are those with whom we do not share any special relation. It is based, rather, in a relationship, in the commitments implicit in existing community. Thus, the same moral principle that calls for parents to spend more time, energy, and other resources on their own children than on other children in the neighborhood also leads citizens of the same town or nation to spend more of their resources on fellow citizens than on persons farther removed. While the responsible Christian nonetheless "cares"—in both psychological and material senses—for persons outside such special relationships, he or she nonetheless "cares more" for those within. The vast mainstream of Christian thought throughout the ages has given moral approbation to this distinction, in spite of and in addition to a continuing appeal for the curtailment of provincialism and nationalistic ethical impulses.[8]

It is difficult to sort out the theoretical requirements from the practical possibilities. The rise of national social welfare programs such as Social Security or unemployment insurance is an example of both the deepening of community and of the universalizing thrust of concern for others, pressing people of one group or class in a nation to invest in the well-being of all other citizens. This is a significant moral achievement. Still, we must recognize that such programs (and many other positive aspects of national life) are only achievable with the existence of barriers to immigration that prevent the system from being overwhelmed with the needs of the many who wish to immigrate. Within the United States, for example, "point-of-entry" states like Florida and California are already bearing significant burdens from current immigration, both legal and otherwise, and "open" borders would swamp the system and dissolve the tenuous political consensus currently supporting a variety of "welfare" programs for the poor.

To extend this principle to international trade, some have argued that just as we owe more to fellow citizens than to others in the realm of education, health, food, and housing, so we also owe more in the realm of shelter from international economic competition in employment. Protectionism here would be interpreted as a strengthening of community, as Cobb and Daly have so eloquently argued.

At the same time, however, the universalizing dimension of the Christian's love of neighbor presses the ethical analysis of international trade to recognize no preference for the advantages of one's fellow citizens over those of people living elsewhere on the globe. Because so much of the debate about trade focuses on its good or bad results, this might be interpreted as calling for a kind of international consequentialism, where the issue in employment, for example, is not whether trade would cause the loss of jobs in one's own nation but whether the worldwide effects of trade on employment

74

are positive or negative as a whole. From this perspective, a job that improves the economic well-being for a citizen in the developing world ought not to be valued as less important than a job for someone living in the industrialized world.

There is a morally important difference between, on the one hand, actions that positively assist others with whom we have a special relation without any direct negative effects on others and, on the other hand, actions that assist those morally closer to us by cutting benefits or increasing costs to others more distant. Raising taxes to fund job training or health services for fellow citizens has no immediate negative impact on citizens of other nations. The inequalities (between the poor of the developing world and the now better-off poor of the industrialized world) created through this process are lamentable in the sense that such provisions would optimally be available for all persons on the planet. However, those inequalities are not morally objectionable in themselves. On the other hand, to the extent that there is a trade-off between jobs in different parts of the world, a moral argument to prefer jobs at home is at least morally suspect.

Although there are authentic ethical differences here, the greater portion of the disagreement seems to be founded on differing empirical estimates of the effects of trade (for example, concerning the number and quality of jobs to be created by trade in the developing world) rather than on different moral assessments of the value of or obligations to persons at home or abroad.

5. THE ROLE OF SCIENCE IN ETHICS: NEITHER MASTER NOR VALET

The single most influential intellectual development over the past five hundred years has been the rise of science. Of course, the ancient Greeks and Chinese had science, but it was more limited in its reach and integrated within broader humanistic studies. In the modern world, science has unlocked the secrets to a multitude of natural mysteries that subsequently allowed the application of technology to transform the world in myriad ways. In fact, the spectacular effectiveness of the physical sciences has raised not only their own stature but also that of their sister social sciences in the minds of both scientists and laypersons alike.

Undergirding an appropriate intellectual respect for science is the instinct which Paul Tillich once referred to as "humility before the fact." In both the natural and social world, it is all too easy simply to presume things are the way we'd like them to be. Thus we might wish that farm chemicals present no risk to ground water supplies (but they do), or we might be inclined to interpret rape as primarily an act of sexual passion (which it isn't), or we might presume that welfare grants to the poor will have no effect on the incentive to work (yet they will). In each case, the role of science, whether physical or social, is to assist us in correcting our own perceptions of how the world around us "works." The three brief answers above in parentheses—that farm chemicals pollute ground water, that rape is an act of violence, and that welfare programs affect incentives—are generally accepted results of careful scientific study. These results can still be disputed, but only the irresponsible would attempt to resolve such disputes without scientific analysis of the factors involved.

Christians should recognize, then, that the world can indeed be shaped, but not in any way we please. Both physical and social life exhibit patterns or regularities that range from the malleable to the unyielding. There are debates within science about the robustness of these regularities and corresponding debates within ethics concerning the moral appropriateness of those which are mutable. It is interesting to note that political "liberals" and "conservatives" exhibit a willingness to challenge or respect regularities on differing issues. For example, "liberals" tend to challenge social regularities which appear to them as oppressive of women or ethnic minorities, but are more likely to respect the natural limits in nature and to call for a curb in the economic destruction of the environment. "Conservatives" often advocate maintenance of what they see as the natural regularities in social relationships like marriage and the traditional family and yet often exhibit considerable confidence that human ingenuity will eventually resolve problems caused by the apparent natural limits of the ecosphere. There is simply no hope of resolving such differences without an appreciation for science as an independent source of insight to which ethics—Christian or otherwise— must at times defer. Moral conviction should not be allowed to substitute for scientific understanding of causal relationships. Science, then, must not be a simple valet, with ethics or religion as its master.

At the same time, however, science should not be perceived as the master. Confidence among philosophers of science in "the scientific method" as the paradigm for all human inquiry peaked early in the twentieth century at a time when the "objectivity" of science received its greatest accolades. More recent decades have seen a growing consensus among philosophers and historians of science that science itself is a social project and its grasp of the "objective facts" a matter of agreement among the scientists involved.

Nonetheless, it is not uncommon for those attempting to shape public policy to run up against social scientists, perhaps most often economists, who have so much confidence in their theories that they view science as the master of social policy, ruling entirely out of court many alternatives which others may wish to pursue. Outside of social science, this arrogance about "what is really causing" our current problems and about "the only hope for true change" appears as a matter of the ideological commitments of the social scientists involved, arrayed on a political spectrum from Marxists on the left to libertarians on the right. Even within social science, all too many attribute their opponents' scientific results (but not their own) to ideological commitments. More helpful is the view that such differences are attributable to alternative choices concerning scientific method and that these choices are themselves not defensible by appeal to scientific methodology alone. Thus, science should not be seen as master, with ethics or religion supplying only the goals for public policy.

The problem for Christian ethics, then, is a complicated one. On the one hand it relies heavily on science for understanding how the world works. On the other, the well-informed layperson must be realistically aware of the competing explanations—particularly within social science—and must adjudicate among them on not only ethical but scientific grounds as well. Although the scope of this inquiry into international trade does not allow for an examination of these broader issues, this volume, as an example of interdisciplinary inquiry, may contribute to a more general assessment of the interaction of science and ethics.[9]

SOCIAL ETHICS AND THE ROLE OF GOVERNMENT

Debates about good economic policy inevitably entail the participants' views of markets and government. The standard "conservative" or pro-market view argues that markets allow individuals the freedom to try to attain their own goals and that the heavy hand of government is always attempting to subvert that freedom and define goals that some other group would endorse. Those on the left see markets as the arena where the wealthy and powerful take advantage of the poor and weak, and they understand government as the only hope for redressing the injustices which self-interest in markets will inevitably effect.

The gap here is obviously wide and the constraints of space permit our treating the topic only briefly. At its best, the Christian tradition has been accurately realistic about the interaction of individuals in institutions, and it will be helpful to reconfigure our thinking about markets and government. Because of a fundamental awareness of the effects of original sin, Christian theologians throughout the centuries have recognized the fundamental insight named by Augustine in the notion of "the city of man." Governments are essential in limiting the injustice to which sinful pride and self-interest lead. Thomas Aquinas taught that right order in institutional life required that the political authority enforce laws because not everyone has a well-formed character leading them to choose a virtuous life. For Luther, the secular order of law and authority rightly used secular, compulsory methods. John Calvin's ideal of a holy community entailed a robust role for government in securing the reasonable welfare of its citizens.

At the same time, the Christian tradition has been vividly aware of the temptation toward excessive power on the part of governments. In earlier eras this took the form of an ethical condemnation of the tyranny of emperors, kings, and princes. In the twentieth century it has taken the form of an affirmation of participatory democracy and an endorsement of the political and economic rights of individual persons. Too much of our public discourse is cast as a choice *between* markets and government. Markets must be structured and limited by communal (governmental) restrictions.

It is helpful to understand government involvement in economic issues as setting the ground rules or boundaries within which individuals and organizations meet with each other in markets. One can, then, understand a market as a "space" where people interact with one another through voluntary agreements (for example, buying and selling, agreeing to contracts, etc.) where it is presumed by all involved that individuals will look out for their own interests.

For nearly all of us, of course, self-interest is not all we will look out for—our moral commitments will lead us to be friendly to strangers, help coworkers, and so forth. The moral character of the people who make up any society is critical for the success of any institutional arrangements: both for the political choice of good ground rules for those institutions as well as for virtuous acts of various sorts in situations where the institutions don't require them.

Still, most know and accept the basic logic of market transactions that individuals enter markets to accomplish their goals. As a result we do not and ought not to feel guilty when we seek a promotion or look for the very best farm produce at the grocery store. Similarly, we expect that the local Ford dealer's "sale price" on a new car is basically an attempt to make a profit without losing customers to the Chevrolet dealer across town.

Whether and to what degree this endorsement of self-interested activity "works" in society depends immensely on "the rules of the game." Though they rarely advert to it, there are a multitude of restrictions on self-interested action without which even "conservatives" would not endorse the interplay of self-interest, because of the evil that the powerful would effect. Thus, for example, we have made it illegal to kill or physically threaten one's competitor as a way of gaining an economic advantage. Large corporations no longer debate the use of such tactics, but commerce has not always been this way. Drug cartels and organized crime syndicates find such procedures quite effective. Rather, the history of commerce shows that it is only when laws against violence eliminate the business advantage of "thugs" that other moral characters take on leadership roles in economic life. A similar story can be told about laws that prevent eight-year-olds from working fourteen-hour days, or require workplace safety standards, or mandate a Social Security system.

It is helpful, then, to think of markets as an arena within which society morally legitimates the self-interested interaction of individuals. The arena itself is bounded by law, and a good deal of the commercial law in industrialized nations amounts to restrictions on activities in which self-interested individuals might otherwise engage, but which are now kept outside the arena of legitimate market behavior.

Michael Walzer has coined a term that aptly describes many of these prohibitions: the blocked exchange.[10] Although most things are fair game for buying and selling, there is a long list of possible exchanges prevented or "blocked" by law. Thus, the laws of most industrialized nations today do not allow the buying or selling of human beings, cocaine, hand grenades, the votes of legislators, the votes of citizens, the obligation to serve in the armed forces, the judgment of the courts, and so on. Ways around some of these prohibitions certainly exist, but they stand blocked in principle, and society regularly attempts to strengthen the barrier to them by better law or more effective enforcement.

In addition, there are a host of other exchanges which, while allowed in some circumstances, are regulated in one way or another. Although it has become popular in recent years to criticize the bureaucratic excesses of regulation, such criticism often clouds the underlying reality that most citizens, including a majority of economic conservatives, would support many of these basic restrictions on activity. Included here are regulation of "insider trading," the sale of prescription drugs, the disposal of hazardous waste, health standards for restaurant kitchens, safety standards for nursing homes and coal mines, and so on.

Interestingly, this understanding of the necessary relation of government and markets not only applies to more or less "capitalist" nations but also describes the economies of totalitarian states. Consider even the Soviet Union before its collapse. That government had far less confidence in individual interactions in the market than was true in the West, but, for example, once the production (or import) of consumer goods was decided upon and consumer prices were set, there were basically market forces at work determining whether and how Russian citizens spent their consumer rubles.

Envisioning markets as an arena bounded by laws within which the assertion of self-interest is morally legitimate does not solve the "real" problem of determining whether any current restrictions ought to be removed or whether any currently legal activities ought to be regulated or prohibited altogether. What this understanding of the relation of government and markets does accomplish is to eliminate the simplistic rhetoric on each side. On the one hand, it contradicts those conservatives who preach against "government" as if human life or even economic life would be better without any "government interference." On the other hand, it calls to realism those Christians who would endorse only altruistic behavior in economic life and who often criticize the activities of large economic actors such as multinational firms or labor unions simply on the grounds that they are acting out of their own self-interest. It does not resolve the issues of power in international trade—of the government, of transnational firms, of the wealthy—but it provides a framework within which conflicting moral and empirical claims about power can be adjudicated.

Critical to all these discussions is the notion of justice in Christian social ethics. A full treatment of this notion lies beyond the scope of this volume, but it is helpful to recall that justice has traditionally included three interrelated dimensions in Christian ethics. The first is that individuals have an obligation to other individuals with whom they have made contracts or agreements. This is the dimension of justice most self-evident in modern society. If I make an agreement with you, I am obliged in justice to fulfill it. The second dimension is an obligation all persons have to contribute to the well-being of the community. Rooted in the covenant of the Hebrew Scriptures, the Christian notion of obligation to the community entails a requirement that the able-bodied both contribute to the community's production and support shared institutions. The third dimension arises from God's gift of creation to humanity: Justice requires that the prosperity of the well-to-do meet the needs of those who are unable to provide for themselves.

Within this understanding of justice, there are many concrete public policy issues that need to be addressed, including the moral status of profit-making firms, labor unions, and governments; the rights and responsibilities of workers and of employers; the responsibility to overcome the evils of racism, sexism, and other injustices. A brief investigation into the rights and responsibilities of property ownership from a Christian perspective will be helpful, both for its importance to issues of trade and as an example of how Christian ethics can provide insight into a variety of public policy debates.

PRIVATE PROPERTY: A LEGITIMATE BUT LIMITED CLAIM

God's creation of the world has dramatic implications for the meaning of private property—implications that conflict with the understanding of property pervasively held in the industrialized world today. A typical view today is that ownership of property grants to the owner an almost absolute control of the item owned and its uses. If I own something valuable and yet choose to destroy it, my neighbors may think me foolish but few will think me immoral for not having given it away instead.

And yet a judgment of immorality would be exactly the verdict handed down by the Christian tradition for such an act. At root here is the biblical doctrine of creation. The world around us has been created by God with a purpose: Moral use of the material world, then, must respect that purpose. We have already seen several restrictions on property ownership characteristic of the Hebrew Scriptures.

The leaders of the early church give ample evidence that this was Christianity's position from the beginning as well. Ambrose of Milan argued that "God has ordered all things to be produced so that there should be food in common for all, and that the earth should be the common possession of all."[11] Calling on the common-sense notion that the earth and human beings existed before human laws about property ownership, early Christians understood that whatever prerogatives the legal system granted to property holders, these ought not to undermine the fundamental intention of the Creator that the world should provide for the needs of all creatures. As a result, Augustine taught that "the superfluous things of the wealthy are the necessities of the poor. When superfluous things are possessed, the property of others is possessed."[12] Elsewhere he added,

"Those who give something to the poor should not think that they are doing so from what is their own."[13] The leaders of the early church left no doubt that the wealthy had an overwhelming responsibility to share their prosperity with those whose needs were unmet. This perspective, of course, openly conflicted with the more absolute view of property that prevailed in Rome during the empire.

This perspective on property was developed even further in the Middle Ages by Thomas Aquinas, in his pairing of Aristotle's notion of the *telos* (goal or end) of life with the biblical understanding of God's purpose or goal in creating the world. For Aquinas, God's goal in creation is "built into" each creature. Thus, the healthy tree grows toward the sun in accord with God's plan and in doing so fulfills its "nature" as a tree. Humans have been granted a free will and thus have a choice whether to fulfill their natures as God intended. Nonetheless, the "natural law" ethic Aquinas delineated allowed the person to use human reason to assess what God's intentions were in creation and then use willpower to act in accord with those intentions. Thus in his discussion of private property, Aquinas observed that private ownership is not required by the natural law (since presumably the initial creation in the garden occurred without private ownership). However, he argued, it is not contrary to natural law and, like clothing, is an appropriate addition to natural law because it is helpful.[14]

When he asked whether private property is morally justifiable, Aquinas distinguished two aspects of the relation between persons and property. The first is the authority to make decisions concerning material goods (the power "to procure and dispense" them) and the second is the actual use of the thing possessed.

Concerning the former, Aquinas cited what we today would call "efficiency" reasons for justifying the procuring and dispensing of material goods by individuals. First, each person is more willing to exert effort to obtain and care for property when it is owned individually than when owned in common. Second, things are more orderly when it is clear who has responsibility for some physical possession. And third, a more peaceful state of affairs will exist in society when there are no disputes as to who has the authority to make decisions about the use of each object.

In regard to the second aspect, however, Aquinas seems—from the modern point of view—to turn the tables. When it comes to the actual *use* of goods, the owner is to respect the intention of God embodied in the nature of those very goods: They are to be used in common. In perhaps the most dramatic conclusion in all of Aquinas' writings, he asks whether a poor person urgently in need of sustenance might simply take food from someone who has an abundance if that is the only alternative. Like the early church and biblical witnesses before him, Aquinas appeals not to the "rights" of the poor person (a modern moral notion) but rather to the plan of God. If I have an abundance of bread in my pantry and refuse to share it with you who are starving, I am violating, in Aquinas' terms, the nature of the bread. That is, God's purpose was that bread should feed hungry people and I am preventing this from happening. As a result, Aquinas argued, when the poor one in dire need takes the bread, it is "neither theft nor robbery."[15]

The great figures of the Protestant Reformation, Martin Luther and John Calvin, objected strenuously to the philosophical arguments of Aquinas and the Roman church. Yet in spite of their rejection of what they saw as an overconfidence in human reason, their view of the limitations of private property was remarkably similar to Aquinas'. In time of famine, and for widows unable to work, Luther recognized the possibility that righteousness would allow a return to the love-communism of the garden and could legitimate stealing bread from the baker.[16] Similarly, Calvin envisioned that within the holy community material benefits are produced by dedication and hard work in order that the basic needs of all be satisfied, with the wealthy contributing to the well-being of the less fortunate.[17] In a similar vein, John Wesley preached three simple rules: "Gain all you can; save all you can; give all you can." Those who lived up to the first two rules but ignored the third were, in Wesley's words, "twofold more the children of hell than ever they were before."[18] The wealthy were to share their abundance with the needy because this is God's design for life.

There are several implications of the Christian doctrine of property for issues related to international trade. The first and most obvious is that the wealth enjoyed by the industrialized nations of the north carries obligations in justice not only toward the poor of their own nations but toward the impoverished of the rest of the world as well. Thus, negotiations about international trade should incorporate "concessions" for developing nations, particularly for those with the most severe problems of poverty. In addition, the limitations on the rights of property owners undergirds the moral claim of communities (and their governments) to legislate particular limitations on property owners, for example, zoning ordinances, eminent domain, income taxes, and environmental regulations. Thus, those persons and businesses involved in international trade stand under an obligation to respect the local decisions of communities in which they operate, and they actually bear the responsibility to *promote* just regulations in nations where illegitimate governments have failed to implement them. Libertarian claims—that each owner deserves complete and autonomous control of all assets—are undercut. National governments are charged with devising policies for trade that promote the common good. Still, of course, this does not resolve all the issues, since the most important debates over trade concern not whether governments have the right to intervene but, instead, how trade should be properly structured.

CHRISTIAN ETHICS AND PUBLIC POLICY

The move from religious faith to ethical foundations to concrete public policy is not a simple one. Diversities in the intentions of the participants, the character of their dialogue, the sources to which they appeal for authority, and a variety of other characteristics obviate any direct transposition of religious principles into obvious policies.

James Gustafson has provided a helpful typology of what he calls "the varieties of moral discourse."[19] He distinguishes prophetic, narrative, ethical, and policy discourse. Each is an appropriate and authentic form of moral reflection and conversation, but they differ immensely in their style and context.

Prophetic discourse takes on two different forms: indictment and utopian vision. Prophetic indictment condemns current failures and vividly illustrates the chasm between human society as it is and what it ought to be. Utopian prophetic discourse sketches the outlines of an ideal human community, engendering in its positive depiction a lure for contemporary believers. Both forms of prophetic discourse employ dramatic symbols and language, evoking a sense of urgency on the one hand and a lure on the other. Prophetic discourse exhibits a capacity for motivation that is lacking in the more abstract forms of ethical and policy discourse.

Narrative moral discourse sustains the traditions of a community through concrete stories about earlier figures and events in that community's history. As narrative theologians have articulately argued, such narratives are constitutive of communities, not simply dispensable additions to them. Narratives can sustain communal life while prophetic, ethical, and policy discourse tend to take such communal foundations for granted.

By ethical discourse, Gustafson refers to "more philosophically self-conscious and rigorous modes of moral argumentation."[20] Ethical discourse attempts to clarify ideas and claims such as "justice" or "rights." It is attentive to philosophical arguments about the foundation for moral decision making (for example, debates about deontological or teleological ethics). It presses each moral argument to "make sense," valuing both its intellectual foundations and its internal coherence. It challenges prophetic, narrative, and policy discourse to be more self-critical and intellectually respectful of diverse points of view.

Public policy discourse, according to Gustafson, "seeks to determine what is desirable within the constraints of what is possible."[21] It is written from the perspective of persons responsible not simply for critique of evils but for the feasible organization of community. Although it does not treat all regularities as permanent, it is attentive to the limits of change in such human and natural patterns. It challenges prophetic, narrative, and ethical discourses to be more "realistic" in striving to achieve only what is possible, particularly in a pluralistic social setting where well-meaning groups differ in their fundamental commitments.

Each of these four plays a critical role in the community's overall moral conversation, and none is sufficient without the others. Although prophetic discourse undercuts pretense and short-range goals, it is less helpful to persons and groups needing to make incremental choices caused by the conflict of goods. Although narrative discourse undergirds communal self-identity, it is far less helpful in the inevitable moral dialogue with others outside that faith community. Although ethical discourse strives to improve the clarity of ideas and moral arguments, it does not provide the motivating capacity or undergirding symbols that communities require. Although policy discourse attends more carefully to the difficult trade-offs required in concrete political action, it is inevitably more shortsighted than the other three modes of discourse and often provides little opportunity for the exercise of moral imagination.

This volume can be seen as straddling the border between ethical and policy discourse with primary emphasis on the latter. It focuses on a number of concrete policy issues related to international trade, highlighting the interaction of economic insight with ethical principles. Attempting as it does to implement the foregoing ethical guidelines in a world where possibilities are constrained in many ways, it remains vulnerable to prophetic critique from those who take one or another of the principles as the nonnegotiable bedrock commitment of Christian faith. Those more inclined to recognize trade-offs among competing goods will find it more useful.

We have just concluded an all-too-brief look at biblical and theological sources and a number of consequent ethical resources relevant to the issue. Ethical judgments about trade need to take into account particular issues. What would be the effects on family farms of increased international trade in agricultural products? How would farmers in the developing world be affected? Would this be just? Does increased international trade further threaten the earth's environment and thus violate the principle of sustainability? Do reduced tariffs on manufactured inputs lead to the transfer of jobs out of the industrialized nations and into the Third World? Will this cause greater economic hardship for those workers in the industrialized world who are already at the bottom of the employment hierarchy? Will it help Third World workers who got the new jobs? How do we weigh these effects against one another?

These and a variety of related issues will get closer attention later. First, however, it will be helpful to recognize that the debate over international trade is heavily influenced by a variety of intellectual convictions which participants in that debate bring with them from the outset.

CHAPTER 5

BACKGROUND COMMITMENTS

We've all experienced a lively disagreement with someone else. At its best, disagreement challenges our lazy assumptions, provides evidence we had not previously considered, and can lead us to reconfigure our notions about ourselves and the world around us.

There are, however, times when disagreements don't seem to be very productive. This happens most frequently when we understand ourselves to be discussing a particular issue with someone holding a different point of view but find that time and again the other produces arguments that seem to us to be extraneous to the topic at hand. Our sense is that, rather than debating the issues we set out to address, our conversation partner is for some reason trying to shift the focus of the discussion toward a different set of issues. We can often, of course, learn from the relationship which the other sees between the two sets of issues. However, the conversation is unproductive for us if we conclude that the issues are not nearly so closely related as the other thinks and yet we never do return to a careful discussion of the original topic.

This shift of focus away from the topic at hand, of course, could be an intellectually irresponsible trick. However, what concerns us here is when the other is acting quite responsibly but judges that some other set of issues "in the background" is so important and the conclusions from them so clear that they must take precedence over the debate internal to the topic.

In discussions where that topic is international trade, various participants to the debate sometimes revert quickly to other sets of issues, such as damage to the environment, the excesses of government, the mistreatment of the poor, judgments about the superiority of capitalism or socialism, and so on. The problem for a book on international trade is that, for all the importance of these other issues, they cannot practically be addressed in the same volume. One possible procedure is simply to ignore them altogether. It is more helpful, though, to acknowledge them and to attempt to identify the underlying differences that participants to the debate bring with them from those background conversations.

In analyzing the sources of disagreement in policy discourse, Ralph Potter has identified four elements of moral arguments: empirical factual data, theological or quasi-theological perspectives, decisions regarding fundamental loyalties, and modes of ethical reasoning.[1] Moral decisions are far more complicated, he observes, than simply applying ethical reasoning to the empirical situation.

Commitments akin to Potter's quasi-theological perspectives and fundamental loyalties can be seen playing powerful roles when brought into the debate over trade. They will here be called "background convictions," and they include a variety of commitments, loyalties, presumptions, perspectives, social analyses, or ideological (not in the pejorative sense) positions that are held at a very basic conceptual level. Of course, no social scientific or social ethical assessment of issues *internal* to the debate on trade can be resolved without reference to larger frameworks, but because some of those larger frameworks so often go unannounced when the narrower issues of trade are debated, it is helpful to identify them separately.

Each of these background issues is a complicated matter worthy of intensive and sustained pursuit independently. Thus, there should be no illusion of resolving them here. At their worst, however, such background convictions can insulate participants to the trade debate from responding to, understanding, or in some cases even listening to the arguments of others about the various effects of trade.

BACKGROUND COMMITMENTS AFFECTING THE DEBATE ABOUT TRADE

1. Markets and Multinationals

It is no surprise that attitudes about the usefulness and appropriate scope of markets correlate strongly with attitudes about the extension of markets across national boundaries. Because large multinational corporations are the primary parties to international commercial agreements, attitudes about such transnational organizations are deeply influential.

At a more fundamental level, of course, convictions about "capitalism" and "socialism" are extremely powerful, particularly among those who understand their opponents' positions simplistically. Examples here include both those on the right who assert that, because of the fall of the Soviet Union, socialism is dead (even though socialists in the rest of the world have for decades rejected the Soviet model), as well as those on the left who acknowledge only the damaging effects of multinationals or attribute to them only the most rapacious of motives.

Even among those less inclined to ideological extremes, background commitments concerning markets often exert excessive influence. Included here are those introductory economics textbooks that never get around to explaining the limitations of the theory of comparative advantage that Cobb and Daly identify. Equally problematic are treatises on the 1989 Canada-U.S. Free Trade Agreement, such as the one where the author's own conviction that transnational businesses are the primary beneficiaries of the agreement leads him to attribute to the advocates of trade the *intention* to "maximize" the profits of multinationals as the only means of increasing economic welfare.[2]

91

2. *Democratic Government: Its Efficacy and Orientation*

Divergent assessments of the capacities of democratic governments also influence perspectives on international trade. Ironically, those on the left and on the right tend to agree that one of the fundamental problems with democratic governments is their susceptibility to control by special interests.

Those on the left tend to view the powerful economic interests of the wealthy (and the multinational firms they control) in all nations as nearly determinative of national policies on international trade. The primary hope on the left is that democratic governments can be influenced to cut the benefits currently going to multinationals and increase protection of the environment and workers in industries threatened by trade.

Those on the right, particularly conservative academics, tend to rely on "public choice theory" to argue that democratic governments will predictably respond to special interests of one sort or another and thus cannot be trusted to intervene wisely in markets. This perspective identifies the distorting effects of special interests of both capital *and* labor that attempt to alter the rules of the game to serve their own goals.

Understandably influential is the national historical experience with democratic governance of any participant to debates about economic policy. Thus it is extremely rare for participants in Canada or the United States—nations with long traditions of peaceful political transition—to consider a violent subversion of the political process. In a number of developing nations, however, a larger proportion of participants feel compelled to consider a violent overthrow of the prevailing political system. Obviously, with less confidence in the ability of the current system of government to act in accord with fundamental values, one will be less likely to conclude that a system of international trade can be justly structured.

Where the left tends to ignore or downplay the benefits of international trade, those on the right tend to do the same to its destructive effects. Ultimately, those on the left have higher hopes for government and call for broader governmental powers in the structuring of trade, even though they are not particularly optimistic about the possibilities of reducing the influence of the wealthy on national and international policy concerning trade.

3. Nationalism: National Identity and Interests

It is no mystery that throughout human history international trade has been viewed by smaller and less powerful nations as a threat to national identity and cultural independence. Economists of the German historical school in the nineteenth century ridiculed the high-minded arguments of classical British economics, which favored free trade, as a disguise for an economic policy that simply served Great Britain's own national economic interests. Similarly, many Canadians today who oppose the Canada-U.S. Free Trade Agreement and NAFTA do so out of a concern that Canadian identity and independence are threatened by these versions of international trade.

The threats come in two general forms. The first and most influential is that foreign multinational firms will have increased power over the lives of domestic workers and consumers and that they will be even less accountable than domestic firms. Included here, for example, is the cultural apprehension of the French in their continued resistance during the Uruguay round of GATT negotiations to opening French markets to Hollywood entertainments.

The second sort of loss of autonomy feared is that brought about by international trade agreements themselves. There have been a number of complaints against the General Agreement on Tariffs and Trade (the GATT) and its successor the World Trade Organization for stressing economic productivity and ignoring environmental and social concerns. An example that has angered many United States citizens is the well-heralded tuna-dolphin decision by the GATT, striking down a U.S. law designed to protect dolphins but which was judged to violate the GATT ban on extrajurisdictional restrictions on methods of production.[3] Critics of the Canada-U.S. Free Trade Agreement argue that many democratically chosen environmental policies in Canada concerning forests, fisheries, and the environment have been and will continue to be challenged by American firms contending that such legislation gives an unfair advantage to Canadian producers.[4]

93

Everyone involved in the debate on international trade begins with *some* assessment of both the importance of national autonomy and the threat to it posed by increased trade. Such judgments inevitably affect the moral evaluation of trade.

4. *Environmental Problems: Severity and Urgency*

As we have seen, concern over damage done to the environment by international trade motivates much of the critique of trade agreements. Assessments of the importance of environmental values and of the current threat to them are critically important ethical elements. In an ideal world, debates over environmental problems would be resolved before a view of international trade were constructed. In practice, the two are interrelated; convictions about the one have important feedback effects on convictions about the other, and vice versa. The diversity of views on the global environmental situation is immense.

Large numbers of Christians, including sizable numbers of Christian theologians and ethicists, have come to a heightened concern about the fate of the ecosphere. Though Christians generally do not count among their number radical environmentalists who would subordinate the life prospects of humans to those of the rest of the natural world, there are many with remarkably strong assessments. Donald B. Conroy, president of the North American Conference on Religion and Ecology, asserts that

> we find ourselves confronting yet another holocaust of unimaginable destruction. The threat is to air, water, food, animal species, forests, in fact to all the ecosystems of the planet on which we and future generations will live.[5]

Conroy not only views such threats as comprehensive but judges them as more important than any other problem we face:

> Compared to these ecological concerns, all other social or economic problems pale. Wouldn't it be tragic if, after ending the Cold War and avoiding the possibility of nuclear holocaust, we citizens of Earth found ourselves on a dead planet—with an uninhabitable moonscape to call home?[6]

94

At the same time, however, critics of the environmentalist movement from the other end of the spectrum accuse it of faulty science and a hidden agenda:

> Modern socialist utopian movements, like much of the environmental movement, stress the need to look into the far future . . . and to impose great present sacrifices to ensure the goodness of the outcome of that distant future. . . . Those movements are willing, by virtue of their fantastic pretensions to knowledge, to grant colossal powers to the state.[7]

In a series of recent books, critics on the right have excoriated environmentalists for oversimplifying science, playing on the news media's penchant for calamity, and pressing for sizable misdirection of public and private funds amidst unwarranted "scares" concerning alar, asbestos, dioxin, and other issues.[8]

Sorting through the competing claims about environmental issues is not an easy task and certainly cannot be undertaken here. Discrepancies in background convictions about the severity and urgency of environmental problems affect and at times seem almost to determine assessments of international trade and the economic growth it encourages.

5. Equity: The Importance and Character of "Distributional" Issues

Economic change brought about by the interaction of self-interest in markets is oblivious to most moral claims unless those claims have previously been integrated into the "rules of the game" within which the interactions occur. The classic example concerning international trade is the decision by a firm to close a plant in one nation in order to move production to another. It is quite likely that many firms will ignore the economic hardship of displaced workers, their families, and the local community unless the legal structure of the economy requires them to attend to it, through advance notice of plant closing and the provision of funds for retraining and relocation.

Participants to the debate about international trade who have by prior commitment very little interest in equity issues (or perhaps hold a view of equity that endorses market outcomes), do not acknowledge equity concerns as evidence against international

95

trade and thus have more reason to favor trade. Some even farther to the right have more simplistically asserted that markets should not be held responsible for injustices arising from "pre-market distribution" of property rights.[9] Similarly, many with strong concerns about improving international equity are aware that powerful economic interests (such as local elites and multinational firms) can often exact concessions from less powerful groups (like workers or even governments). This conviction leads some to assert that multinationals *inevitably* exploit Third World peoples, rendering international trade by multinationals inherently unjust. Others who favor greater international equity recognize that historical patterns of unjust income distribution in developing nations are, unfortunately, highly robust, but they conclude that the lot of the poor there is unlikely to improve without the dynamism of economic growth.

It is no surprise that background convictions about equity heavily influence debates about international trade.

6. Employment and Unemployment

Employment issues loom large *within* the debate about international trade. Still, however, there are two critically important background issues concerning employment that deeply affect the debate.

The first concerns the relation of workers to owners of capital. Those who oppose international trade out of concern for working people tend to share a single view about employment relations. They tend to picture an adversarial relationship between firms and employees and tend to value highly trade unions as a countervailing power against large corporations. Many argue that workers' economic well-being can be substantially improved by law, in effect forcing a transfer of power from owners to workers. This perspective interprets the growing rates of unemployment in most industrialized countries over the last thirty years as evidence of the growing success of large firms in their struggle with working people. In this view, unemployment and wage-stagnation in nations such as the United States and Canada are proof that wealthy corporate interests can prevent national governments from undertaking national economic policies that would benefit working people.

The mainstream economic view of the same set of circumstances interprets the interests of firms and employees as largely coincident. From this perspective, workers do better when the firms that employ them do well and do worse when those firms incur losses. Most economists argue that the basic determinate of workers' income is their productivity and that governments can make only minor improvements in workers' economic well-being by trying to force a transfer of power from employers to employees.

The second background issue related to employment concerns national macroeconomic policy related to unemployment. Most mainstream economists believe that above certain levels of unemployment, the inflationary pressures caused (by employee groups pressing for higher wages and firms pressing for higher prices) will lead not simply to higher inflation but accelerating inflation, with successively higher levels of inflation each year. As a result, economists talk about the "NAIRU," the non-accelerating-inflation rate of unemployment.[10] Although stable inflation can be tolerated, they argue, the unpredictability of accelerating inflation is both economically destructive and politically untenable. From the mainstream economic perspective, wise central bankers will not attempt to reduce the unemployment rate below the NAIRU, although the nation might wisely try to reduce the NAIRU itself. This might be accomplished through certain changes in labor markets, such as more education, particularly for low-skilled and unemployed groups, better services in assisting the unemployed in finding available jobs, and (from a laissez-faire perspective) even a cut in unemployment benefits and in the number of labor unions.

Critics of this perspective tend to view a nation's rate of unemployment as a policy variable over which national policy, at least in large economies, has sizable control. Current historically high rates of unemployment are understood as the outcomes of policy choices made to further the interests of the wealthy rather than to protect the interests of workers ready and able to work but unable to find employment.

It is no surprise that background convictions here powerfully orient arguments on trade.

7. Economic Growth and the Welfare of the
Poor in the Developing Nations

Particularly among Christians and others committed to reducing world poverty, one of the most influential of background commitments concerns the presumed effects on the world's poor arising from economic growth in developing nations, with or without increased international trade. Those divided on this background issue often differ on their concrete expectations of the patterns of growth and adjustment in developing nations. They can also disagree about the prospects that Third World governments will adopt the proper strategies for equitable growth and thus differ on the question of the most appropriate political stance to take to influence continuing growth.

Those who take the position that trade-induced economic growth will not help the poor in the developing world generally argue that it is multinational firms and local elites who will direct the course of economic growth and be its primary beneficiaries. If a particular sector of the economy, whether agriculture or industry, expands, that sector becomes more attractive to owners of capital, who will move quickly to buy up newly valuable assets and leave the poor worse off than before. This prospect for Third World agriculture in particular has often been argued in opposition to increased agricultural trade.[11] While a few of the poor gain as a result of somewhat higher wages, a larger number are seen as excluded from the process. Vast numbers migrate from the rural areas to urban slums and live in a deeper and more dehumanizing poverty than before.

Those on the other side view economic growth as the best single hope for increasing the economic welfare of the poor. From this perspective, an increase in prosperity for the owners of capital, whether agricultural or industrial, coincides with an increase in the aggregate wages paid to workers and most frequently with an increase in the number of jobs as well. In many parts of the world the poor themselves are landholders and benefit directly from higher land values. Disruption of traditional patterns of employment and indeed some migration is seen as an unfortunate side effect which inevitably attends such economic growth. In the longer term, it is argued, the greater prosperity for those employed in the now-expanded sectors will spill over to other areas of the nation as these workers spend their now higher incomes. This is the basic approach of the World Bank, the International Monetary Fund, and most other international agencies related to economic issues.

The two sides also often disagree in their presumptions about the prospects for politically responsible decisions by national governments and international agencies. Those who are skeptical about the positive effects for the poor of economic growth tend to hold the view that Third World governments are far more responsive to their middle and upper classes than to the poor and more responsive to urban interests than rural. They tend to presume that international agencies cause at least as much harm as good and that the most beneficial thing First World governments can do is to slow down the nearly inevitable steamroller of economic growth and marginalization of the poor. Many on the other side share the skepticism about Third World governments' interests in attending to the welfare of the poorest classes, but they conclude from this that general economic growth in the nation is the single best hope for those currently most disadvantaged. The first group points to the example of Brazil, where significant economic growth has occurred with very little of it assisting the poor, and the second group looks to the model of Spain since its entry into the European Union or to the newly industrialized nations of the Far East, where general economic growth has significantly benefited the least advantaged groups.

8. Technology: Promise and Risk

Over the past century, technology has changed so rapidly and has had such a pervasive influence that just about everyone can agree on two dimensions of our technological future. The first is that it is nearly impossible to predict what technological advances will occur. The second is that our common human fate will depend more and more on the influences of technology, be they good or ill.

There is a panoply of current and anticipated problems in which technology plays a pivotal role. These are the focus of daily newspaper reports and scientific studies: greenhouse gas emissions and global warming, developments in land and air transport and the congestion these cause, acid rain, carpal tunnel syndrome, nuclear proliferation, the depletion of world petroleum stocks, and the

99

prospects for commercial nuclear fusion. The list goes on. While each of these issues involves complex technological processes and judgments, one can hear within the debate about international trade (as well as in many other particular debates) general presumptions about the prospects and risks of technology that seem heavily influential.

Some approach every issue with a strong technological optimism, downplaying the physical limitations of the planet in light of the creative productivity of the human intellect. The optimists see the world as getting better and better, and they judge from history that optimism about technology's ability to solve our problems is the only reasonable course.

At the other end of the spectrum are those who see modern technology as the primary cause of the list of world-threatening problems we face. In a market system where profitability rather than benefit to humanity or the planet is the criterion for technological development, there is no wonder that we have created as many problems as we have. From this point of view, the technological optimists base their naive extrapolations on two centuries of recent good fortune, a brief span of geological time in which we have consumed much of the earth's store of resources and absorptive capacity, which took untold eons of planetary history to produce. From this perspective, it is simply human arrogance to count on uncertain technologies or to hope that further scientific study will show that large threats like global warming really won't materialize after all. Instead, this approach recommends a technological humility and immediate changes in public policy and lifestyle to anticipate the possibility that outcomes may be bad and irreversible.

Although most people are at neither end of the spectrum, an overall judgment about the promise or threat of technology in the future is often heavily influential in debates about international trade.

9. A Spiritual Assessment of Economic Growth and Consumption

As indicated in the first step of Adam Smith's argument about market exchange, central to the economist's view of international trade is the conviction that more economic goods are good for people. Christian ethics has in each age taken a nuanced approach to this issue, affirming that economic goods are good and a part of God's plan for the benefit of humanity, while at the same time warning of the distracting and religiously deadening effects of excessive wealth, particularly in the presence of the poverty of others. Arising from this latter danger is an argument against more international trade because it promises to increase consumption levels and consumerism in the industrialized world.

While many Christians share this concern, few have themselves opted to forgo all or even most modern conveniences, rendering morally ambiguous any vigorous condemnation of trade on these grounds. Aware that their restrictions on international trade and finance will indeed have an impact on material living standards, Daly and Cobb explicitly advocate "a frugal and disciplined life" in recognition of the spiritual challenges ahead. Although they do not anticipate a radical drop in living standards, they cite the Amish as responsible examples for their readers.[12]

Obviously background convictions concerning the possibility for responsible Christian living by the world's well-to-do will powerfully influence narrower judgments about trade and economic development.

10. Models of Change: Crisis or Marginal Change

Mainstream economists generally presume that nearly all change is incremental (i.e., "marginal") change and that only very rarely is there the sort of abrupt, all-or-nothing change that leaves no room for adjustments in response. On the other hand, some critics of international trade tend to employ a crisis model, pointing to severe problems now or soon to come that must be dealt with definitively. Describing the differences a bit simplistically, we might observe that while some have never in their lives employed the language of "crisis," others rarely make an argument without it.

Obviously, proponents of these two general approaches to change can each point to many individual events and policies for empirical support. That is, neither side begins simplistically with a model of change and then imposes it on the facts of international trade. Yet it seems more than coincidental that those who regularly see crises in other arenas of life perceive the negative effects of trade as creating a crisis. Similarly, it is no surprise that those who recognize only incremental change in life also anticipate a smooth adjustment to any dislocations caused by trade. Presumptions about change influence perceptions of trade.

CONCLUSION

What has been accomplished by naming and briefly examining these ten background commitments? On the one hand, very little. Each of these topics is itself an immense issue concerning which tomes have been written and debates continue. On the other hand, if any one of us entering the debate about international trade can first acknowledge the existence of these background commitments, particularly those about which we hold strong opinions, it may assist us and others to differentiate among the various reasons, evidence, and conceptual commitments that we bring to the debate about trade. Without this effort we may, in Roger Hutchinson's words, be insisting on "a framework for discussion" which itself "predetermines the outcome of the debate."[13]

No claim is being made here that it is inherently wrong to take strong positions at one or the other end of the spectrum on any one of these background issues. Each requires a separate and extended conversation. If one does ultimately settle into a strong position on one of these background issues, that "commitment" will likely have a strong effect on one's assessment of increased international trade and a host of other issues. All this can occur in an intellectually responsible manner.

Still, strong background commitments bring significant dangers in train. These can be seen if we consider the effect of political alliances between diverse groups who hold similar practical policy positions concerning international trade, or for that matter, concerning any significant policy question. The political process of democracy regularly brings together persons of diverse intellectual and cultural commitments when they share a common political goal. Such *political* alliances can be quite morally responsible on the part of both groups and are not the focus of attention here.

The problem arises when strong background commitments lead to an *intellectual* alliance without responsible consideration of the issues. Persons who bring very strong background commitments to the debate on trade—in the sense that their position on trade depends completely or heavily on their position concerning some particular background issue—too often succumb to a destructive temptation. They often uncritically accept, support, or at times even extol the intellectual arguments of political allies concerning the strong background commitments that brought those allies into the alliance. A few examples will illustrate.

Many whose commitments about environmental problems lead them to a negative assessment of increased trade have allied themselves with other opponents of trade who have strong background commitments concerning employment. While any one person might come to a series of careful judgments in each of these areas that links them together, all too often the environmentalist who opposes trade on environmental grounds simply accepts the intellectual arguments of the other group without responsible attention to the alternative points of view in the debates on the extent and causes of job loss. Likewise, when persons on the right hold strong background convictions about the need to reduce the influence of government, they may not only endorse a deregulation of trade but uncritically accept the intellectual arguments of anti-environmentalists simply because they are on the same side of the trade issue politically. These two examples focus on the interplay of trade with background commitments concerning the environment, government, and employment. Any number of permutations among the various background issues is possible.

It is no easy intellectual task to arrive at a responsible position on any one of these background issues. Yet, once we have come to a very strong conviction about one of them, it takes an even greater intellectual discipline—as well as an unusually strong moral commitment to dialogue—to challenge our political allies for not having thought through their own positions carefully enough. When we hold a strong position on a background issue central to our view of the world, we all face the strong temptation either to ignore the writings of those who oppose us or to read them solely to find and later expose their weakest arguments. The need to budget our time and psychic energy renders nearly irresistible the temptation to ignore the writings of our allies' strongest critics. In a world where most people live with and talk to people much like themselves and where those who read about public policy issues tend to read magazines, books, and journals espousing opinions much like their own, careful attention to the intellectual diversity on each of these background commitments is sorely needed.

This much said, the issues internal to international trade still need examining. We now turn to the three main clusters of issues most at stake in debates over international trade: agriculture, the environment, and employment.

CHAPTER 6

TRADE AND AGRICULTURE

The debate over international trade in agricultural products is dominated by the changes that have occurred in agriculture in industrialized nations over the past two centuries.

Christian faith has always cherished community and the trust that people have in one another based on ties that bind. Many urban residents are unsure of their own physical security and relate throughout the day to a long list of anonymous clerks, attendants, and voices on the phone. In contrast, the shared familial histories and pervasive mutual familiarity typical of small rural communities stand as vital though endangered reminders of the loss of community in modern urban life. Because of such concerns, articulately expressed in the work of Daly and Cobb and others, many participants in the debate about international trade share a commitment to the preservation of "the family farm." From this perspective, the trend in agriculture is not a healthy one, and further international trade in agricultural commodities can only accelerate it.

Proponents of international trade tend to take the line we saw Adam Smith endorse in an earlier chapter: If consumers can buy food more cheaply from foreign sources, they should do so. Economists, well known for their support of expanded trade, have been opposing government efforts to restrict trade in farm products at least since David Ricardo's opposition to the British Corn Laws.

Those who object to expanding international trade point instead to the loss of the family farm and the transformation of rural life in industrialized nations. The vibrant network of small towns, each a few miles apart, each supporting scores of small farms, has disappeared. Countless rural towns have dried up altogether, and many others are commercially threatened as intermediate-sized cities forty or more miles apart become the commercial centers for most of the economic activities of farm families today.

A critically important part of this process has been the move to larger and larger farms, bringing about what economists refer to as "the economies of scale." But this, of course, entails fewer farmers as more and more small farms are bought up into larger ones. As figures 6.1 and 6.2 indicate, in the late nineteenth century approximately 50 percent of all jobs in Canada and the United States were in agriculture. The absolute number of jobs in agriculture peaked early in the twentieth century, but by then represented only about one-third of all jobs in each nation. Today, agricultural jobs make up about 3 percent of the total.[1] The picture is quite similar in Western Europe and Japan. Although everyone still needs to eat, the economic importance of agriculture as a provider of jobs has dramatically declined.

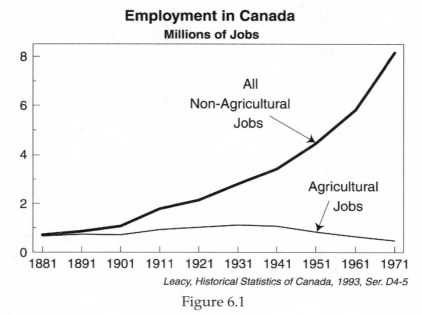

Employment in Canada
Millions of Jobs

All Non-Agricultural Jobs

Agricultural Jobs

Leacy, Historical Statistics of Canada, 1993, Ser. D4-5

Figure 6.1

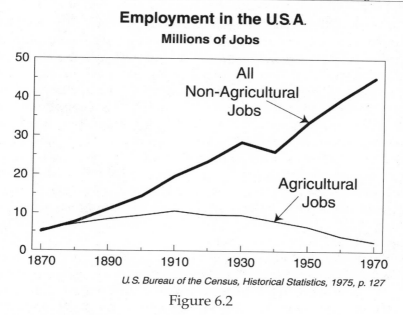

Employment in the U.S.A.
Millions of Jobs

U.S. Bureau of the Census, Historical Statistics, 1975, p. 127

Figure 6.2

With fewer farmers, there is need for fewer grocery and hardware stores, fewer seed and implement dealers, fewer cafes and clothing stores, and even fewer churches and towns.

Those attempting to reverse or at least slow this process and ensure a future for the family farm generally support the current system of government subsidies for agriculture in the United States, Canada, and other industrialized nations. They are aware that such programs unfortunately tend to help large-scale farming operations more than those smaller farmers they would prefer to assist,[2] but such subsidies appear to many as the only politically feasible means of stemming the tide that is otherwise certain to swamp smaller farms and the rural communities they sustain.

Critics of increased international trade in agriculture tend to attribute the demise of the small family farm to one of two causes, each pressing farming to become "monocultural agribusiness." The first of these is the influence of large agricultural commodities firms, who purchase farm products and market them at home and abroad. Small farmers often feel they are at the mercy of the profit-maximizing price structure of these giant traders. More frequently, attention is directed toward a second cause: the influence of national policies,

107

particularly in the United States but in Canada as well, in developing technologies and structuring advantages for large-scale farming operations. These include agricultural support programs and tax policies as well as the research orientations of U.S. land grant universities and Canadian agricultural colleges, which have invested huge sums over the past century in "high tech," large-scale agricultural research and have worked hard to disseminate the techniques developed there throughout the countryside.[3] As Daly and Cobb have phrased it, "It is federal policy that has destroyed family farms in so much of the country, not any inherent weakness in the family farm system."[4] Many groups seeking greater justice in the United States and Canada have lamented the number of bankruptcies of hardworking farm families in recent decades and have sought national policies to counteract them.

Christians need to be concerned with the future of community and with injustices done to families, whether urban or rural. However, it is a mistake to attribute the main trends in agriculture over the last century to national policies. Such policies—along with large commodities firms—have assisted in this progression, but they have been a secondary force.

It is a far worse mistake to claim, as one justice-oriented publication does, that "such hard times are even more morally unacceptable because they happen despite the high productivity" of modern farmers.[5] This position is not only inaccurate but actually gets cause-and-effect completely backward. The growth of farmers' productivity is one of the two primary *causes* for the drop in the number of farmers from a vast majority to a tiny minority in industrialized nations today.

TWO POWERFUL ECONOMIC FORCES

Debates over international trade in agricultural products cannot be resolved on scientific grounds alone: Important moral and political decisions are at stake. Still, participants in this debate will continue to joust with phantom opponents until they come to a greater appreciation of the causes behind the transformation of modern agriculture. There are two that stand out: rising agricultural productivity and the character of consumer demand for food.

Rising Agricultural Productivity

Much of what is now the agricultural center of Canada and the United States used to appear far less promising. In the early nineteenth century, Major Stephen H. Long, on a mission to explore the Great Plains of the Louisiana Purchase, wrote that the region between the Missouri River and the Rocky Mountains was "destined by the barrenness of its soil, the inhospitable character of its climate, and by other physical disadvantages, to be the abode of perpetual desolation."[6] Today, large parts of that region, and of many others in Canada and the United States of similar promise at the time, yield a bountiful harvest that was previously unthinkable. Why is that?

The single most important force in the transformation of agriculture over the past two hundred years has been the dramatic increases in productivity of farmers themselves. When the first farm families arrived on the edges of the Great Plains of Canada and the United States early in the nineteenth century, they typically tilled a few acres and kept some livestock, all to provide adequate food for the coming winter. Before the construction of the railroads, very little of their farm produce was sold, and that was marketed locally to cover the cost of those few supplies—like salt, sugar, and oil—which had to be purchased from the outside. It was a rewarding but a difficult life.

Nearly all the families who moved out onto the Great Plains in the nineteenth century were accustomed to farming on land that first had to be cleared of trees. Although the clearing itself was hard work, the availability of nearby timber for buildings, fences, and fuel, and the supply of drinking water from creeks and springs were considered necessities of farming life. Farmers poised to move onto the Great Plains saw a land without trees for heating homes, with roads that turned to mire in the spring rain, with a need for deep wells, without abundant rock and timber for construction, and with a rich but difficult soil that the familiar horse-drawn plow couldn't handle.[7] Looking back on that era, we can see that changes in technology were immensely influential.

The cast iron plow was developed in 1797 and improved twenty years later with interchangeable parts. These were effective in well-drained soils, though their brittle parts too often broke. The larger problem was that even once polished, cast iron surfaces were covered with small cavities, which increased friction and prevented the moldboard, the large curved blade of the plow, from releasing sticky soils and turning the furrow.[8] When John Deere developed the steel plow in 1837—and further improved it a number of times subsequently—he enabled farmers to deal with the rich and sticky Midwest prairie soils.

The first mechanical reapers were developed in the 1830s, but it was only with continuing improvement that they became widely used. Labor conditions as well made an important difference. Canada's preferred trade position with Great Britain created something of a Canadian agricultural labor shortage in the 1850s, during the Crimean War, when Canadian farm products were in great demand overseas. With increased demand for labor in the building of the railroads and even departures for the Pacific gold rush, Canadian farmers faced a sizable rise in the price of labor and as a result, turned to labor-saving farm equipment far more rapidly.[9] With the improvement of the threshing machine, corn planter, grain drill, mowing machines, and revolving disk harrows throughout the nineteenth century, agricultural productivity rose dramatically.

Just as important, however, were improvements in technology outside agriculture proper. Developments in well-drilling machinery not only made water for habitation easier, but in arid regions made water for range animals a possibility. Changes in transportation were even more important. Slow improvement in road construction helped local transportation, but it was the building of the railroads in Canada and the United States that truly transformed nineteenth-century agriculture. Prior to the arrival of the railroad, it was not uncommon for farmers in western Canada or the United States to raise four bushels of wheat as cheaply as an Eastern farmer might raise one. Yet without a market in the West, the Eastern farmer's one bushel sold for more.[10] With the spread of railroads

110

throughout the Great Plains in the second half of the nineteenth century, farmers not only had access to markets farther afield but had the incentive to invest in improvements to their land and in more productive horse-drawn machinery, allowing them to till and harvest more acres per year.[11]

Improvements of agricultural technology in the twentieth century were even more revolutionary. The single most important of these was the farm tractor. Manufacturing enterprises had gained the advantage of steam-powered machines nearly two centuries earlier, but it was not until the invention of the internal combustion engine that a practical alternative to the horse became available to farmers. The widespread use of tractors began after World War I. Following the Second World War electricity became widely available on Canadian and United States farms through government-subsidized rural electrification programs. The electric motor transformed myriad farm chores, and electricity came to be depended on to light the barn, chill the milk, and "candle" the eggs.

We should not bear any illusion that all of these technological changes held only positive effects. Farmers are human like everyone else, and they tend to overlook social costs—problems felt by others but caused by the farming operation—when making production decisions. In deciding how much fertilizer to use, the farmer is inclined to compare the cost of fertilizer with the increase in revenue it brings about. Overlooked in the process are the effects of nitrogen and phosphorus runoffs into streams and nearby lakes, often causing overgrowth there. Environmentalists have decried the nutrient-rich runoff from the great sugarcane fields of Florida that are endangering the Everglades. Runoff from pesticides and herbicides into groundwater has effects felt far from the farmer's home. Large irrigation operations are dramatically lowering the levels of irreplenishable underground aquifers, threatening to use up in a century waters that have taken millennia to accumulate. Removing windbreaks to make way for larger equipment and plowing up and planting threatened soils has led to dramatic increases in wind and water erosion, causing sizable losses where the soil is deposited as well as significantly decreasing the fertility of the farmer's land for future generations.

Twentieth-century farmers operate at much larger scales than their nineteenth-century predecessors and thus have indeed harmed the environment more severely. However, we should recall that many a nineteenth-century farmer was guilty of nonsustainable methods. Some would sow wheat year after year until the field returned only half a crop. Historical records show British visitors well versed in agricultural practice standing scandalized by the cropping methods of many Canadian farmers, whom they accused of mining the soil. Slipshod tillage, a lack of crop rotation, and in many cases not even applying animal manure back on the land had led to the exhaustion of some soils in Ontario as early as 1820.[12]

Nonetheless, whether new or old, farming practices that exploit the environment unsustainably ought not to be tolerated. The many advantages caused by improving productivity through new technologies do not in any way legitimate the damages caused along the way. As with pollution caused in manufacturing, it will take governmental regulation to prevent such abuses. Responsible farmers, like responsible factory managers, will remain at a competitive disadvantage until communal restrictions prevent irresponsible farm operators from despoiling the environment.

At the same time, these changes in the productivity of modern farming have had a number of positive effects. The single most important of these is a rise in the economic welfare of farmers themselves. Almost everyone understands the reason that today's manufacturing workers are economically better off than the manufacturing workers of a hundred years ago: Workers today produce more and better products every hour. Picture the tool-and-die worker today who operates computer-controlled equipment capable of machining carbon steel tools with an accuracy of thousandths of an inch. The analogous process a century ago required great skills (some of which workers today no longer possess), but it was slower and the equipment far less precise. The capital goods produced by the modern worker are far more powerful, in part because of the increased precision which has come alongside an increase in units produced per hour. As a result, today's tool-and-die worker has an income far higher than that of earlier such workers and far higher than similar workers today in, say, developing countries where

112

older processes may still be used. The key here is that an increase in hourly productivity is the primary reason for increases in hourly wage and economic welfare.

The same has been happening in agriculture. Farmers today are far better off economically than their forebears of a century ago, not simply because they live in a richer nation—though that helps—but because they themselves produce more during each growing season. A brief but telling vignette is provided by one study of the changes experienced by an Ontario farm family between 1850 and 1860.[13] Grain and hay harvests improved, more of the wooded land on the farm was cleared, the open fireplace gave way to a cooking stove and candles to coal-oil lamps. The always clean farmhouse floors began to be covered with carpets, and the spinning wheel and loom were displaced by purchased cloth and a sewing machine. The economic welfare of farm families was rising because farmers were producing and selling more.

This dramatic increase in productivity has been accompanied by larger and larger average farm sizes in United States and Canadian agriculture. It is true that some farms formerly owned by a family are now nonfamily "corporate" farms (about four-tenths of 1 percent of all farms in Canada,[14] about three-tenths of 1 percent in the U.S.[15]), but the vast majority of small farms that have "disappeared" have simply been bought up by a neighboring family ready to farm more acres than before. It is also true that nationally funded agricultural research and the dissemination of information on techniques to improve farm productivity have encouraged farmers to move to larger-scale farms in order to reap the benefits of the economies of scale available with larger machinery and new techniques. Yet to attribute this choice of larger-scale, higher-productivity techniques to such outside forces is to miss the underlying decisions that farmers themselves have freely made.

Farm families have appreciated the advantages of rural life, but they have also valued most of the amenities that a higher standard of living earlier brought to their urban counterparts. Thus, with the availability of more education, better seed varieties, labor-saving farm machinery, and a host of other developments, most farmers, generation after generation, have chosen higher-skilled, higher-technology production methods to increase their productivity and their incomes.

113

Some technological developments have increased productivity per acre, as figure 6.3 shows, for some crops. Most farmers in the United States and Canada own the land they farm and have a clear incentive to increase productivity per acre. In fact, if government policy were driving changes in agriculture, it might reasonably be a policy strongly directed toward increased production per acre—in order to get as much as possible out of the farmland acreage of the nation. But as figure 6.4 indicates, far more dramatic changes have taken place in the number of hours that farmers tend each acre.

Why has the number of labor hours per acre decreased? Farmers didn't simply become less attentive to their crops. Clearly, the ability to tend more acres per hour is the primary cause. This, in general, comes from the use of larger-scale machinery, allowing a farmer to plow or disk or plant or harvest more acres per day than was possible with older technologies. As figure 6.5 indicates, increases in productivity per hour have vastly outstripped increases in productivity per acre. It is difficult to look at that graph and to deny that farmers themselves (the primary beneficiaries of increases in productivity per hour) are the driving force behind this historic change in agriculture.

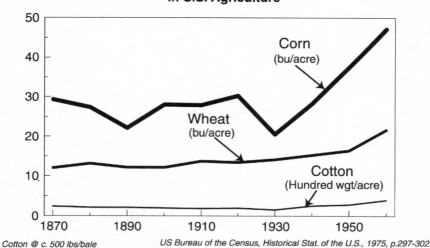

Figure 6.3

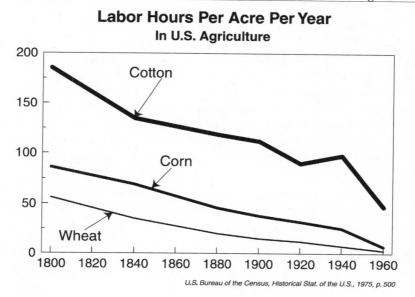

Figure 6.4

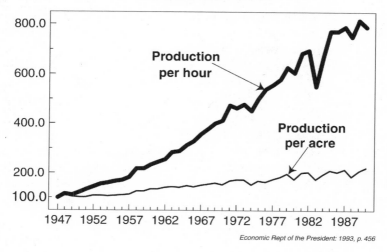

Figure 6.5

The interest of farmers in being about as prosperous as urban workers has been the main force leading to larger farms, fewer farmers, and fewer rural towns to support them. Of course, rising farm productivity isn't the only force at work. Simultaneous developments in transportation have made greater mobility possible. In the time that their great grandparents needed to drive the buggy a few miles into town for supplies, today's farmers can take the pickup truck thirty or forty miles to buy groceries and will often travel much farther to find a better selection or price on larger purchases.

The Character of Consumer Demand for Food

The second important economic force affecting modern farming is, strictly speaking, a characteristic of consumer demand for food. Even most well-educated citizens today are ignorant of what economists refer to as "the income elasticity of demand for food," but this notion is essential to understanding what has happened to agriculture in industrialized nations and what will most likely occur in the developing world as well.

Consider what happens when, because of an increase in wages at a typical job in a typical city, a family experiences a 10 percent increase in annual income. The family now has more money to spend and will tend to spend more on most things they are already purchasing: groceries, family recreation, their automobile or refrigerator (at least when they next replace them), and a variety of other things. Both careful empirical study and common sense indicate that when a family's income rises by 10 percent, they increase their expenditures on some items by more than 10 percent and on other items by less than 10 percent. Thus, they may increase their expenditures on such "luxuries" as recreation or "eating out" or new kitchen appliances by more than 10 percent and may increase their expenditures on "necessities" such as light bulbs, salt, or bread by less than 10 percent. That is, the purchase of luxury goods is more responsive to an increase in income than is the purchase of necessities. In fact, this is one of the basic meanings of the words "luxury" and "necessity" themselves.

This responsiveness, or "elasticity," of consumers' demand for various products when incomes rise has been extensively studied and its effects carefully chronicled. Economists have devised a numerical measure of this responsiveness: the ratio of the percent change in quantity purchased to the percent change in income. Thus, if a 10 percent rise in income is accompanied by a 20 percent increase in purchase of movie tickets each year, "the income elasticity of demand" for movies would be 2 (i.e., 20 percent divided by 10 percent). If demand for bread rose by only 3 percent, its income elasticity of demand would be .3 (i.e., 3/10: 3 percent divided by 10 percent). Those goods for which market demand increases more than income (both measured in percentage terms) have income elasticities of demand greater than 1.0, a "relatively high" elasticity or responsiveness of demand to a change in income. Figure 6.6 indicates the income elasticities of demand for a number of products for United States consumers.

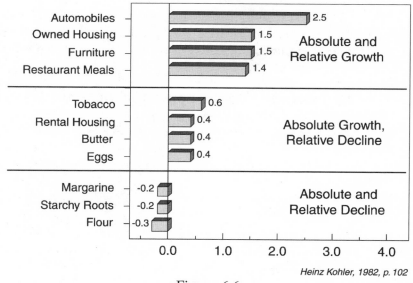

Figure 6.6

For goods with income elasticities of demand greater than one, as incomes in the nation rise, production will grow faster than incomes, which means production will not only grow in absolute terms but will also grow relative to the production of other commodities on average. Those production processes in the middle group (with elasticities

117

between zero and one) will experience absolute growth (people will spend more money on them as their incomes rise) but will be in relative decline (production growing slower than the average), and they will be a shrinking proportion of the national economic pie. Those products in the third group (negative elasticities) will show an absolute decline (with *fewer* dollars spent on them as people's incomes rise) and, of course, a decline relative to other production processes.

Figure 6.7, indicating Canadian per capita consumption for beef, milk, flour, and potatoes, shows more concretely what this means. Over the fifty years covered by these statistics, per capita personal income and expenditure in Canada grew almost fourfold.[16] As the graph indicates, consumption of beef rose by about 80 percent, meaning that beef production expanded but not as fast as the fourfold expansion of the economy as a whole. The other three farm products saw sizable decreases in per capita consumption as Canadian incomes rose, implying a negative income elasticity of demand. We should note that because the population of Canada rose by nearly 150 percent over this fifty-year period the *overall* demand for each of these products expanded. Nonetheless, all four of them, including beef, fell in importance as a proportion of overall Canadian production.

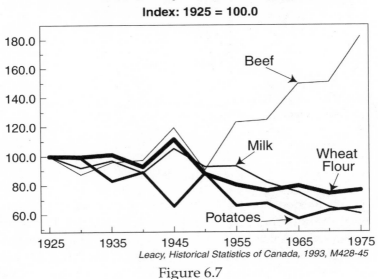

Canadian Per Capita Food Consumption
Index: 1925 = 100.0

Leacy, Historical Statistics of Canada, 1993, M428-45

Figure 6.7

People do indeed increase their spending on "meals" by more than their increase in income—note in the table that the income elasticity of demand for dining out is 1.4—but most of that goes to restaurants and food processors, who sell convenience, and very little increase in consumption of farm products is entailed. As figure 6.8 indicates, even considering only dollars consumers spend at the grocery store, the proportion of those dollars going to farmers has been dropping over time.

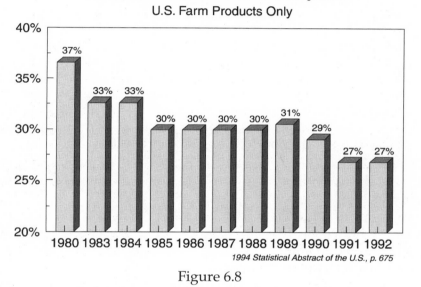

Farm Portion of U.S. Grocery Bill
U.S. Farm Products Only

1994 Statistical Abstract of the U.S., p. 675

Figure 6.8

People are surprised to hear that nearly three-quarters of their grocery outlay doesn't go to farmers. But even in 1913, the earliest date for data on this matter in the United States, less than half the grocery outlay went to farmers for the products they sold.[17] Today there are more than six times as many people employed in processing, transporting, and selling that food we buy in the grocery store than there are farmers growing it.[18]

There are at least two complexities in this measure of income elasticity of demand that should be noted. The first is that it represents a generalization about consumer behavior in a particular nation at a particular time. It is completely dependent on human choices; it obviously does not have the "natural" validity of regulari-

119

ties of physics or chemistry. It is an empirical generalization of how most people do in fact make consumption choices when their incomes rise. It *could* change. At the same time, however, these regularities in consumer behavior seem to be pervasive and robust. Although there are many cultural differences among the industrialized nations of the world, the income elasticities for other industrialized nations, including places as different as Japan and Western Europe, are not substantially different.

The second complexity is that the income elasticity of demand for products changes as people's income rises. More simply put, what are luxuries for poor people are necessities for rich folk. In nations with low income, the income elasticity of demand for food products is relatively high, even though in more advanced industrialized nations it is relatively low. Hungry people, the poorest of the poor, will spend nearly all of any increase in income on food (income elasticity of, perhaps, 9). Poor people with adequate diets tend, as their incomes rise, to increase expenditures on "higher quality" foods, usually substituting meats for grains, which greatly increases their (indirect) demand for feed grains (elasticities of 2 or 3, for example). The income elasticity of demand for food drops lower than 1.0 when average incomes are high enough that most people in a nation have already made those substitutions.

Returning to the effects of this characteristic of demand on farming, we start with the fact that throughout most of the last two hundred years of Canadian and United States history, economic productivity has been rising and the average income of citizens has risen in train. Thus we can picture a long series of annual increases in income where people spend more money on a multitude of products, but tend to have smaller increases in their purchase of farm products than in their purchase of most other goods. Thus, although more money is spent on farm products than before, this larger amount is annually a smaller and smaller portion of the total number of consumer dollars spent on all products in the nation. Agriculture expenditures grow but become a proportionately smaller slice of a larger national economic pie. Put in the most general terms, the share of national expenditures (i.e., the share of GDP) going to the agricultural sector drops (in percentage) as a nation becomes wealthier. Figure 6.9 gives a sort of "moving picture" of this long-term trend over the last two centuries for a number of now-industrialized nations. In every case, the importance of agriculture as a share of national production has fallen over time. Figure 6.10 gives a "snapshot" picture of the differences among a number of developing and industrialized nations in 1992, illustrating the effects of differences in income during a single year. Agriculture is a far larger share of national production in poor nations than in wealthy. The forces at work here are not the decisions of policy-makers in Ottawa or Washington, D.C., nor of grain traders at Cargill. It is a social fact of consumer choice that as average incomes in a nation rise, the farm sector in that nation shrinks as a proportion of the national economy.

What does this mean for farmers? To simplify thinking through this matter, let us presume that there is no change in the nation's population as the national income rises. If the number of farmers in the nation remains exactly the same each year, then as long as the number of dollars going to buy agricultural products rises the average income of farmers in the nation will rise.[19] At the same time, however, the number of nonfarm jobs and average income of nonfarmers will be rising much faster since a far higher portion of the annual increase in national income is going to nonfarm products. It is possible, of course, that farmers could be satisfied with their rising incomes, but the fact that incomes tend to rise faster (and thus are higher) in nonfarm employment leads to a migration from the farm sector to other employment in the nation. Many a farm family has seen most of their children move to the city—whether willingly or reluctantly—because of better economic prospects there.

Government investment in agricultural research—just like individual farmers' investments in more education or new technologies—tends to raise farm productivity and reduce the income gap between farm and nonfarm incomes. This research must be faulted for its historical ignorance of environmental degradation and must be redirected to include sustainability among its goals. Nonetheless, without government research and dissemination of information to farmers, rural incomes would lag even farther behind urban than they currently do. The transformation of agriculture might have been slowed somewhat if the Canadian and United States governments had spent nothing for agricultural research; however, it seems undeniable that a minority of farmers would have begun using more productive techniques, even if those at first had been developed in other nations. Without government efforts to promulgate such information to all farmers, however, it is likely that income disparities among farmers would have been far greater than actually resulted.

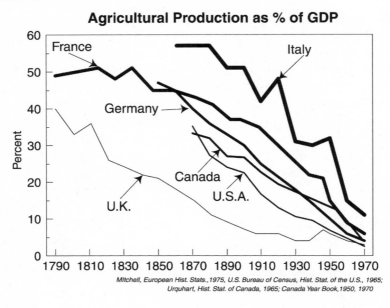

Agricultural Production as % of GDP

Mitchell, European Hist. Stats.,1975, U.S. Bureau of Census, Hist. Stat. of the U.S., 1965;
Urquhart, Hist. Stat. of Canada, 1965; Canada Year Book,1950, 1970

Figure 6.9

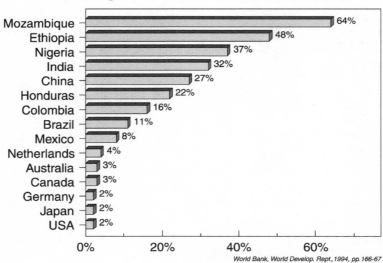

Agriculture as % of GDP: 1992

World Bank, World Develop. Rept.,1994, pp. 166-67

Figure 6.10

Of course, not all departures from farming are taken voluntarily. Even though many young adults choose to leave rural areas to seek their fortunes in the city, the more noticeable and far more painful experience of bankrupt farmers deserves careful attention. Every farm operation has to choose a particular mix of crops and the technologies to grow them. This involves a substantial risk, more than in most other occupations, with a family's life savings. The ordinary ebb and flow of agricultural production, due largely to local weather patterns, and of agricultural prices, due largely to more distant patterns of weather and public policy, bring about large fluctuations in profits and losses for farmers over the years. Even reasonable loans, usually increasing the mortgage on farmland itself, may turn sour if agricultural prices are bad for an extended period of time. When bankruptcy occurs, a somewhat better price for agricultural products could usually have averted the calamity, or at least postponed it by allowing for continuing payments on the mortgage. Aware that higher agricultural prices and less price volatility would allow many hardworking farm families to survive, many citizens, both rural and urban, have pressed for governmental supports for agricultural prices.

GOVERNMENT SUPPORT OF AGRICULTURAL PRICES

It was out of a concern for the fate of the small family farm that agricultural support programs in Canada, the United States, and the other industrialized nations of the world began. It will be helpful first to review such programs generally and then to look more closely at one particular program: price supports for sugar.

Overview of Farm Support Programs

It is helpful to begin with a brief survey of governmental subsidies to agricultural producers today, for there are a wide variety of types of subsidy, and different nations subsidize different products to different extents. Figures 6.11 and 6.12 give an estimate of the annual subsidy to farmers in Canada and the United States for some of the products currently subsidized.

123

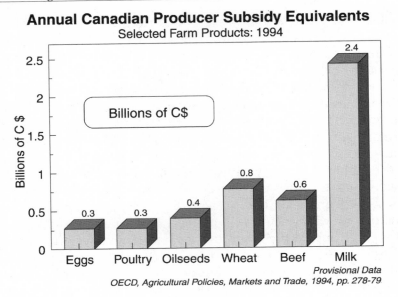

Figure 6.11

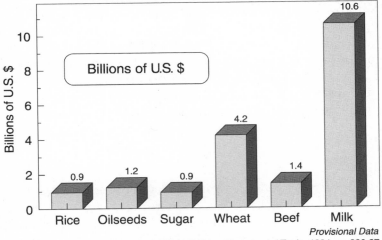

Figure 6.12

The U.S. total producer subsidy equivalent for grains and live-stock products was approximately $28 billion in 1993, while the total for Canada—with a farm population about one-tenth as large—was about $6 billion.[20]

Estimates of actual subsidies are a bit tricky because only a portion occurs as direct government cash payments to farmers. The simplest form of subsidy is a guaranteed minimum price: If farmers have to sell at a lower price in the market, the government makes up the difference between the market price and the "support price" in cash payments. Somewhat more complicated is the system of guaranteed loans frequently used, where the farmer pays back the loan if farm prices are good but has the option to hand over the farm commodities themselves if prices turn sour. California farmers of all types benefit from highly subsidized water produced through large government dam and diversion projects and sold at rates far below market value. Canadian wheat farmers benefit from the coordination and marketing facilities of the Canadian Wheat Board and from indirect subsidies in the transportation and sale of grain provided by the Board. "Set-aside" programs attempt to improve farm incomes by paying farmers not to plant certain acres, leading to smaller supplies and, thus, higher market prices. In the case of sugar in the United States, a small quota of duty-free imports is allowed each year, after which imports are effectively blocked by a stiff tariff. Canadian dairy, egg, and poultry producers similarly benefit from import quotas.

It is difficult to compare and analyze such diverse programs. However, the Organisation for Economic Co-operation and Development (OECD) conducts an annual survey of agricultural production and trade and has devised a thorough, though complicated, procedure for translating each of these subsidies into a dollar amount, a "subsidy equivalent." The literature on farm supports traditionally distinguishes between a "consumer subsidy equivalent" and a more comprehensive "producer subsidy equivalent."

Because it is rare for there to be a law declaring that consumers must pay higher farm food prices, the subsidy from consumers to producers is often invisible to the consumers themselves. The OECD's measure of consumer subsidy equivalent for, say, wheat, is the difference between the price of wheat as it is sold inside the nation and the price of wheat as it is sold in international markets. If the international price is lower than the domestic price, then consumers are paying more than they would otherwise have to, presumably because of some sort of governmental intervention in food markets. To compute the overall annual value of the consumer subsidy equivalent for wheat, one would multiply the difference in the two prices by the number of bushels of wheat sold in the nation.[21]

The producer subsidy equivalent measures all subsidies going to farmers and begins with the basic consumer subsidy represented by the difference in domestic and world prices for farm products. This base number is then adjusted for the additional direct payments from governments to farmers.[22] The data in figures 6.11 and 6.12 were given in terms of producer subsidy equivalents.

Figure 6.13 indicates for a number of industrialized nations the total of agricultural supports, including as a group the twelve nations of what is now the European Union.

Subsidies for Agricultural Products
in Billions of U.S. $

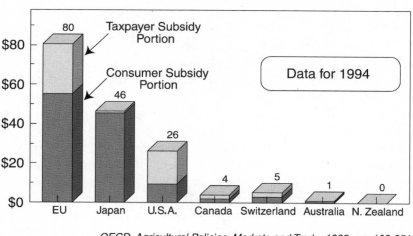

OECD, Agricultural Policies, Markets and Trade, 1995, pp. 193-251

Figure 6.13

The chart distinguishes between the taxpayer subsidy portion, which consists primarily of direct government payments to farmers, and consumer subsidy portion, which is largely invisible since consumers ordinarily do not know that food could be purchased more cheaply abroad if it were not for governmental restrictions. The amounts of money involved are substantial and have grown significantly in the past twenty years. As figure 6.14 shows, they also represent a sizable portion of farm income. This chart indicates producer subsidies as a percentage of the total value (quantity produced times domestic price) of the farm products in the survey (grains, oilseeds, sugar, meats, milk, eggs, and wool).[23]

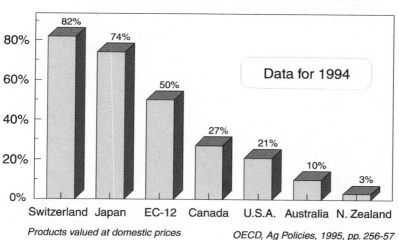

**Subsidies for Agricultural Products
As % of the Total Value of Those Products**

Products valued at domestic prices   *OECD, Ag Policies, 1995, pp. 256-57*

Figure 6.14

The chart gives a vivid picture of the sizable amounts of money involved in agricultural policy, but it does mislead somewhat because of the dramatic differences in the overall population of these nations and in the number of farmers in each. Figure 6.15 takes scale into account, showing the producer subsidy equivalent per hectare of cultivated farmland. Although the United States grants more subsidies in the aggregate than any other individual nation, when account is taken of the size of the agricultural sector, the United States and Canada are comparable—and are clearly overshadowed in subsidy per hectare by Japan and the nations of Europe.

127

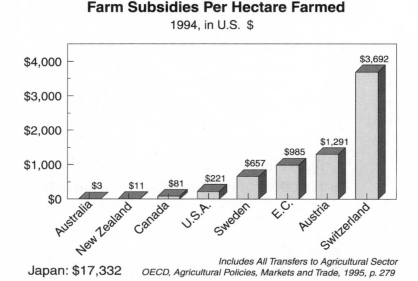

Farm Subsidies Per Hectare Farmed

1994, in U.S. $

Japan: $17,332

Includes All Transfers to Agricultural Sector
OECD, Agricultural Policies, Markets and Trade, 1995, p. 279

Figure 6.15

The most prevalent rationale behind national governments' support of agriculture is the difficulties caused for farmers by the fluctuation of world agricultural prices. Every business has its risks, but farming has more than most. From the point of view of each individual farmer, a good year is one when the harvest is large, usually due to ideal weather conditions, and a bad year is one when it's small, usually due to drought or hail or other extreme weather. Because farmers' livelihoods depend on the sale of their crop, the farmer's overall income depends not just on the number of bushels of a crop to be sold but on the price as well. Good weather and ideal growing conditions in nearly all the growing areas of the world bring about a supply far greater than average, and the surplus drives down the price per bushel.

Of course, any one group of farmers will benefit in a "bumper crop" year for their local area when overall world production is below average, so that world prices rise at the very time this particular group of farmers has more bushels to sell. The worst situation is the opposite: when the farmers in a particular area are hit hard by bad weather during a year when most farm areas around the world

128

are booming due to excellent growing conditions. In this situation, prices are low from the bumper crop around the world, but these particular farmers have even fewer bushels than usual to sell.

In general, agricultural prices are highly responsive to changes in supply: They often drop more than the increase in quantity produced, leaving farmers with less money in a bumper crop year than in a normal one. At work here is what economists describe as "the price elasticity of demand." This notion is parallel to the income elasticity of demand we saw earlier in the chapter, but addresses instead the responsiveness of consumers to a change in price (rather than to a change in income). It asks: What will be the percentage of change in the quantity consumers demand when there is, say, a 10 percent change in the price? It turns out that consumers' demand for agricultural products tends to be unresponsive ("inelastic") to changes in price. When prices fall, people don't consume much more than before, and when prices rise, people don't consume much less. Thus, when a bumper crop occurs, slightly lower prices don't really induce much extra consumer demand for agricultural products, and the price has to drop rather severely in order for the whole crop to be sold. This is why, for example, a 5 percent rise in production during a bumper crop year might lead to a 10 percent drop in the price and thus leave farm incomes actually lower in spite of the rise in production. Similarly, relatively large jumps in price will occur when there are shortages, because higher prices don't induce much of a drop in consumer demand. The result is sizable price volatility in agricultural prices.[24]

Because the well-being of domestic farmers is so heavily dependent on the vagaries of weather not only at home but elsewhere in the world, the governments of nearly all industrialized nations now support agricultural prices. However, it is one of the ironies of the price support system that this very effort on the part of some nations to insulate their farmers from the volatility of international prices actually tends to increase that international price volatility itself—and this can only harm the unsubsidized farmers of the developing world. Consider how this occurs.

The primary purpose of agricultural supports is to keep domestic agricultural product prices high even in a year when international agricultural product prices are relatively low. That means, of course, that domestic consumers will be paying the higher "supported" price and cannot benefit from lower international prices.[25] Thus domestic consumption does not rise in response to lower world prices. The home market is "insulated" from international price fluctuations. As a result, an international bumper crop (which caused the low prices in the first place) can only be sold if prices drop even more than they would have to if consumers in the insulated market had actually increased their consumption in response to lower prices. Thus, those farmers in unprotected farm sectors (for example, in the Third World) will face even more price volatility and will suffer the most. In a time of low world agricultural prices, agricultural support programs in the industrialized nations make life even harder on farmers in the developing world than it would otherwise be.

This penalty arising from price volatility, however, is not the only damage done to Third World farmers by agricultural price supports in the industrialized world. More important is the regular, year-after-year effect of excluding Third World agricultural products from sale in First World markets through the supported prices for First World farmers' products.

To understand this effect, it is important to realize a critical anomaly in the relationship between the governments of the world and their agricultural sectors. While nearly all industrialized nations support their farmers, protecting them from low international prices, most developing nations actually penalize their farmers.[26] The rationale behind this varies extensively. Most important is a "cheap food policy," attempting to improve the standard of living of urban people. Although most Third World residents are rural people, the political reality is that governments respond most to the better-educated, politically active urban classes. In some countries, national policy for economic development deliberately penalizes agriculture in an attempt to promote a manufacturing sector, intending to provide jobs and to produce goods which would then not have to be imported from the industrialized world.

Particularly in Latin America (with the exception of Mexico), in most of sub-Saharan Africa (except Nigeria), and in Asia (except for rapidly industrializing Pacific rim nations), Third World producers of specific agricultural commodities face explicit taxation. In addition, many developing nations have official exchange rates that are overvalued, artificially raising the price of their farmers' exports in world markets, making them less competitive.[27] This lowers domestic food prices, helpful to urban dwellers, both rich and poor, but harmful to farmers—again, both rich and poor. Lower prices also cut domestic food production. Thus the combination of industrialized nations' support of agriculture (tending to lower world food prices) and developing nations' effective taxation of agriculture is a critical force harming the economic well-being of the poor farmers of the world, the vast majority of the Third World poor.

Predicting what would happen if First World nations ended their farm price supports is a tricky business, and a variety of economic studies have come up with varying estimates of the ultimate effect on world farm prices. Two outcomes, however, do seem to be quite clear. The first is that world agricultural prices would have less volatility than they do now, due to the effects we have cited. This would help the Third World poor, both urban and rural. The elimination of subsidies would mean that the average consumer-taxpayer in the industrialized world would pay less for food, but would be more exposed to the price fluctuations in world agricultural markets. The second is that world agricultural production would shift somewhat toward developing nations. World agricultural prices would tend to rise (because the industrialized nations would buy more food in the world market), but the end of subsidies would mean lower per-unit revenues for farmers in the industrialized world than they currently enjoy. A number of First World agricultural producers would stop farming, and Third World farmers would grow and sell more basic foodstuffs on the world market.

Short of abandoning farm price support programs, First World nations could still assist the Third World poor by simply eliminating the subsidies currently provided (largely through tax dollars) for the export of farm products from the First World to the Third. Except in time of crop shortages, eliminating poverty in developing nations will require that Third World farmers be encouraged through the price system and other methods to produce and sell more.

Of course, it would be a mistake to overrate the negative effects of agricultural supports in industrial nations. Although these do harm the rural poor of the world, there are more influential forces.

131

The plight of the poor in the developing world is *most* directly affected by the policies undertaken by their own governments. In addition to land reform, badly needed in many countries, one of the best things those governments could do for the rural poor of their nations is to end the many subsidies of the urban classes. However, an examination of that sort of policy lies beyond the scope of this inquiry into international trade.

This overview of farm price support systems has been quite general, and it will be helpful to take a look at a particular commodity support program, in this case one that has perhaps the weakest moral case underlying it.

Supporting U.S. Sugar

United States government policies have been affecting the sugar market since 1789, when the fledgling government imposed tariffs on sugar, and other imports, as a means to generate revenue.[28] A small sugar industry grew up and by 1894 a 40 percent tariff on sugar imports had been imposed. World sugar production expanded rapidly in the 1930s and prices were driven to historically low levels, rendering the 40 percent tariff too small to protect domestic sugar production. Producers and refiners appealed for protection from the vagaries of price fluctuations in the world market, and Congress passed a series of "Sugar Acts" and eventually incorporated these sugar tariffs into the umbrella "Farm Bill" now enacted every five years. The effect of substantial tariffs on sugar imports within the industrialized nations is to reduce Third World production in favor of that in the industrialized world.

As figure 6.16 indicates, the price of sugar in the United States has in most years been substantially higher than the world price. In accordance with the 1990 Farm Act, a small quota of duty-free sugar imports is allowed but a 16¢ per pound tariff is imposed on any additional imported sugar.

Thus the effective price of imports in the United States is the world price of sugar plus 16¢, allowing U.S. sugar producers to sell sugar at any price up to approximately 15¢ more than the world price without fear of competition.

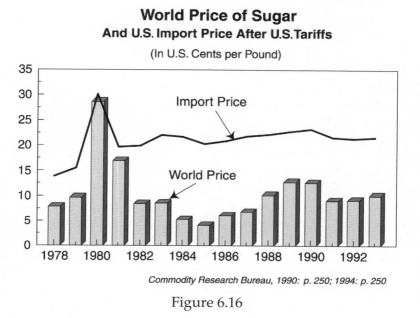

World Price of Sugar
And U.S. Import Price After U.S. Tariffs

(In U.S. Cents per Pound)

Commodity Research Bureau, 1990: p. 250; 1994: p. 250

Figure 6.16

As a result, the growing of sugarcane or sugar beets in the United States is far more profitable than it would otherwise be. It is, in fact, far more profitable than the next most profitable alternative use of the land used to grow them.[29] By one estimate, the six large firms that own all of the sugarcane farms and mills in Florida received a total benefit of approximately $329 million in 1984–85.[30] Farming is not as concentrated in the sugar beet growing regions, but even there neighboring farmers who are not members of the sugar beet cooperatives aren't allowed in and can't grow sugar beets because they would be denied access to the co-op's beet processing facilities.[31] The co-ops themselves limit production among their members by a cartel-like allocation process. Federal farm policy also aims to limit production through marketing allotments to producers.[32]

The United States is, of course, not alone in subsidizing sugar production. European nations have been doing the same at least since the days of Napoleon, who, in the face of a British sea blockade cutting off cane sugar imports from the Caribbean, began extensive sugar beet cultivation.[33] The European Union today employs a complicated system of price supports directed at increasing the economic

133

well-being of sugar beet growers.[34] Japan has even higher subsidies for its sugar beet growers.

Both the United States and the European Union allow some importation of sugar from Third World nations, the U.S. admitting from the Caribbean an amount equal to about 15 percent of domestic production and the EU importing from former British colonies an amount equal to approximately 10 percent of European production.[35] These few, select developing nations do benefit from the higher, protected price. Nonetheless, the primary losers from the protection of sugar by industrialized nations are sugar consumers there and the large majority of sugar producers in the developing world, whose products are effectively excluded.

It is a tricky business to estimate what would happen to world sugar prices if all such subsidy programs were ended. Estimates for the rise in world sugar price (due to the extra demand for sugar in the industrialized world) have ranged from 65 percent[36] to 50 percent[37] to 22 percent[38] to 5 percent.[39] It is also not completely clear what would happen to sugar production if subsidies were ended and the world price of sugar rose, say, 30 percent or 40 percent. Some efficient sugar producers in the industrialized world would likely still remain in business at that price, with a number of less efficient operations ceasing. What is clear is that the production of sugar would expand significantly in the primary sugar-producing nations of the world: Thailand, India, Cuba, Brazil, and Australia. These nations would not only benefit from a higher price for the sugar they sell but would also face a significantly greater demand for their products. With the exception of Australia, these are developing nations, a majority of whose poor are rural farmers.

A MORAL ASSESSMENT

Any moral evaluation of the issues concerning international trade and agriculture must begin with current agricultural support policies. To do this we will briefly examine three morally critical economic effects of those policies, consider the morally problematic political effects of those policies, and conclude with a moral evaluation of the loss of rural communities.

Three Morally Important Economic Effects

Agricultural support policies have a dizzying number of effects, but three stand out here.

The first is the impact of farm programs on farmers themselves. The primary motivation behind farm subsidies from the perspective of most citizens, and certainly from the perspective of Christian ethics committed to love of neighbor and a concern for the poor, has been an intention to help endangered family farmers stay in business in the face of severe economic difficulties. The policies have had some effect because domestic farm prices have been higher than they would otherwise be.

However, because the mechanism for transferring such subsidies to farmers is an indirect one—particularly those parts of the subsidies that come from consumers paying higher prices—in the United States it actually costs about $1.20 on average for every $1 gained by farm producers[40] (and the cost per dollar gained seems to be rising over time). In addition, because the primary moral argument focuses on helping marginal farming families, even greater inefficiencies are entailed by using subsidies that go to farmers in proportion to their output—which happens when farm prices are raised, whether indirectly through import restrictions or directly through government-guaranteed minimum prices. If we rank farms by the size of their annual sales, in Canada the largest 42 percent of farms are responsible for more than 89 percent of all farm sales,[41] while in the United States, the largest 35 percent of all farms produce 90 percent of all farm products sold.[42] As a result, these farms will receive 89 percent and 90 percent, respectively, of all farm subsidies when such subsidies are paid in proportion to a farmer's output. It seems to be a reasonable moral judgment that these largest farms do not deserve farm subsidies intended for struggling family farmers. If that's true, the cost of providing $1 of subsidy to those farmers producing the other 10 percent or 11 percent of farm products actually comes to approximately $12 because so much of the aid is misdirected to the prosperous.

The moral argument for crop subsidies focuses on assisting smaller farmers to remain in business. Just which farmers deserve such subsidies is a debatable issue, but it might be safe to say that these would be farms in the bottom half or bottom two-thirds of the distribution of farms by size. A more efficient and far more just use of national resources to help

135

marginal farm families would be to send payments directly to quali-
fying families, unrelated to the amount of production.

The second morally important economic effect of agricultural support
programs is their impact on poor citizens in nations attempting to assist farm
families. Domestically, attention is usually focused on the benefits that go to
farmers. However, the consumer subsidy (basically the difference between
the lower world price and the higher domestic price) is substantial. For sugar
alone, it has been estimated at approximately $55 per year for a family of four
in the United States.[43] The fact that poor people in industrialized nations face
significantly higher food prices is a sizable argument against such policies.
Figures 6.17 and 6.18 indicate for a number of products in Canada and the
United States the increases in the price of such products for everyday
consumers caused by government agricultural support programs. For example, Canadian dairies pay 155 percent more for their milk than they would
have to if Canada were unilaterally to abandon its price supports for milk.
United States dairies pay more than double what they would if an analogous
unilateral change took place in U.S. farm policy. The change in prices for
consumers would be smaller, but few who advocate agricultural subsidies
to help low-income farmers seem to be aware of the burden higher food
prices put on even lower-income consumers.

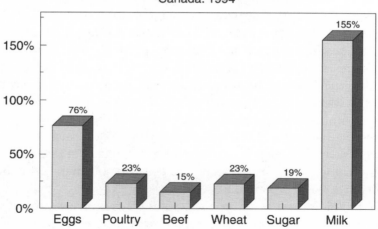

Permanent Price Hikes Caused by Policy
Canada: 1994

Based on Consumer Subsidy Equivalents/Nominal Assistance Coefficient on Product
OECD, Agricultural Policies, Markets and Trade, 1995, pp. 210-11

Figure 6.17

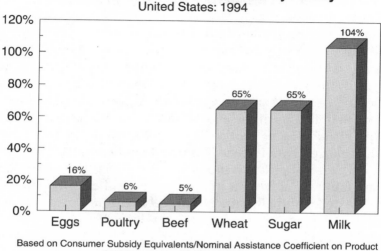

Permanent Price Hikes Caused by Policy
United States: 1994

Based on Consumer Subsidy Equivalents/Nominal Assistance Coefficient on Product
OECD, Agricultural Policies, Markets and Trade, 1995, pp. 250-51

Figure 6.18

These figures, however, are a bit misleading because they presume that if one nation eliminated its price supports, it would then import those farm products paying the lower international price. However, if all nations of the world ended their farm support programs, it is likely that the international price of farm products would rise. The domestic prices of farm products which consumers face may be higher or lower (depending on the form of the terminated subsidy for each particular farm product), but any higher prices for poor families in the industrialized world could and should be offset by a small portion of the national savings from ending the support programs.

A third set of effects of agricultural subsidies—their results for developing nations—is in nearly all cases their most morally objectionable. When Canada or the United States subsidizes, say, grains or dairy products, North American farmers are encouraged to produce more than they would otherwise.[44] Thus these farmers (or the governments that subsidize them and often end up holding farm commodities) have extra quantities of such farm products to sell,

137

lowering prices throughout the world—something that occurs even if the national government buys the extra grain and *gives* it away to developing nations.

Even more directly harmful are the export subsidy programs created more recently by many industrialized nations. These are explicitly targeted at making farm products of industrial nations cheaper in the rest of the world. Thus, they lower farm prices in developing nations. U.S. and Canadian farmers and policy makers often seem oblivious of the effects such subsidies have on the rural poor in the developing world. Relatively prosperous farm families in industrialized nations feel victimized by the vagaries of international agricultural prices. But it is surely the case that Third World farming families, making a living by selling their products to the urban residents of their nation, will feel far more threatened when the international price of farm products drops because of subsidies paid for by the wealthy nations of the world helping out their own farmers. Christian ethics defends the expenditures of tax dollars to provide a higher standard of economic welfare domestically than can be guaranteed internationally. However, ordinary farm subsidies exceed this standard and directly harm Third World farmers. It is certainly the case that export subsidies do so.

Those lower prices have a beneficial effect for nonfarmers in the Third World, including the sizable numbers of urban poor families. However, the majority of poor people in the Third World are farmers themselves. Low farm prices, driven lower by subsidy programs, can only hurt rural farmers in the developing world.

If for the reasons listed here, Canada, the United States, and the other industrialized nations of the world phased out their various programs that support domestic agriculture, the effect in the Third World would on balance be positive for poor people, but that is an average result and one not true for every group. In addition, as is often the case, policies within developing nations are even more influential for the welfare of the poor there than are changes in the international economy.

It turns out that it is remarkably difficult to construct adequate economic models to predict the effects of various policy changes. The multitude of current forms of policy support for particular farm products in the industrialized world and for penalty or support of particular products in various Third World countries makes modeling such changes a daunting task.[45] Such estimates are even more severely complicated by uncertainty as to the response of governments in developing nations to the termination of farm supports in industrialized nations. Nonetheless, there seems to be general agreement that if industrialized nations removed their agricultural supports and developing nations their agricultural penalties, the well-being of rural populations in the developing world would improve significantly.

The Moral Capacity of the Political Process

Any moral evaluation of policies designed to increase farm incomes should include an evaluation of the political process which produces and sustains those policies. In the case of farm subsidies in the industrialized world, the very forces which brought about these subsidies have been strengthened by the subsidies themselves, making morally appropriate changes to the policies more difficult. Of course, all subsidies create vested interests which will predictably apply political pressure to continue the subsidy in existence, and agricultural subsidies are no exception.[46] This is a commonplace of political life. Nonetheless, other, more subtle forces are also at work.

As we see, the political impetus to subsidize agriculture comes from the risks farmers face from the volatility of world market prices and from a long-standing though poorly informed perception that farm incomes are "unfairly low." The political discussion today about the appropriateness of the farm program, separate from any budgetary stringencies that might bring about changes, is hampered because in two important ways the farm policies themselves have created additional political support for themselves.

The first of these is that farming, like other ways of life requiring substantial capital investments, is characterized by high costs of adjustment. The shift from one crop to another is a costly one, given the investment in machinery, in related technologies, and in the farmer's own expertise. Subsidized farmers have strong incentives to attempt to influence the political process to prevent the loss of wealth and income that they would suffer if they had to cease producing a currently subsidized crop because of international competition. In addition, some food processors (such as sugarcane mills, sugar beet factories, and dairy co-ops) have strong incentives to support the subsidies to protect the value of their own assets. Such organizations of farmers or processors often tax their members a few cents per ton and "invest" the money in lobbyists to protect the value of the subsidies they currently enjoy.

The second characteristic increasing the political support for commodity subsidies is the effect of policy-induced technological change. Sugar is a good example here because the high price of sugar in the United States has encouraged the development of new technologies to produce alternative sweeteners from corn: high fructose corn syrups. Corn syrups have almost completely replaced sugar in soft drinks and now represent more than half the overall natural sweetener market in the United States. Although corn syrups can be produced at a price slightly below the (supported) price of crystal sugars from cane and beets in the U.S., it is unlikely that this new industry would have grown up if the far lower international price of sugar had been available. The incentive structures created by the farm subsidy programs have created this new industry.

From an economic perspective, once the sugar subsidy is in place, this new industry is an improvement because it provides sweeteners at a lower price. U.S. consumers will then have more money to spend on other things. Politically, however, the result is less happy. Sugar subsidies are now supported not simply by those regions involved in producing and refining cane and beets, but now by the far broader constituency of those producing corn, for corn growers now benefit from a higher price of corn whether their own corn is used for corn syrups or other purposes. Thus a national policy of dubious moral merit has, by inducing technological change, increased political support for itself.

Christians need to be realistic about the public policy process and the vested interests which inevitably arise around the incentive structures created by policy itself. In this case, for example, a move to a system of subsidies applicable only to smaller-scale farmers or tied to environmentally sustainable agricultural techniques would be morally preferable but has become politically far more difficult because of the alignment of vested interests unintentionally created by current farm support programs.

140

A Moral Evaluation of the Loss of Rural Community

If it were not for the broader issue of the loss of rural communities, it is unlikely that Christian ethicists and others interested in greater justice would have viewed changes in agriculture as significantly different from changes in other industries transformed by new technologies. The kinds of technological changes that have occurred in agriculture have occurred and will continue to occur elsewhere. The U.S. Bureau of Labor Statistics estimates that an additional 20 percent of farmers will move to other occupations in the next decade and a half.[47] Although this is a large number, there are 28 other occupations listed by the Bureau which are estimated to lose during that same period a higher proportion of jobs than farming, including railroad switch maintenance workers, directory assistance operators, billing and posting clerks, typesetters, motion picture projectionists, and switchboard operators. Saying this does not make such losses any easier, nor does it exempt the nation from an obligation to assist significantly in the transition to other jobs. It does say, however, that farmers are not alone.

Improvements in productivity through technological advance are not easy to accomplish, but, once discovered, they are even harder to resist. In essence, such changes improve internal efficiency—stretching inputs to produce more output—and a moral objection to them must be based either on a violation of the producers or on negative externalities. If a well-founded moral discernment leads to a negative judgment about particular technologies, Christians should undertake resistance to them. The question, therefore, is this: Should such technological changes in agriculture be resisted on moral grounds?

Leaving farming requires a far more severe shift in occupation than leaving most of those other jobs that will be lost. Because rural community life is heavily dependent on a single kind of production, changes in farming entail radical changes in how people organize their lives together. This raises a critically important issue for Christian ethical reflection on the meaning of community life in the modern world.

What should we make of the changes in rural life? If the causes for these historical transformations were the greed of multinational firms or the misguided hopes behind a national agricultural policy,

141

Christians might understandably object to the loss of vibrant community and work hard to counteract such forces. If, however, as has been argued here, the primary forces behind the transformation of modern agriculture have been the decisions of farmers (to improve their own productivity and well-being) and the decisions of consumers (to spend most additional income on nonfarm products), then an ethical analysis of the transformation of rural life must take into consideration the moral standing of those decision makers—farmers and consumers—who stand behind such changes.

We should not forget, of course, that small, incremental changes can sometimes add up to large nonincremental effects. In fact, it is a critical weakness of mainstream economic analysis that it focuses so predominantly on "marginal" (i.e., incremental) changes. Such a focus is very helpful in analyzing behavior in many situations, but it tends to overlook the long-term, cumulative effect of marginal choices, something to which Christian ethics must always attend. In addition, focusing on incremental changes and individual decisions tends to overlook what in public choice theory is called the problem of "isolation": that the results of many individuals' decisions made in isolation may be worse than a single decision those same people would make if they gathered into a group.[48]

Encouraging farmers or consumers or citizens to make all decisions from an individual's perspective is, indeed, morally inappropriate, and communal decisions are morally necessary in many areas. Thus a Christian understanding of property ownership and of stewardship for the earth warrants communal (i.e., governmental) regulation of environmentally damaging farm practices from high-erosion tillage to irrigation to the use of fertilizers, pesticides, and herbicides. No one farmer does much harm, but collectively much damage is done.

However, from the perspective of a Christian endorsement of individual creativity and the goodness of the material world (and of the increase in economic welfare farmers and consumers seek), it seems unlikely that the nation should intervene to prevent farmers from tilling another hundred acres or planting a better variety of seed or to prevent consumers from spending a smaller and smaller portion of their growing incomes on farm products. In addition, the Christian option for the poor argues explicitly against agricultural

142

trade flows *into* developing nations (further impoverishing the rural poor there) and in favor of flows in the other direction.

Does this mean that the loss of community in rural areas is of no consequence? Not at all. Knowing your neighbors, trusting others, gathering for community celebration, caring for elderly relatives, feeling responsible for others' children, helping rebuild another's barn, worshiping weekly in the church where you were baptized—all these and more represent the rich integration of life and faith in rural community. Of course, those same rural communities do tend to have traditional shortcomings: provincialism, resistance to outsiders and to diversity among their own members, and subordination of the life prospects of women to those of men. Nonetheless, the disappearance of rural communities is, on balance, a true loss from the perspective of Christian ethics. The problem is that once one understands the causes behind that loss, the moral cost of reversing this trend is simply too high.

Although critics of increased international trade in farm products cannot, by this argument, sustain a verdict in favor of agricultural price supports, much of their criticism is actually directed at environmentally unsustainable farm practices and is completely on target. Canada and the United States need to work hard to bring to farming the sort of environmental standards and general ecological consciousness that has begun to be applied to many areas of industry. Forcing farm operations to internalize their social costs will cost large operations more than small ones. This will tend to lower the cost advantages of large-scale farming and may do more to preserve smaller farm operations than current price support programs ever could. A recent World Resources Institute study has shown that agricultural support policies themselves, by basing payments on a multi-year average of land planted in the supported crop, strongly discourage crop rotation, an environmentally benign technique for increasing productivity per acre.[49] But whether large or small, it is quite likely that the environmentally responsible farm of the future will be more "high tech" than today. For example, one of the primary prospects for cutting fertilizer use—which will both lower costs and reduce environmentally damaging runoff—is the use of geo-positioning technologies, which tailor the application of nutrients and other soil additives to the particular needs of each small section of the farmer's field.

In addition, Christian commitment may indeed lead to attempts to subsidize marginal farm families, either to allow them to remain in agriculture or to assist in the transition into other work. Current farm programs could be transformed into income supplements for low-income farmers, "decoupling" subsidies from production, as this proposal is known in policy debates. This would help poorer farmers without creating incentives for increased production in industrialized nations or disincentives for Third World farmers. However, this would cost the political support of the well-to-do farmers and would turn the program, more explicitly, into a "welfare" program, something which even economically marginal farmers have often said they do not want.

Because one of the greatest concerns expressed in the moral evaluation of changes in rural life is the appearance of "corporate farms" owned by outsiders, land ownership laws could be changed, requiring that federal farm subsidies go only to owner-operated farms. A more radical possibility is the requirement that all farms, perhaps beyond a few recreational acres, be owned by resident farmers. Although Libertarians would object in principle to such a proposal, the Christian economic ethic could support it out of a view of property as a limited claim. However, even here there would be at least two important negative effects. Retiring farmers would no longer be able to sell to the highest bidder: Farm land would be worth less. Second, it is possible that farmers requiring outside financing (as most businesses do) would find the costs of that financing somewhat higher because such a law would restrict the investment of nonfarmers in the farm sector.

CONCLUSION

This chapter has reviewed the arguments about international trade in farm products, beginning with an analysis of the transformation of agriculture in the United States and Canada as primarily dependent on the choices farmers and consumers have made. It has argued that farm price-support programs are inefficient, costing as much as $12 for every $1 that goes to a "needy" farmer. Even more important, agricultural supports have unintentionally harmed poor farmers in Third World nations, through lower international prices for food they grow. By reducing demand for food grown in developing nations, lower prices have lowered incomes and raised unemployment among the rural poor.

We have also seen how such farm support programs structure incentives for farmers that contradict the need to move to alternative patterns and technologies for crop production due to the environmental damage modern agriculture currently causes. Additional laws will be needed to internalize the social costs of farming, similar to those applying to manufacturing and other production processes in the modern world. In fact, it is quite likely that removing the advantages that large farm operations currently gain from the various crop support programs and from the absence of adequate environmental legislation would do more to help small farm operations survive than current price support programs themselves.

We should be realistic here, however, because very small farms are not likely to be economically viable under any policy regime. In the United States, 54 percent of all farms have annual gross sales of less than U.S. $20,000;[50] in Canada, 42 percent of farms have annual gross sales of less than C $25,000.[51] Even morally appropriate efforts to assist low-income farmers should be directed at those whose future can realistically be sustained. Farming is a way of life but it is also an occupation and business. Even small farms have relatively high capital costs (largely for land and equipment), and there is no hope that $20,000 or $25,000 in overall sales can pay farm expenses and still support a family.

An immediate end to agricultural support programs is not only politically impossible but unwise as well. It would lead to abrupt adjustments that would harm the most vulnerable in both industrialized and developing nations. However, a program of gradual cuts in agricultural price supports, perhaps over the next decade, could allow for a more orderly transition in food production. Some small progress was made in this regard in the "Uruguay round" of the GATT talks. Signatory nations committed themselves to reducing agricultural price supports, beginning with a "tariffication" of current price supports, a process of translating all current import restrictions into their financial equivalent in a tariff to make them more visible.[52]

There remain, of course, many questions about the effects that such a shift would actually have on poor people in the Third World. Among the background assumptions we saw in chapter 5 was a presumption about the character of economic development. There is, of course, a danger that domestic policies in the developing world will so favor the rural wealthy over the rural poor that the advantages accruing to developing nations from a cessation of agriculture support policies in the industrialized world may not help poor rural people much. In most parts of the world, however, this seems quite unlikely. It is difficult to devise a credible story whereby the increased demand for Third World agricultural products would on balance harm the rural poor. Those who own their own land are almost certain to benefit, and even those who are farm employees will face an increase in demand for their labor. It must be recognized, however, that such issues raise a host of others that lie beyond the scope of this volume. As is always the case, domestic political and economic institutions—such as national policies on land reform and on the freedom of workers to organize—will be far more influential forces than international trade.

For now, however, our inquiry into the ethics and economics of international trade leads us to recognize the critical importance of attributing causality accurately and of tracing effects more carefully. The largest single stumbling block in the moral conversation about the future of agriculture seems to be the misattribution of causes, which we have reviewed. There will remain critical moral judgments to be made, but we must begin with an accurate understanding of what is happening and why.

CHAPTER 7

TRADE AND THE ENVIRONMENT

Christian faith requires a commitment to sustainability and to the integrity of God's creation. As a result, an assessment of the severity and urgency of anticipated environmental damage stands as a crucial background conviction in the debate over international trade. In an ideal world, controversies about environmental problems might be resolved before a view of international trade were constructed. It is no surprise that controversies around trade abound when some commentators anticipate cataclysmic problems or attribute a moral status to the biosphere (or even "biotic rights"),[1] while others anticipate smooth adjustments or ascribe no more than an instrumental value to the non-human natural world.

Many critics of increased international trade see environmental problems as not only vastly serious but immensely urgent, due to both the severity of the coming damage and the irreversibility of the natural and social processes involved. John Cobb has employed as a symbol for our environmental situation today the image of a train hurtling down a hillside toward an anticipated but nonexistent bridge over a deep gorge.[2] With this sort of assessment of environmental problems, it is understandable that growth-producing international trade makes little sense. Instead, Daly and Cobb call for steady-state "development," but not growth.[3]

Some trade proponents on the right openly deride environmentalists for extremism and faulty science, and they accuse the environmental movement of covertly statist goals aimed at political control of the economy.[4] More frequently, economists and other proponents of increased trade acknowledge the existence of environmental problems caused by economic growth, but tend to view those problems as less severe than do critics of trade. Of course, economists differ significantly among themselves, but it seems clear that most share a position fundamentally opposite that of Daly and Cobb. To some extent this may be attributable to a history of cataclysmic predictions within economics that have proved to be unfounded. Thomas Malthus was neither the first nor the last economist to predict dire consequences, only to be proved wrong because of later, unanticipated adjustments in the system.

FIVE ENVIRONMENTAL CHALLENGES TO TRADE

Those opposing increased trade out of concern for the environment tend to object on the basis of five distinct mechanisms of interaction between trade and damage to the ecosphere.

The first objection is that trade contributes to an unsustainable depletion of the planet's natural resources. The second is that trade accelerates the unsustainable use of the earth's absorptive capacity. Each of these is a particular form of the more general objection that trade promotes economic growth, which is the primary cause of environmental destruction.

The third sort of relation between increased trade and more responsible environmental policies arises from the competitive advantage of firms located in nations with weak environmental laws. Many critics of trade have predicted that curbing import restrictions in industrialized nations will simply encourage large corporations to move their manufacturing operations overseas to escape the costs of mandated pollution abatement which they currently face.

The fourth objection to increased trade focuses on the environmental effects of international agreements designed to increase trade (e.g., the GATT/WTO, the Canada-U.S. Free Trade Agreement, NAFTA, etc.). From this perspective, trade is not simply an activity between nations; it has become an international legal force which

148

threatens national sovereignty. Individual nations have surrendered authority to international trade organizations, which then have the power to overturn national environmental laws.

The fifth point of contention between advocates and opponents of increased trade concerns the unilateral use of restrictions on imports as a lever to get other nations to improve their own environmental regulations.

These five points of tension between trade and the environment provide a helpful typology for the remainder of this chapter.

1. Using Up the Earth's Assets: Trade and Resource Depletion

Each year the nations of the world export to one another total merchandise trade in excess of three and a half trillion dollars ($3,500,000,000,000), a number so large that it overwhelms even an active imagination.[5] Not only is the dollar value immense, but the amount of materials shipped internationally is equally stunning. Careful record is kept only on the mass of materials loaded and unloaded in maritime shipments, but as figure 7.1 indicates, mountains or, in some cases, lakes of raw materials and processed goods are transported by ships between nations, more than four billion metric tons each year.

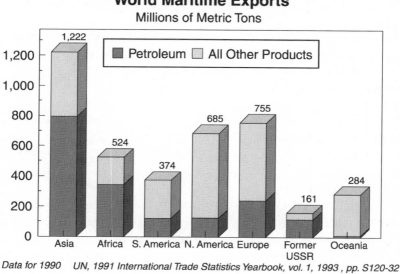

World Maritime Exports
Millions of Metric Tons

Data for 1990   UN, 1991 International Trade Statistics Yearbook, vol. 1, 1993, pp. S120-32

Figure 7.1

149

Although much of that amount includes manufactured products and renewable primary products such as food and timber, a large portion consists of nonrenewable natural resources that are consumed by production processes and people far distant from the point of origin. The scale on which human activity is transforming the planet is astounding. Is this a problem? if so, how big?

Depleting Nonrenewable Resources

Environmental concerns about resource depletion first came to general awareness in 1972 with the publication of *The Limits to Growth,* a report of the Club of Rome. The report was pathbreaking, though because of its novelty it contained a number of methodological limitations. Most important was the tendency to extrapolate contemporary trends into the future without considering the effects of price changes on patterns of consumption. For example, the study reported that the price of mercury had gone up 500 percent in the previous twenty years and the price of lead 300 percent in the previous thirty.[6] In summary, the report asserted,

> Given present resource consumption rates and the projected increase in these rates, the great majority of the currently important nonrenewable resources will be extremely costly one hundred years from now.[7]

This sort of prediction took more concrete and visible form in a celebrated wager between environmentalist and population specialist Paul Ehrlich and futurist Julian Simon. In 1980 the two agreed to a ten-year bet on which direction the real (i.e., inflation-adjusted) price of raw materials would move. The two drew up a futures contract requiring Simon to sell to Ehrlich ten years later the same quantities of five metals (copper, chrome, nickel, tin, and tungsten) which could be purchased for $1,000 in 1980. If the prices rose over that ten-year period, Simon would pay the difference; if they fell, Ehrlich would ante up.

Economists have generally refrained from Simon's optimism about a drop in resource prices. Yet for another reason, they almost always meet predictions about "running out" of natural resources with skepticism. Economic theory predicts that resource depletion will never occur completely (because that last unit will be too expensive to extract) and will occur very slowly, far more slowly than simply extrapolation of current trends would indicate. The reason for this is that as the price of resource A rises (due to higher extraction costs as the most convenient sources are used up first), users of A will have an incentive to switch to a "backstop technology," an alternative resource B which *had* been more expensive but which is now cheaper than A. The process is an iterative one, in that this increased demand for resource B tends to raise its price and, in turn, some users of resource B may find it economically attractive to substitute yet another resource C in place of B. There is a good bit of technological optimism in this presumption, for it assumes that as the price of any one resource rises there *will be* other resources that are close technological substitutes for it.

Just how much of this substitution can occur? This is a critically important issue but no one really knows the answer. One's position on the long-term result of this iterative substitution process stands as a part of a background commitment concerning technology generally: Some are optimistic, some pessimistic.

Even if we don't know how much substitution *can* occur in the future, how much has already occurred? Although economic theory encourages a reliance on higher resource prices to trigger this iterative substitution, it is one of the ironies of the twentieth century that this process has not much been in play in recent decades. No poll was taken in the early 1970s, but it is likely that, along with the Club of Rome and Paul Ehrlich, a large majority of people concerned about the environment would have predicted sizable increases in the price of metals and minerals over the subsequent twenty years. However, as figure 7.2 indicates, real raw commodity prices for metals and minerals, as well as for petroleum and raw agricultural products, were actually lower in 1992 than they were in 1975.

Copper prices were down 22 percent, bauxite 46 percent, zinc 69 percent, nickel 35 percent, and iron ore 23 percent.[8] The price of metals and minerals overall dropped by approximately 40 percent over those seventeen years. Real petroleum prices dropped by a third, though the influence of the OPEC oil cartel in raising prices in the 1970s renders this change less telling. Agriculture prices dropped by more than 50 percent, though as we have seen, part of that is due to subsidies by the industrialized nations. Incidentally, the record shows that in October of 1990, when the ten-year wager was up, Paul Ehrlich sent a check for $576.07 to Julian Simon.[9]

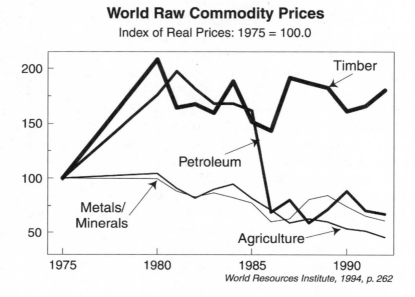

World Raw Commodity Prices

Index of Real Prices: 1975 = 100.0

World Resources Institute, 1994, p. 262

Figure 7.2

Of all this data, the information about the price of metals and minerals is the most critical. Part of the drop in prices comes from more efficient production processes. Just as important, there has actually been an increase in the reserves of nearly all such resources in the meantime. It remains true that such natural resources are in a finite and "fixed" supply on the planet; this is a geologic fact. From the point of human activity, known reserves (those physical supplies which are economically feasible to extract) depend on the effort of humans to find them and to devise more effective ways to extract them.

Optimists on the right have been excessively exuberant in their conclusions. Ronald Bailey has summarized the depletion issue in glowing terms:

> There are no permanent resource shortages—future food supplies are ample, world population will level off before overcrowding becomes a problem and pollution can be controlled at modest cost.[10]

152

Those less optimistic about long-term shortages of natural resources warn that the impact of humanity on the resource base is
approaching, if it has not already reached, a maximum sustainable
rate. Herman Daly argues that we now live in a "full world," quite
unlike the empty world of the past where natural resources were
considered to be "free" goods.[11] Daly warns that economists and
many others have overlooked the complementarity between human
capital and natural capital (that the productivity of the former depends on the presence of the latter) and instead have stressed their
substitutability (which is true to a degree but not without limit). The
value of human capital is in many situations threatened by a dimin-
ishing flow of natural capital (for example, in fishing and forestry in
some parts of the world), and this leads to unsustainability because,

> In the era of full-world economics, this threat is real and is met by
> liquidating stocks of natural capital to temporarily keep up the flow
> of natural resources that support the value of man-made capital.[12]

Glib optimism in the face of broad scientific uncertainties is not
available to Christians committed to respect for the integrity of
creation. Nonetheless, trends in resource prices do make a difference. Although no one doubts that there is a finite amount of all these
materials in the earth, in a recent edition of its environmental source-
book, the World Resources Institute has in effect downplayed the
significance of natural resource depletion in the face of these
changes: "Evidence suggests however that the world is not yet
running out of most nonrenewable resources and is not likely to, at
least in the next few decades." In addition, when that process of
"running out" begins to raise prices, the Institute argues,

> New technology is increasingly making possible substitutes for many
> traditional natural resource-based materials. Technology develop-
> ment is also yielding to more efficient means of providing light,
> motive power, and other energy-related services. Such changes are
> paving the way to economies less dependent on natural resources.
> When shortages do emerge, experience and economic theory suggest
> that prices will rise, accelerating technological change and substitu-
> tion.[13]

An investigation and ultimate evaluation of this debate cannot be undertaken here, but it is clear that the uncertainties about the future call for a morally induced caution in public policy.

One of the most important changes required in such public policy is ending subsidies for the production and consumption of nonrenewable natural resources. Examples are numerous. Oil companies receive indirect tax subsidies through depletion allowances and, as we will see in more detail presently, consumers of petroleum products in North America pay far less for the externalities they generate than consumers in the rest of the industrialized world. We have earlier noted the shift of a sizable portion of U.S. dairy production to semi-arid regions of California where water is priced far below its governmentally subsidized cost of production. Such unsustainable stress on water resources has led, among other tragedies, to the demise of the Colorado River long before it flows to the sea; except in years of unusually high precipitation, it is simply used up. Similarly, in many regions of the world, irrigation projects are depleting irreplenishable aquifers. In the Ludhiana District of the Punjab in India, the water table fell nearly a meter during the 1980s, the result of government subsidies that had reduced the cost of irrigation to the farmer.[14] Both irrigation and the logging of forests are important to the economic development of the Third World, but subsidies in the use of natural resources are shortsighted and counterproductive.[15] They give producers and consumers false signals, implying that resources cost less than is both economically and morally true.

The nonrenewable resource perhaps most important economically is the supply of carbon-based fuels, particularly natural gas and petroleum (which make up about half the world's international maritime trade). As these two energy sources are depleted, there are three alternative backstop technologies available. The first is coal, abundant in supply but threatening even more global warming per unit of energy than do petroleum and natural gas (a problem to which we will soon turn). The second is nuclear power, an energy source growing in world importance but whose long-term waste storage problems remain an unresolved threat (and entail a background judgment concerning which huge disparities of opinion exist). The third is really a cluster of renewable energy sources

154

including energy generated from wind, from solar photovoltaic cells, and from geothermal or solar heat collection. As we shall see in the discussion of pollution problems, a carbon tax designed to internalize the social pollution costs of commercial energy sources would render these renewable sources of energy more commercially competitive, given technological improvements in recent decades.[16]

Depleting Renewable Resources: Forests

As figure 7.2 indicated, the one type of raw commodity whose price *did* rise between 1975 and 1992 was timber, a thoroughly renewable resource. Combined with the loss of millions of acres of forest through land use changes (e.g., the burning of vast areas of the Amazon rain forests), consumer demand for wood presents a serious environmental threat to the sustainability of forests in many parts of the world.

Trade has indeed played a role in this process. Figure 7.3 charts a number of industrialized nations of the world, Japan in particular, that have been annually importing immense quantities of wood, for both construction and the production of paper products.[17]

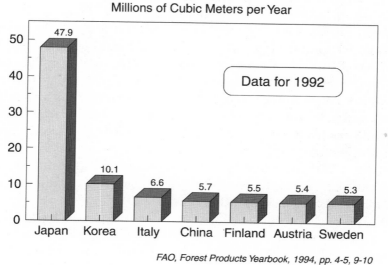

Leading Wood Importers
Millions of Cubic Meters per Year

FAO, *Forest Products Yearbook*, 1994, pp. 4-5, 9-10

Figure 7.3

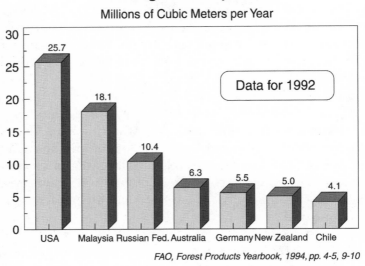

Leading Wood Exporters

Millions of Cubic Meters per Year

FAO, Forest Products Yearbook, 1994, pp. 4-5, 9-10

Figure 7.4

Yet as figure 7.4 shows, with the critically important exception of Malaysia, the leading exporters of roundwood in the world are more advanced economies. Forests in the industrialized world certainly need careful environmental attention, and public policy must be developed to preserve critical portions of the now mostly logged "ancient" forests. Still, a recent study done by the FAO (the United Nations Food and Agriculture Organization) and data gathered by the World Resource Institute suggest that the total forested area of the industrialized nations of the temperate zone (Europe, the Soviet Union, Canada, the United States, and Japan) actually increased between 1980 and 1990.[18] The primary problem of unsustainable forest use in the world occurs in the developing world, primarily with tropical and subtropical forests.

As is clear from the chart, Malaysia stands out as a sore thumb among the world's leading exporters of wood. In many ways, Malaysia's case is an extreme one. Numerous reports and studies have been done both within Malaysia and abroad documenting the devastation of forests, particularly in the provinces of Borneo, and the government corruption, collusion, and flouting of both true national interest and international law that characterize the high-profit mining of Malaysia's forests.[19] A number of steps have been taken internationally to rein in such practices, in particular, the International Tropical Timber Agreement (ITTA). Entering into force in 1985, the ITTA has been approved by most of the world's leading importers and exporters of tropical forest products, including Malaysia. Its fundamental aim is to ensure that by the year 2000 all tropical timber sold in international trade will be taken from forests under sustainable management.[20]

Although bad public policy and venal private interests play important parts in the world's current unsustainable use of its forests, the most important force in this process is far more ordinary, though sometimes overlooked by environmentalists.[21] As figure 7.5 indicates, in those parts of the world where forests are most severely threatened—Asia, South America, and Africa—the vast majority of wood harvested becomes fuel, almost exclusively for domestic use.

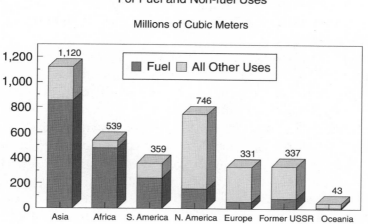

World Wood Production: 1992
For Fuel and Non-fuel Uses

Millions of Cubic Meters

FAO, Forest Products Yearbook, 1994, pp. 2-39

Figure 7.5

157

Much world attention has rightly been focused on the loss of rain forest in recent decades, but other types of forests have seen even more rapid losses worldwide.[22] Consider the example of Sudan, home to more of the world's "very dry" forests than any other nation. It annually produces more than twenty-four million cubic meters of wood, exports none of it, and consumes 90 percent of it as fuelwood or charcoal,[23] resulting in a loss of 81,000 hectares (more than 300 square miles) of very dry forests each year.[24]

This is not an isolated case. About half the people on the planet use wood, charcoal, or a biomass substitute (such as crop residues or dung) to cook all or some of their meals.[25] The stoves traditionally used are terribly inefficient, consuming six or seven times more energy than modern stoves using commercial fuels. The gas range in the typical kitchen of the industrialized world is a sizable capital investment but is not simply a great convenience; it is more frugal with the earth's energy resources than traditional cookstoves.[26]

We should be careful to note that such comparisons are in no way an indictment of the poor of the world for their necessity. Their behavior is perfectly reasonable and morally justifiable. The point here is that an environmentally superior alternative can be made available, even within the budgets of the vast majority of the poor.

Considerable effort is being exerted to introduce more energy-efficient biomass stoves in the developing world.[27] Improved design reduces indoor smoke and dramatically cuts fuel consumption, making these newer stoves an attractive option. Consumers can often pay for the stove with the fuel saved during a few months' use.[28] Convincing large numbers of people to change even to lower-cost technologies is difficult; traditional practices change only slowly.[29] Nonetheless, considerable success has been achieved where the introduction of improved stoves has been undertaken with proper reliance on local producers and the reactions of local consumers. Reducing household biomass smoke reduces disease; cutting fuel consumption by up to 50 percent means a significant rise in economic welfare: a dramatic reduction in the time necessary to collect daily fuelwood in rural areas and substantial increases in effective annual income for urban dwellers who must purchase their charcoal or fuelwood.

The unsustainable use of the world's forests is a critical concern for a Christian ethics committed to the principle of respect for the integrity of God's creation. Trade plays a role in that unsustainability, and existing treaties on illegal timber trade need to be enforced and strengthened. Nonetheless, in addition to the threat to forests from land use changes, it is the consumption of wood for fuel that most threatens the world's forests. In fact, the availability of commercial fuels, often provided through international trade, will be an important step on the way to dependence on renewable energy sources that can sustain the annual energy demand of the increasing prosperity of developing nations.

Biodiversity

Threats to global biodiversity from indiscriminate economic growth are severe. How to value losses in the variety of species and in the genetic variety within individual species stands as an important background assumption that cannot be examined here. Although the Christian's commitment to the integrity of God's creation is the driving force behind concern about biodiversity, a careful specification of precisely what losses in biodiversity are morally acceptable is a matter of great debate. Far less debatable is the conviction that humankind has been all too casual in mining the biological resources of the world and that strong efforts need to be made to reverse the trend.

In many ways, the interplay of science and biodiversity remains at a critical threshold. We still suffer from large deficiencies in knowledge about the range and character of uncounted species on the earth. In addition to the value any species possesses in itself as a part of God's creation, the very diversity of species hosted by, for example, tropical ecosystems represents a critically important source of genetic material in an era of genetic manipulation. Though for a long time drug companies and other users of such genetic material took it for granted as a part of "the global commons," more recent agreements between pharmaceutical firms and peoples indigenous to those ecosystems have begun to recognize and repay the debt these firms and their customers owe.[30] More public pressure to continue this trend toward strengthened international agreement

159

for the equitable treatment of indigenous peoples and host Third World countries is needed.

The single most important threat to biodiversity has been the loss of habitat, in nearly every type of ecosystem on the earth. International trade plays a role in this process, and international agreements about a host of issues affecting pollution, overexploitation of plant and animal species, agriculture and forestry, and the loss of habitat are critical.[31] The Convention on International Trade in Endangered Species of Wild Fauna and Flora (CITES) has been in force for some twenty years. It has helped curtail inappropriate trade in endangered species, even though stronger compliance by signatory nations is still required.[32] The Global Environment Facility, a joint program of the U.N. and the World Bank, has made protecting biodiversity a high priority, and though successes have been limited, such cooperative international efforts show promise.[33]

Looking back on this cluster of issues related to trade and resource depletion, it becomes clear that, like purely domestic economic activity, international commerce requires a framework of rules. In most cases these must be rooted both in national legislation and in international agreement. Because of the importance of background assumptions concerning technological optimism in evaluating the depletion of nonrenewable resources and of the value of species diversity in assessing prospects for biodiversity, participants to these debates have unusually wide differences to negotiate in structuring such agreements. Significant progress has been made in the daunting task of establishing a scientifically rigorous definition for global biogeophysical sustainability,[34] but far more work has yet to be done.

2. Overtaxing the Earth's Absorptive Capacity: Trade and Pollution

The second reason trade is often accused of threatening the environment is the concern that more economic growth will further overwhelm the earth's capacity to absorb the wastes which humankind annually generates. Two central distinctions are critically important. The first concerns the difference between primarily "local" environmental problems (such as air and water quality) and the more clearly "global" environmental problems (such as greenhouse

160

warming and upper-atmosphere ozone depletion). The second distinction is between increased international trade and increased economic growth. Economic growth without increased trade can have impacts on the environment discernibly different from growth accompanied by increased trade.

Trade and Primarily Local Environmental Problems

At an elementary level it is obvious that environmental problems grow as economies shift from being predominantly agricultural to predominantly industrial. Atmospheric emissions from motor vehicles and factories, to take simply one sort of pollution, cause deteriorating health conditions. If the environment were the only value to which Christian ethics needed to attend, international trade might appropriately be condemned simply because it leads to greater economic growth and, therefore, to more pressure on the planet's absorptive capacity. However, Christians must also attend to other values, like the need for an increase in economic welfare for the world's poor; moreover, Christian ethics must take a more careful look at the relation between increasing environmental problems and increasing prosperity.

The impact of international trade on local pollution problems is notoriously difficult to assess against the background of pollution problems arising from local economic activity alone. Nonetheless, it is clear that firms involved in international trade, like those which operate only locally, regularly exert political power to resist local or national regulations aimed at reducing pollution, because of the increased costs of production they entail. We postpone until later in this chapter the treatment of one critically important question here: to what extent "dirty" industries tend to migrate from nations with strict environmental laws to others where environmental regulation is more permissive.

Of all the forms of international trade that may cause greater pollution, the international waste trade stands out. Solid and liquid wastes from production and consumption are ultimately deposited back into the biosphere in one particular location or another. These range from very low-risk wastes that can be composted or landfilled to high-risk wastes that are highly toxic, persistent, mobile, and bioaccumulative. Examples of the latter include cyanide wastes, chlorinated solvent wastes from the degreasing of metals, and dioxin-based wastes.

Concerned about environmental damage, the industrialized nations of the world have imposed stricter regulations on the disposal of toxic wastes, greatly raising the cost of disposition. This has led to the rise of hazardous waste disposal firms and an international trade in toxic wastes. In principle there is good reason to allow the transport of toxic wastes across national boundaries. Particularly for hazardous wastes generated in developing nations, transport to other nations with more adequate disposal facilities makes both economic and moral sense. The problem, however, is that far greater quantities of hazardous wastes have flowed in the other direction, not because of adequate disposal potential but rather because the governments of developing nations may be willing to provide disposal sites for wastes in return for money, even though this may not serve the long-term interests of the nation. For example, the African nation of Guinea-Bissau negotiated—and later under public outcry rescinded—a $120 million-per-year deal to store industrial wastes from the north. Such amounts of money are simply part of the cost of doing business to large industrial firms, but this sum represented nearly 75 percent of Guinea-Bissau's annual gross domestic product. The prospects for graft and other forms of governmental corruption in the presence of large amounts of money will predictably threaten democratic accountabilities. However, the issue is even more complicated than that.[35]

To understand the decision from the point of view of developing nations, it might be helpful to consider the possibility that an imaginary and vastly wealthy trading partner offered a very lucrative hazardous waste contract to the government of Canada or the United States. What would occur if the Canadian government received an offer for, say, $300 billion, or if the U.S. government received an offer of $3 trillion? These dollar amounts, of course, are completely unrealistic. Nonetheless, the scale of these offers is the same as that sometimes presented to small Third World countries, and it helps to recognize that more than a few legislators and citizens in even the wealthy industrialized nations would likely advocate accepting such a hazardous waste contract even if that meant rendering some portion of the country permanently uninhabitable.

The Basel Convention on the control of transboundary movements of hazardous wastes and their disposal is a critically important development. Although representatives of nearly all the industrialized nations signed the convention, a number of these nations have been slow to ratify and move toward strengthening the convention. The agreement prohibits the export of wastes for disposal in Antarctica and requires the acceptance in writing by the nation of import for any transboundary hazardous waste shipments. This attempts to prevent bribery of local government officials in contravention of national laws. Because national governments themselves can be corrupted or simply shortsighted, waste exports are permitted under the convention only if the exporting nation does "not have the technical capacity" or "suitable disposal sites," and only if the country of import has appropriate facilities for environmentally appropriate treatment and disposal.[36] Although it is in principle possible for a developing nation to be technically ready to accept, treat, and store the results of hazardous waste, the risk of corruption or myopic self-interest of the current generation is so high that a Christian moral commitment to the integrity of creation would seem to require that each nation agree to treat and dispose of its own hazardous wastes as the usual procedure. Although such an agreement is "paternalistic" and rejects the economies of scale that international trade promises, the risks arising from the vast disparities of wealth between nations render it prudent.

Shifting attention to more "ordinary" kinds of pollution, we should recognize that it is both empirically and ethically incorrect simply to indict trade and economic growth because of local pollution problems. As one researcher has put it, "The air is harder to breathe, the water is dirtier and the sanitation and health conditions are poorer in Calcutta, Lagos, or Mexico City, than in New York, Tokyo, and London."[37] This relation of wealth and environmental health is illustrated in figure 7.6, depicting the "intensity of environmental wear hypothesis."[38]

Researchers studying environmental problems in developing countries have found that increases in national per capita income beyond $4,000 or $5,000 tend to alleviate a number of particular local environmental problems, because of growing pressure on governments for environmental relief once economic growth has provided for other basic elements of economic welfare.[39] The "intensity of environmental wear" hypothesis proposes a more general though unproved intuition: that the overall environmental cost caused by an extra dollar of gross domestic product rises during the early stages of national economic development, peaks somewhere around $5,000 or $6,000 per capita income, and then falls thereafter. We should be careful to note that this does not claim that total environmental wear actually decreases at higher income levels; each additional dollar of GDP still adds environmental wear. What it says, however, is that the increase in environmental wear caused per dollar of growth is more severe in nations where per capita incomes are low than where per capita incomes are already high.

Intensity of Environmental Wear Hypothesis
Damage per $ GDP as Incomes Rise

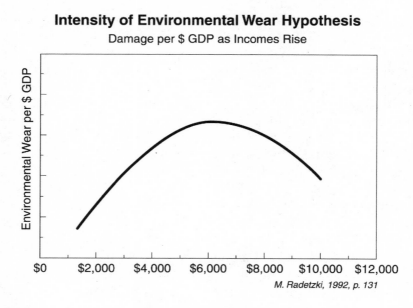

M. Radetzki, 1992, p. 131

Figure 7.6

As always, it is important to understand the causality here. A number of conservative critics of the environmental movement have misread the fact that local pollution problems often improve with national economic growth. Indur M. Goklany has asserted that "anything that retards economic growth generally also retards environmental cleanup and consigns millions to squalid and untimely

164

deaths."[40] Without explaining the causality involved, he observes that "countries undergo an environmental transition as they become wealthier and reach a point at which they start getting cleaner." Goklany makes but one reference to "more stringent clean air legislation" in a lengthy account of the history of the improvement of air quality in the industrialized world, and that is largely to downplay the role of government.[41]

Although the development of cleaner technologies has been essential to stemming air and water pollution problems in wealthier nations, those technologies have been necessitated by environmental regulations, which do indeed "retard economic growth" because they increase the costs of production. They are, in effect, a national decision to "spend" a portion of national income to offset the environmentally damaging effects of economic growth. In the United States, this amounts to more than 2 percent of GDP.[42] What conservative critics of environmentalists so often overlook is that most environmental regulations were and often still are opposed at nearly every turn by the corporations affected (and at times by their workers).

To a large extent, lower-income nations spend a smaller portion of their national income to alleviate pollution problems because there are other more pressing needs to be addressed first. A contributing factor in this slower response to pollution problems in developing nations is clearly the resistance of powerful economic interests to regulations that increase costs and lower profits, just as it is in the industrialized world. Though this problem is more severe in the developing world, many reputable Third World policymakers have described the decision as concerning what a nation judges it "can afford."

There is still much work that needs to be done to reduce local pollution problems in the industrialized world. Nonetheless, significant progress has been achieved, as was discovered in the joint U.N. study of twenty of the world's "megacities," published in 1992.[43] Compared with other urban centers, cities in industrialized nations have significantly lower levels of sulfur dioxide, nitrogen oxides, and volatile organic compounds. Although problems remain (for example, ozone levels remain high in Los Angeles and Tokyo), the large investments in pollution control technologies in wealthier nations have made a significant difference.

Of course, it is not simply urban areas that face pollution. One of the charges against increased trade in agricultural products, for example, is that this will lead to greater use of pesticides and herbicides in developing nations, where runoff will damage the local environment. However, as figures 7.7 and 7.8 indicate, in both fertilizer and pesticide use, it is the highly subsidized farms of the industrialized nations that are the world's heavy users.

Although a shift of agricultural production to the developing world is likely to bring about an increase in the use of fertilizers and pesticides there, it would most likely bring about a net reduction in their use worldwide. While energy use and energy-related pollution problems in agriculture pale in comparison with those in the industrial sector, a shift of agricultural production toward the developing world would also tend to decrease the energy intensity of agriculture worldwide, as figure 7.9 indicates.

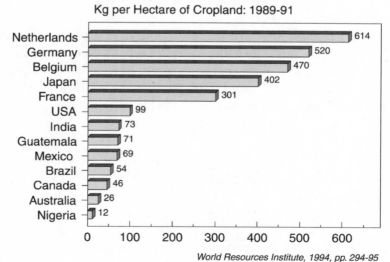

Fertilizer Use in Agriculture

Kg per Hectare of Cropland: 1989-91

World Resources Institute, 1994, pp. 294-95

Figure 7.7

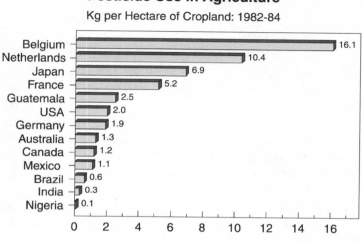

Pesticide Use in Agriculture
Kg per Hectare of Cropland: 1982-84

Only Active Ingredients Measured
World Resources Institute, 1992, pp. 274-75

Figure 7.8

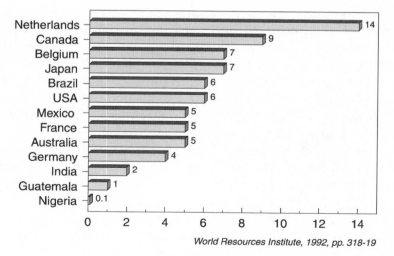

Energy Use in Agriculture
Megajoules per U.S. $ of Farm Output: 1989

World Resources Institute, 1992, pp. 318-19

Figure 7.9

167

Trade and Global Pollution

Although even local pollution problems have global effects eventually, it is helpful to distinguish them from pollution threats that are predominantly global.

The actual conveyance of merchandise in international trade does itself lead to pollution of the world's oceans. Oceangoing ships have been notoriously casual about dumping wastes at sea, including petroleum wastes, perhaps the single most environmentally damaging kind. Although oil tanker accidents receive the most publicity, they represent, by one estimate, only about 5 percent of the oil annually entering the world's oceans.[44] Nearly four times as important is the discharge of bilge and fuel oil and the operational (i.e., "business-as-usual") losses from oil tankers.

The MARPOL Convention (the International Convention for the Prevention of Pollution from Ships) came into force in 1983, and has been ratified by most of the chief trading nations of the world.[45] MARPOL aims to eliminate pollution of the sea by oil, chemicals, and other hazardous substances discharged from ships, whether accidentally or through normal operations. In the face of resistance from some shippers, considerably more progress needs to be made here. But even perfect compliance wouldn't end petroleum pollution, since more than half the oil entering the world's marine environment comes from a combination of land-based discharges and atmospheric deposition.[46] Considering not just oil but all forms of pollution annually affecting the oceans, a recent U.N. report estimated that only about 12 percent comes from maritime transport.[47] Strengthening MARPOL and more rigorously implementing it is very important, but even if all ships disappeared from the high seas tomorrow, only a small decline would take place in the continuing pollution of the world's oceans.

The two most pressing global pollution problems result from the everyday activity of humanity in the twentieth century: a rise in the accumulation of "greenhouse" gases and the depletion of the ozone in the upper atmosphere.

The scientific analysis of global warming—the progressive warming of the atmosphere due to increasing concentrations of "greenhouse" gases such as carbon dioxide—is incomplete. There is close to scientific certainty about the insulating effect of increasing levels of CO_2 and other greenhouse gases in the atmosphere: They will without doubt tend to hold in heat that is now radiated off into space. However, a number of significant scientific questions remain. The first set of uncertainties concerns the effects on atmospheric temperatures from not-yet-understood dynamics in cloud cover, ocean currents, and atmospheric chemistry. The second concerns the particular effects of rising temperatures on agriculture and other weather-sensitive human activities in different parts of the planet.[48]

Annual anthropogenic (i.e., "man-made") emissions of CO_2 represent about 5 percent of the natural CO_2 released into the atmosphere. This is not a large proportion, but it is significant enough to alter the balance of the carbon cycle, raising the proportion of CO_2 in the atmosphere. What do we know about greenhouse emissions and their relation to international trade?

Figure 7.10 lists the top thirteen nations in overall emissions of greenhouse gases, predominantly carbon dioxide. Figure 7.11 gives data on a few of the top fifty nations in the world ranked in order of per capita emissions.

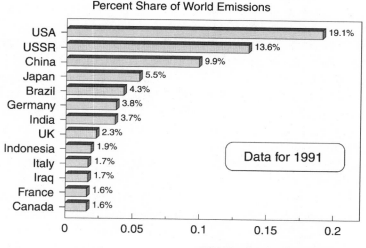

Greenhouse Emissions: Top 13 Nations

Percent Share of World Emissions

Nation	Percent
USA	19.1%
USSR	13.6%
China	9.9%
Japan	5.5%
Brazil	4.3%
Germany	3.8%
India	3.7%
UK	2.3%
Indonesia	1.9%
Italy	1.7%
Iraq	1.7%
France	1.6%
Canada	1.6%

Data for 1991

World Resources Institute, 1994, p. 201

Figure 7.10

169

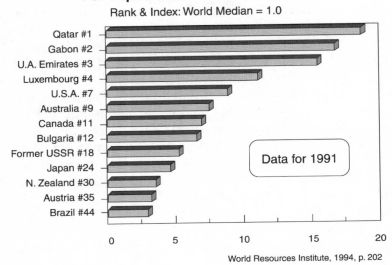

Per Capita Greenhouse Emissions

Rank & Index: World Median = 1.0

World Resources Institute, 1994, p. 202

Figure 7.11

There is no doubt that economic growth brings about more greenhouse gas emissions. However, the second chart makes clear that it is not simply overall economic growth alone that contributes to such pollution. Nations that produce and export petroleum (for example, Qatar, Gabon, and the United Arab Emirates) and nations where national policy keeps energy costs low (for example, the U.S.A. and Canada) tend to rank higher on the list.

Do nations that engage in more international trade emit more greenhouse gases because of it? Environmental critics of trade have argued that if nations became more economically self-sufficient, goods would not have to be shipped so far, cutting energy consumption and greenhouse emissions. Thus, it is helpful to ask how the actual transportation of goods in international trade contributes to the buildup of greenhouse gases. Unfortunately, no one can answer this question. Much international trade (for example, most trade between European nations or between Canada and the U.S.) takes place by rail or truck, and current national mileage figures for

170

aggregate trucking or railroad hauling do not accurately distinguish between domestic and international destinations. Nonetheless, international accounting for CO_2 emissions does keep track of maritime "bunker fuels," those consumed by ships in international transport. These represent about 1.5 percent of CO_2 emissions from all industrial processes.[49] This is not a small number in absolute terms (more than 250 million metric tons of CO_2 emissions each year!), but is certainly small relative to the other sources of CO_2 emitted from industrial processes. In addition, about half the tonnage transported by ship in international trade consists of petroleum or petroleum products, pointing the finger toward domestic consumption of commercial energy.

Thus we might then ask: What are the *sources* of greenhouse gases and how are these related to trade? Figure 7.12 illustrates estimates of worldwide emissions from the four principal anthropogenic sources. There are some other limitations in the data,[50] but the chart gives a rough estimate of most world greenhouse gas emissions brought about by human action.[51]

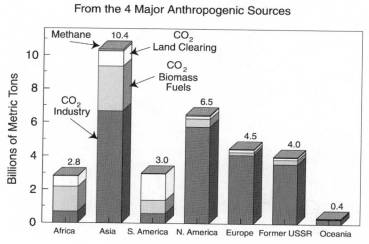

World Greenhouse Gas Emissions: 1991

From the 4 Major Anthropogenic Sources

World Resources Institute, 1994, pp. 362-65; Krause, et al., 1992, p. 119

Figure 7.12

171

The land clearing indicated in the chart represents conscious human efforts to change land use, from which approximately 3.4 billion metric tons of CO_2 are released annually in the world, largely in the burning of forests. This is a substantial impact, but the more important environmental result is the loss of forests, which would otherwise perennially absorb substantial amounts of CO_2 from the atmosphere. Annual global methane emissions (from, in order of importance, livestock, rice growing, municipal wastes, coal mining, and oil and gas production) amount to some 250 million tons, very small in relation to the greenhouse effect of CO_2 emissions. As is quite clear from the chart, the two most important anthropogenic sources of greenhouse gas emissions are industrial production, which is responsible for more than 22 billion tons of CO_2 per year (about 70 percent of the worldwide greenhouse emissions from these four principal sources), and biomass fuels, which give off nearly 6 billion tons (about 17 percent). And as figure 7.13 indicates, nearly all CO_2 emissions from industrial sources come from the burning of

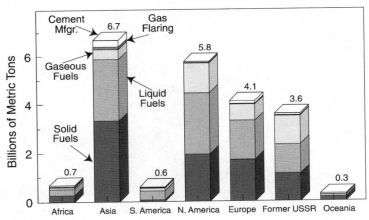

World Industrial CO₂ Emissions: 1991

From the 5 Major Industrial Sources

World Resources Institute, 1994, pp. 362-63

Figure 7.13

commercial fuels, distinguished here as solid, liquid, and gaseous (which are almost entirely coals, petroleum products, and natural gas).

A small but significant proportion of anthropogenic CO_2 emissions arises from the burning of biomass fuels, mostly firewood, predominantly in the developing world. The policy options we saw earlier concerning forest sustainability apply here as well. Increasing the efficiencies of biomass stoves is a first step; this reduces CO_2 emissions while improving economic welfare. International assistance is important in that process, and international trade will likely prove essential in the move from biomass to cleaner-burning fuels, particularly renewables, as Third World incomes rise.

The primary threat of greenhouse global warming arises from the use of commercial energy—throughout the world, but especially in industrialized nations. Commercial energy consumption per person is by far the highest there. Figure 7.14 illustrates the differences among several industrialized countries, converting all forms of energy into their equivalent in oil for comparison.

Our question, then, is, "Do nations that trade more consume more energy?" Figure 7.15 illustrates one measure of how much various industrialized nations trade: the ratio of the value of exports to the value of gross national product for the same countries.[52] If trade were a dominant factor in energy consumption, we would expect to see some correlation in these two charts. However, efficient energy users appear at opposite ends of the trade scale as do the two least-efficient industrialized users of commercial energy, the United States and Canada.

The importance of trade to any national economy depends heavily on geography—in particular, the proximity of international trading partners. This explains the heavy international trade of most European nations. Although a glance at the globe would indicate that Canada and the U.S. are similarly situated in this regard, the critical difference is that all principal Canadian cities are located relatively near the border with the United States, making international trade more likely than intra-Canadian trade at a greater distance. If the United States comprised only the northern tier of states

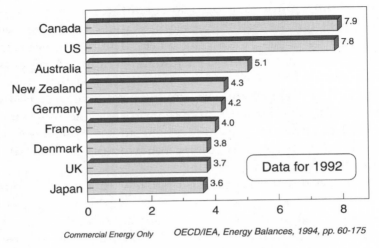

Figure 7.14

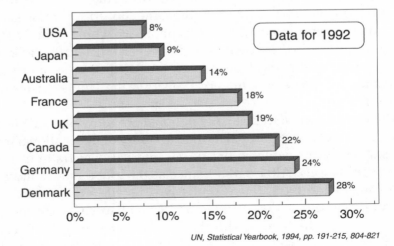

Figure 7.15

along the Canadian border, it would no doubt show as high a percentage of exports as does Canada. However, the U.S. also includes many cities much farther from an international border, thus rendering trade considerably less important for the United States than for Canada.

If the importance of international trade doesn't explain the differences in energy efficiency among the industrialized nations, what does? To some extent, of course, geography is the answer. Nations with colder average temperatures must use more fuel for heat during the winter, and both people and goods in geographically larger nations travel greater distances on average than people and goods do in small countries. Nonetheless, most of the difference in energy efficiencies among industrialized nations is directly attributable to differences in the prices users of energy must pay. Although the data sets for many energy types are incomplete, we can get an idea of international differences in energy prices by examining the data for gasoline. Considering both gasoline supply costs and gasoline taxes, figure 7.16 depicts the differences in price in the industrialized world.

As the chart makes clear, the gasoline prices consumers face in Japan and several European nations are two to three times higher than those faced by Canadian and U.S. consumers. Although every nation's taxes are higher on gasoline than on other forms of energy—to help pay for the costs of highways—similar ratios exist for other types of energy.

Figure 7.17 is a reprint of one we just saw depicting energy consumption per person—enabling a visual comparison with national energy prices. Economic theory predicts that consumers facing higher prices for a good will consume less of that good. The data in these two charts illustrate this strong inverse correlation between energy prices and energy consumption. This provides the most persuasive explanation for energy use patterns in North America. Because United States and Canadian energy users—both individuals and businesses—face significantly lower energy prices than their peers in other industrialized nations, they are less frugal in their use of energy. Of course, the explanation for lower energy supply costs *and* lower energy taxes in Canada and the United States is that both have large domestic energy stocks, politically powerful energy com-

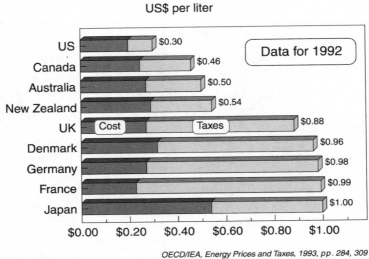

Gasoline Supply-Cost and Taxes
US$ per liter

OECD/IEA, Energy Prices and Taxes, 1993, pp. 284, 309

Figure 7.16

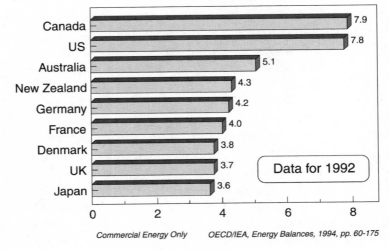

Per Capita Energy Consumption
Metric Tons of Oil Equivalent Per Capita

Commercial Energy Only   *OECD/IEA, Energy Balances, 1994, pp. 60-175*

Figure 7.17

panies, a heavy dependence on the automobile, and a citizenry culturally accustomed to all of the above. It is, for example, far easier in a nation like Japan to build a national consensus supporting higher energy taxes and better energy efficiency when practically all energy is imported and very few citizens have vested interests in energy firms.

The way to reduce energy consumption is to raise energy prices. This will no doubt occur in the coming decades as petroleum stocks decline, but a prudent concern about global warming requires a quicker response. Because any tax on basic commodities such as energy causes serious hardship for the poor, a concern for justice requires offsetting subsidies for low-income people, though these should be general income supplements and not directly related to energy consumption rates, so the poor also experience the incentive to conserve energy.

Different forms of energy release different amounts of carbon, so the single best way to reduce CO_2 emissions is to raise the price of commercial energy in proportion to the amount of CO_2 each form of energy emits: a "carbon tax." As figure 7.18 illustrates, a $100 tax for every metric ton of carbon emitted in the United States or Canada would raise oil prices about 39 percent, natural gas prices by 46 percent, and coal prices by 187 percent. These figures, and those for a $300 tax, come from a study by the International Energy Agency[53] designed to predict the effect of carbon taxes on energy consumption in the year 2010. For simplicity, they presume a currently untaxed market for these three products.

Of course, what producers and consumers respond to will be the prices they face for the kind of energy they need. Thus, as figure 7.19 indicates, a $100 carbon tax would bring about sizably different percentage changes in the prices of different forms of energy in different nations. Several factors are at work here. On the whole, because Japan and Europe already have higher energy taxes, an additional $100 carbon tax would be a smaller percentage change in the current price of energy there than it would be in Canada or the United States, where current taxes are quite low. In addition, commercial purchasers of fuel (oil used directly by industry, or gas, oil, or coal used to produce electricity) face a price reflecting little more than the underlying energy source, plus a small fee to cover trans-

Price Effects of a Carbon Tax: Canada & the U.S.
Projected Cost-plus-Carbon-Tax as a % of Projected Cost

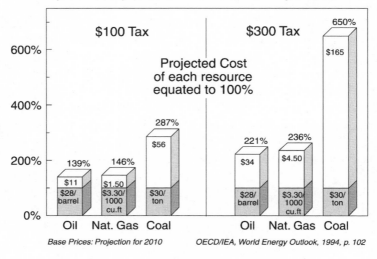

Figure 7.18

Price Increases from $100 Carbon Tax
% Change in 2010 from Business As Usual

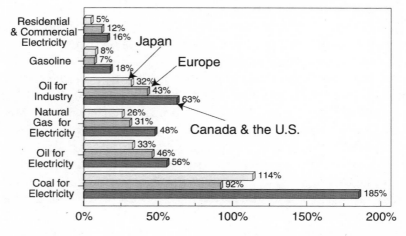

OECD/IEA, World Energy Outlook, 1994, p. 107

Figure 7.19

portation. Thus the carbon tax on the price of the underlying energy source represents a substantial percentage increase in the effective price facing these commercial buyers. The prices of residential and commercial electricity change relatively little because fuel costs are a much smaller portion of the overall cost of electricity, due to the much larger expense incurred by utility companies for capital investment and maintenance. Because gasoline is already heavily taxed relative to other forms of energy in all nations, the carbon tax would have a far smaller impact on retail gasoline prices.

The IEA study predicts that without a carbon tax, CO_2 emissions from the industrialized world will rise by about 30 percent over the next fifteen years, largely due to economic growth. It is a well-established fact that with higher prices for any good, in this case carbon-based energy, consumers will consume less of it and will also seek out substitutes. With a $100 carbon tax, emissions would grow approximately 20 percent.[54] The models developed to estimate such changes are quite sophisticated, and yet they are rudimentary in comparison with the daunting challenge of predicting the future. Nonetheless, they indicate that returning CO_2 emissions to the 1990 level—the goal articulated at the Rio environment conference— would require truly substantial carbon taxes, in the area of $300 per metric ton, bringing about percentage increases in prices about three times those indicated in figure 7.19.

Left out of this study, however, is the quite likely shift toward renewable energy sources that any sizable carbon tax would encourage.[55] Due to recent technological advances, producing electricity from wind, geothermal, and solar heat collection is becoming commercially more attractive even at current energy prices,[56] with government subsidies playing an important part in this process.[57] Substantial permanent increases in the price of carbon-based fuels would cause strong shifts toward renewable energy sources. Petroleum fuels would remain longest used in transportation, because of the need for portability, but even here the use of nonpolluting renewable energy sources to produce hydrogen remains on the horizon as a backstop technology.

How much help to the CO_2 emission problem would higher energy prices be? Even without shifts to backstop technologies, if higher energy prices in the United States brought its average per

179

capita energy use down to the level of Japan's, the amount of commercial energy consumed in the U.S. would drop by 57 percent, a savings two and a half times the total amount of commercial energy currently used annually in Africa and South America combined. In fact, the U.S. economy is so large and its per capita energy consumption compared with Japan is so high that this energy savings would also amount to two and a half times the total annual energy consumption of Japan![58]

Unfortunately, because cheap energy is good—at least in the short run—for consumer pocketbooks and corporate bottom lines, the political climate in the United States and Canada has been largely hostile to energy taxes, and thus the institution of a worldwide carbon tax will not be easy. In addition, it must be admitted that even with substantial taxes it is unlikely that U.S. and Canadian per capita consumption will ever fall to that of Japan, given differences in geography and culture.

Nonetheless, increasing energy taxes (like rising energy supply costs, when those eventually occur due to greater scarcity) would reduce energy consumption and thus CO_2 emissions. In the short run, a price increase from a carbon tax would induce us to drive somewhat less, leave fewer electric lights burning, and adjust the thermostat at home a bit. In the longer run, larger savings would occur. As people changed residences or jobs, they would try harder to shorten commuting distances and would insulate new homes better to save energy on heating and cooling. These and myriad other short-run and long-run adjustments would mean that CO_2 emissions could be cut more extensively and more efficiently through a carbon tax than through any cuts in the scale of international trade. Even if a complete elimination of trade were feasible, its impact on global warming would be tiny in comparison.

In addition to greenhouse warming, the second pressing threat to the global environment is the depletion of ozone in the upper atmosphere, which would increase ultraviolet radiation on the earth's surface, endangering the health and well-being of humans and much of the nonhuman natural world. As with greenhouse emissions, international markets will no more solve the global problem of ozone depletion than local markets will solve local pollution problems. In both cases communal governance is required. To this point, largely because of the resistance of the United States, only slim progress has been made on greenhouse gas emissions, but more has been accomplished on ozone-depleting chlorofluorocarbons (CFCs). The Montreal Protocol, adopted in 1987 and strengthened in 1990, sets timetables for the elimination of most CFCs and a number of other ozone-depleting substances by the year 2000, and permitting a longer transition for developing nations.[59] In many ways the complexity of CFC reduction typifies the ethical complexity of international trade more generally.[60]

Most of the cost (by some estimates 90 percent) of complying with the Montreal Protocol will be due to the conversion of refrigeration equipment, the world's biggest user of CFCs. This causes a dilemma for economic development policy. The arrival of electricity and refrigeration in the homes of more and more ordinary people in the developing world represents a morally important increase in economic prosperity. It will improve nutrition and reduce disease. In China alone, the number of home refrigerators rose from 4 million in 1985 to nearly 35 million in 1991—an eightfold increase in six years.[61] China and India together could easily account for more than 100 million additional refrigerators in the next decade. With or without international trade, these two nations and many others will vastly increase their use of consumer refrigeration and their production of CFCs.

Industrialized nations are likely to take advantage of substitute substances (so-called drop-in technology) to replace CFCs in current refrigeration equipment, but their price at three to five times that of CFCs will make them much less attractive in the developing world, where patent protection has lapsed on most CFC-based technologies. Newer technologies, or improved versions of older technologies based on ammonia or propane, may be possible, but the path of least resistance for many developing countries will still be based on ozone-threatening CFCs. Financial assistance for developing nations was built into the Montreal Protocol, but it was not adequate to the predictable need and a sizable increase is badly needed. Certainly, opposing increases in international trade on the basis of a concern about the ozone layer may not be the most appropriate step, because it would likely slow the needed transfer of non-CFC technologies.

In sum, it would seem from the perspective of both Christian ethics and secular policy analysis that too strong a focus on the detrimental aspects of international trade in the pollution problems of the world actually draws attention away from steps that are far more likely to reduce environmental problems. Even ending all trade tomorrow morning would not make much difference in the local or global pollution problems we currently face. Local problems will continue to require the expenditure of local resources (usually mandated through government). Although the industrialized world has far to go in the control of local pollution problems, experience to date indicates that such strategies are indeed effective. Global problems require global solutions. International agreements to reduce chlorofluorocarbons have been effective, though far more needs to be done to provide incentives to developing nations to adopt ozone-friendly technologies. The threat of global warming, in spite of its uncertainties, calls for an international agreement on a sizable carbon tax to reduce energy consumption, to channel it away from the most carbon-intensive fossil fuels, and, simultaneously, to channel it away from carbon fuels as a group toward alternative, renewable energy sources. For both CFCs and greenhouse gases, continuing international trade relations may prove essential to the dissemination of cleaner technologies in the developing world.

3. Trade and the Competitive Disadvantage of Environmental Laws

Following the concerns that increased trade accelerates the depletion of resources and the pollution of the biosphere is a third issue: Trade transforms local environmental laws into an international competitive disadvantage because of lax environmental laws in other nations. Paul Hawken, for example, predicted that

> the inevitable result of the present GATT treaty is that the rewards of international trade would go to the cheapest producer, not the most responsible producer. . . . International economic advantage would go to the companies that were best able to externalize environmental and social costs; companies that internalized those costs and took full

responsibility for their environmental impact would be placed at a disadvantage.[62]

We saw in the foregoing section that many local pollution problems—in particular air and water quality—actually tend to improve as national incomes rise because nations begin to spend more of that income to alleviate environmental problems once more basic needs are met. This "expenditure" usually comes through government regulations that raise the cost of production in industries that cause pollution. Thus both standard economic theory and everyday common sense predict that firms in nations with high pollution abatement costs will be tempted to move production facilities abroad if more permissive environmental regulations are available there.

For example, numerous reports have documented the environmental degradation brought about by the hundreds of maquiladora plants built in the 1980s in a "free trade zone" along Mexico's northern border: Toxic wastes have been openly dumped into the air and water. There seems to be agreement, even among the critics of increased trade,[63] that Mexico's environmental law is not the primary problem here; enforcement is. Nonetheless, whether it results from weak environmental laws or lack of enforcement, a cost advantage available to firms that migrate would be an incentive for them to do so. The question, of course, is *how prevalent* is the flight of dirty industries from First World nations to the developing world? How *strong* is the tendency to migrate?

Consider the United States. Pollution abatement costs brought about by federal regulations have been substantial, with estimates for 1988 accounting them to be in excess of $14 billion for all U.S. industry. Still, that amount is being paid out of the total value of U.S. industrial production for that year of about $2.6 trillion, resulting in perhaps a .5 percent cost for pollution abatement on the average.[64] Even "dirty" industries (those with the highest pollution abatement costs as a percent of total costs) still have relatively low abatement costs, ranging from a high of 3.2 percent of total costs for cement production to 2.2 percent for industrial chemicals to 1.8 percent for iron and steel foundries. Even if such industries were assured of zero pollution abatement costs for the long run in developing nations (an unlikely prospect), such cost differentials of 2 or 3 percent are not of a magnitude that ordinarily leads to plant relocation, though it would make it more likely for firms at the margin.[65] In addition, of course, firms *might* estimate that pollution abatement costs in the industrialized world will rise faster than in the developing world and thus might expect the cost differential to widen, though this, too, is unlikely given the increase of environmental concern worldwide.

A number of researchers have undertaken empirical investigations to detect any migration of dirty industries toward the developing world. Consider one recent study in Latin America.[66] There has indeed been an increase in dirty industry production and in the trade of dirty industry products in Third World nations, but it remains unclear whether any sizable portion of that comes from plant relocation. The reason for this is that developing nations predictably expand their industrial sectors, including "dirty" industrial sectors, as development proceeds. In any case, there seems to be a clear difference in the choice of "clean" or polluting technologies among developing nations. Figure 7.20 indicates the results of a study of "toxic intensity" (the pollution caused per unit of output) in Latin America.[67]

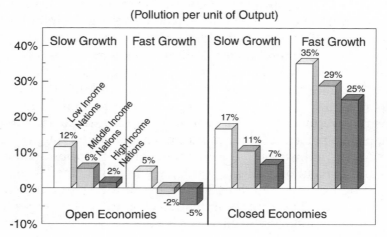

Pollution Growth in Latin America: 1980-89
Imputed Annual % Growth in "Toxic Intensity"

(Pollution per unit of Output)

Birdsall & Wheeler, 1992, p. 166

Figure 7.20

The study found significant differences between open economies (those more oriented to international trade) and closed economies. It also distinguished between low-, middle-, and high-income nations and between nations that were experiencing slow and fast economic growth during the 1980s. As the chart indicates, lower-income nations had higher growths in toxic intensity during the decade than higher-income nations, but there was a dramatic difference in nations that were more open to international trade. For open economies, faster economic growth moved in tandem with *lower* rates of growth in toxic intensity. For closed economies faster economic growth entailed *higher* growth rates of toxic intensity regardless of the initial level of income. Why?

The primary explanation for this difference seems to be that open economies generally, and fast-growth open economies in particular, benefit from faster transfers of clean production technologies from the developed world. It seems that because the newest and most economically efficient production technologies were developed to include cleaner processes (mandated in the industrialized nations), the relatively small costs of pollution abatement included in the new technologies often lead transnational firms producing in both places to invest in the cleaner technologies when producing in the developing world. In contrast, where trade is curtailed and investment decisions are made by local firms subject to more lax environmental law, plant expansion is more frequently a simple replication of older, "dirty" technologies. There are "pollution havens" in the Third World, but there is reason to believe that they occur primarily in closed economies.

A 1995 survey of existing empirical research on the topic concludes that "overall, the evidence of industrial flight to developing countries is weak, at best."[68] Such studies are not definitive. Nor do they contradict the fundamental presumption of trade critics *and* mainstream economists that firms in dirty industries will make relocation decisions to further their own interests, not to reduce global pollution. They do show, however, that such theory-based presumptions identify only one force among many which shape the effects of trade on environmental problems.

185

4. The Rules of Trade and National Sovereignty

The fourth point of conflict between environmental values and trade concerns the authority of some trade agreements to overthrow national environmental laws if they conflict with the principles of trade. Thus, for example, environmentalists were irate that U.S. laws (requiring tuna sold in the United States to be caught using environmentally superior nets, to prevent the death of dolphins) could be overthrown by the GATT after an appeal from Mexico (whose fishing fleets chose to use the more "economical" but environmentally more destructive fishing nets for their tuna catch). Similarly, many Canadians resented the threat to Canadian provincial decisions (to invest tax dollars in reforestation) after a U.S. challenge under the 1989 Canada-U.S. Free Trade Agreement. What appears to Mexican fishers as an unfair trade restriction and to U.S. loggers as an unfair production subsidy appears to others as sorely needed government decisions to offset environmental damage caused by business as usual. The nations of Europe have found a similar problem with the trade rules of the European Union. In the current international scheme of things, trade agreements have more legal clout than environmental agreements, and this leads many environmentalists to become critics of continuing efforts to increase trade. Though each of these agreements is worthy of analysis, it will be helpful to focus on the most critical one, the World Trade Organization, the successor to the General Agreement on Tariffs and Trade (the GATT).

If it were not for its narrow focus on trade and growth, the WTO might universally be recognized as a much-needed communal structure to prevent individual nations from choosing communally destructive policies of protectionism in a kind of "prisoner's dilemma" situation. (If my nation imposes tariffs and yours does not retaliate, I will be better off. However, since we both know that, we may both impose tariffs and both be worse off than if neither had.) Still, it is morally irresponsible to grant authority over the rules of trade to the WTO when only one goal (economic growth) of the many held by member nations is incorporated into its mission. Both religious ethics and secular policy analysis require a change.

There have been a number of good analyses of controversial GATT decisions, in particular the tuna-dolphin case, where the GATT ruled that a U.S. law discriminating against tuna caught with dolphin-endangering nets contravened the GATT agreement and had to be rescinded.[69] The central issue in the case from the perspective of the GATT was that this law entailed a restriction not on the kind of *product* to be allowed into the nation but on the sort of *process* used prior to bringing the product to the border for sale. There were other issues involved,[70] but the most controversial was that the GATT historically allowed nations to ban only particular products, and then, only as long as the ban applied equally to those inside and outside the country. The underlying reason why *process* restrictions were outlawed under the GATT was that it is all too easy for a nation to decide that the dominant process within its own borders is preferred and to erect protectionist barriers against processes used predominantly in other nations.

In the years since the founding of the GATT, nations throughout the world have come to understand the importance of the environmental effects of alternative production processes. Protectionism is no longer the dominant reason that a nation importing a product would care about the process that produced it. In fact, a "product life cycle" analysis is necessary to render production and consumption environmentally responsible—from the extractions of raw natural resources to the wastes released during and at the end of the product's life. As Daniel Esty has phrased it, "This differentiation between products and production processes cannot be sustained in an ecologically interdependent world."[71] Some argue that the WTO's own internal logic requires such an extension: The WTO now holds antitrust as a goal in its prevention of "dumping" and supports human rights in at least a limited way by treating differently products made by prison labor. Thus it could consistently hold environmental quality as a similar goal.[72] Others have proposed steps such as opening WTO sessions to public scrutiny (its dispute resolution panels are notorious for their secrecy) and involving nongovernmental organizations in WTO deliberations as a means of moving toward a "greener" WTO.[73]

There is, of course, another possibility besides transforming the World Trade Organization. The nations of the world could establish a separate and parallel international umbrella agreement, a "Global Environmental Organization," for all environmental issues. This organization could bear an authority parallel to the WTO, and these two international treaty bodies would work out the inevitable conflicts between trade and the environment by negotiation.[74] However, there seem to be, at least in the near term, insurmountable political difficulties in establishing so strong an international organization for the environment. As a result, efforts must continue to transform WTO standards to include environmental sustainability as one of its fundamental commitments.

Those who decide ultimately to oppose the rules of trade of the WTO or other international organizations rather than attempt to improve those rules, tend to take this stance after concluding that such an attempt to change the rules will bear little fruit. Although such a stance is morally defensible, it is at least as morally ambiguous as a commitment to changing the rules. It seems quite unlikely that the environmental problems before us can be solved without international cooperation through binding agreements. Any selective use of the sovereignty argument against rules we do not like will quite likely come back to haunt us when others choose selectively to flout the rules we have worked hard to establish. In fact, a similar form of "unilateralism" (as it has come to be called in the literature) makes up the fifth environmental argument for restricting trade.[75]

5. Import Restrictions as International Environmental Leverage

The last of the five forms of conflict between those who would oppose increased trade and those who would encourage it concerns the active use of trade restrictions as leverage to induce other nations to change their environmental policies. A single nation or group of nations might unilaterally place environmental conditions on imports in an attempt to address ecological problems. To cite simply one example, the United States threatened Japan with restrictions on its animal product exports to the U.S. if Japan did not stop trade in products made from the shell of the rare hawksbill turtle.[76]

At first hearing, it may seem contradictory for environmentalists to propose such a tactic and at the same time complain about the power of the WTO to overthrow national environmental legislation.

However the issue here is different, particularly from a moral perspective. Rather than appealing to an international legal authority with the power to *force* changes, proponents of this approach argue that they are simply stating the conditions under which their own nation will engage in trade, leaving other nations with a free choice: They can either accept those conditions and trade with us, or reject them and find somewhere else to sell their products.

For example, Denmark instituted regulations on containers for mineral waters, soft drinks, and beer, requiring that they be reusable within a system of deposit and return. Because this in effect required glass containers, foreign firms supplying those beverages to Denmark objected. The extra weight (compared with plastic or aluminum containers) significantly increased transportation costs for beverages imported into Denmark, and mandatory reuse required an expensive shipping of empty bottles back across international borders, eliminating the simpler recycling of aluminum or plastic containers at Danish recycling centers. This issue was litigated through the European Commission and not the GATT, but the arguments would have been similar. The Danes defended their law as necessary to minimize packaging waste. Outsiders argued that the laws gave Danish beverage firms an artificial advantage by raising production costs for foreign firms.[77] A similar issue arose under the Canada-U.S. Free Trade Agreement when American beer producers objected to a 10¢ levy on all metallic beer cans sold in the province of Ontario.[78]

Critics of such import restrictions respond in three different ways. The first is that although this process may seem fair enough between nations that have roughly the same economic power, it is all too easy for larger and economically more successful nations to, in effect, "force" economically less influential nations into compliance. In such cases, the distinction between a legal requirement (which many environmentalists oppose as a loss of sovereignty) and a "free" economic choice is simplistic.[79]

The second objection is that this use of trade restrictions to accomplish nontrade goals would open Pandora's box. For every nation that may take this approach for a laudable environmental goal, there may well be a number of others that threaten trade restrictions to further protectionist or geopolitical objectives far less benign. As a result, proponents of trade usually want to "depoliticize" trade decisions. More accurately phrased, they want to insulate trade policy from other political or economic goals of the nation.

The third response by critics against the use of import restrictions to further environmental goals is that they usually don't work. Relations among nations are enough like those among individuals that the use of threats and unilateral mandates to accomplish even morally appropriate goals usually brings about a resentment that threatens not only the goal at hand but a number of others on which nations must cooperate. As Robert Repetto of the World Resources Institute put it,

> Even if legal under international rules, these policies are problematic because they rely on one welfare-reducing measure (trade restrictions) to discourage another (non-cooperation in environmental protection). . . . The use of trade *concessions* to elicit international environmental *cooperation* is an approach much more likely to generate economic and environmental gains and an overall improvement in welfare.[80]

From the perspective of Christian ethics as well as secular policy analysis, the issue here concerns the relative advantages and disadvantages of any nation's claiming the right (and thus allowing others the right) to act unilaterally in trade issues that affect the environment. It seems clear that the best solution would be an international agreement covering such issues, and the nation's effort to achieve such a multilateral agreement might be a "moral test" of the sincerity with which the environmental regulation was initially enacted. For example, it would be obviously duplicitous if Ontario wanted to penalize U.S. brewers for exporting cans, but defended the right of Canadian brewers to export metal cans to the United States without penalty. While helpful, this test does not guarantee moral rectitude, since a nation might decide that its protectionist self-interest (rather than an environmental value) is best served by an internationally recognized trade restriction. Because of the potential for insincere environmental concern to cloak underlying protectionist self-interest, international trade agreements should include in their dispute-resolution processes a judgment about the ultimate social and scientific legitimacy of environmental claims.

190

Nonetheless, it is undeniable that the environmental health of the planet will depend on more ecologically benign production and distribution processes, and, as we have already seen, future trade agreements will need to provide for life-cycle regulation of production. Because progress on environmental issues will require strengthening both international trust and the institutions on which such trust is founded, unilateral actions—even for good causes—should be a last resort, not a first step.

CONCLUSION

The Christian commitment to respecting the integrity of God's creation presents severe challenges to believers today, living within an economic system that will, if unchecked, profligately abuse that gift. In an economy based primarily on markets, the individual decisions of a multitude of economic actors, and in particular the highly influential decisions of the most powerful, will tend to ignore the long-term environmental costs of their actions. Only a community decision through government can channel those forces toward less environmentally destructive outcomes. At the same time, the widespread environmental problems throughout the former Soviet bloc demonstrate that markets are not the only source of threats to the ecosphere.

In this chapter, we have addressed environmental concerns about international trade. The two most fundamental charges against trade are, in effect, charges against economic growth: that it leads to the depletion of the earth's storehouse of resources and simultaneously overwhelms the earth's capacity to absorb wastes. Implicit here, as we have seen, are a number of "background" issues especially concerning the likelihood and severity of future environmental problems. Those more convinced that the likelihood is high and the severity extreme will be more likely to insist on restrictions on economic growth, and on trade. Nonetheless, it would seem that there are more effective and politically more feasible options for reducing each of these long-term problems than trying to do so by restricting trade itself.

Local pollution problems have been mitigated significantly through concerted political decisions to do so, even though much work remains to be done even in wealthy nations such as the United States and Canada. Worldwide pollution problems are critically important. Significant strides in reducing ozone depletion have been made through the Montreal Protocol and related agreements. Trade and increased aid look to be absolutely essential in persuading the developing world to adopt ozone-friendly technologies since CFC refrigeration processes are more cheaply available. Global warming remains a tremendous uncertainty and threat for the world. Nonetheless, restricting trade in an effort to reduce CO_2 emissions will be less effective, politically more difficult, and more likely to stunt the aspirations of Third World people in poverty than would be alternative strategies. These include increasing energy efficiency (particularly in the United States and Canada) through tax policies as well as working toward improving the sustainability of Third World forests through enforcement of timber trade treaties and subsidies for forest preservation and for the dissemination of environmentally friendly technologies such as improved biomass stoves. The single most important step to be taken will be internalizing the social costs of commercial energy through some form of carbon tax. Not only would a substantial carbon tax slow the growth of consumption of carbon-based fuels through higher prices, but perhaps even more important, those higher prices would make backstop renewable technologies more and more economically feasible. While a "soft landing" in the ultimate switch to renewable energy sources is by no means ensured, it is a definite possibility.

This chapter also dealt with three additional points of conflict between advocates of trade and environmentalists. Common sense and economic theory would predict that tighter environmental laws in some nations would create an incentive for firms to move to other countries with looser regulations. However, the empirical record indicates that this cost advantage is small in comparison with other costs of production and that in fact there has been little capital migration due to governmentally imposed pollution abatement costs.

Ultimately, of course, international agreements on pollution standards and other environmental concerns represent the best hope for an ecologically responsible economy worldwide. Thus Christians and others concerned about the environment ought to be more cautious in their assertions of national sovereignty as a defense against rules of trade that currently have too much international legal force. We will return to the question of improving international trade rules in a later chapter; here, the moral danger in the sovereignty argument should be recognized: It undercuts the ultimately necessary deference of local, case-by-case decisions to an international body with the capacity to engender worldwide compliance with higher environmental standards.

All this should not be taken to mean that nothing but good things comes from international trade. It remains true that powerful firms engaged in trade will attempt to subvert efforts to improve the environment because these raise their costs of production. Hard political work will continue to be needed to bring about such improvements. In addition, trade by definition increases the geographic separation between environmental costs caused in production and the economic benefits enjoyed in consumption. Inevitably this causes a greater psychic distance between consumers and the environmental problems their consumption entails, a highly unfortunate result from the perspective of Christian ethics. Even further, as Herman Daly has argued, to the extent that trade allows industrialized nations to exceed their domestic limits on resource generation or waste absorption (by depending on other nations for these), the gradual tightening of biophysical environmental constraints will be felt more simultaneously around the planet than would otherwise have been the case.[81] The result, of course, will be less opportunity for one nation to learn from another's experience with environmental problems and less time to alter behavior when those constraints begin to bind more tightly.

Such dangers are real and too often overlooked by glib advocates of "free trade" on the right. Nonetheless, the moral risks identified in these concerns, though different in scale, seem analogous to those faced domestically by Christians who have a good job, own a car, use a dishwasher, or take a summer vacation at some distance from their home. The environmental threats arising from such "nonexcessive" activities are real and illustrate an important tension implicit in Christian faith today. On the one hand, Christians remain convinced that God sees the material world as good and intends a fulfilling life for everyone. On the other hand, even a moderate modern lifestyle harms the environment—threatening the integrity of God's creation—and of itself does little to address the grinding poverty of so many of our fellow inhabitants on the globe. There is great moral risk in such a lifestyle, as there is in international trade. It is only with hard work to offset those threats to the integrity of creation and to better the prospects of the world's poor that Christians can (conditionally at best) justify such a lifestyle and the patterns of exchange that support it.

In addition to this integration of moral ambiguity within our view of the world, however, we must also acknowledge the positive effects of trade in the transfer of environmentally necessary technologies and in its potential to increase the economic well-being of the poor of the developing world. This recognition has led many in the environmental movement to part company with those who would reduce international trade because of its threat to the environment. A number of environmental organizations have come to share the view articulated in the Worldwatch Institute's *1993 State of the World* report:

> Trade can be a tool for shaping a world that is ecologically sustainable and socially just. . . . Now policymakers must get on with the task of determining how the rules of trade can be revised to help achieve it.[82]

CHAPTER 8

TRADE AND JOBS

For Christians, the religious importance of daily work is rooted in the doctrine of creation: God's original and continuing creation of the material world is an endorsement of its goodness. Ordinary daily work to provide goods and services for people is religiously important and is a limited but real human participation in God's creative plan. Thus, when public policy discussions address issues of employment, moral questions deeply important to Christian faith are involved.

At the same time, however, moral conviction alone is not sufficient to sort through the issues. Participants in the debate about increased international trade necessarily hold theoretical perspectives on the world of economics and jobs. Even those who sharply criticize economic theory still need some theoretical presumption about the interaction of workers and employers in a global economy.

It is no surprise that critics of trade (who often fault the discipline of economics for misunderstanding the effects of trade on employment) tend to complain that economics has too large an influence in the debate, while proponents of trade (who usually think economics is correct in its assessments of these issues) judge that economics is too often ignored. We saw earlier the critique of mainstream economics offered by Herman Daly and John Cobb. While more articulate in this matter than most critics of trade, their arguments about the misplaced concreteness of economic models and the threat to community which mainstream economics represents are widely echoed by others.

On the other side are examples such as Paul Krugman's critique[1] of recent forays into international economics by the historian Paul Kennedy.[2] Krugman argues that Kennedy—simply one example of a sizable group of influential authors—has expounded international trade irresponsibly: readily wading into economic policy issues without any apparent effort to become fluent in the continuing economic conversation. Kennedy attempts to provide a thoroughgoing critique of international trade theory, but along the way confuses Adam Smith and David Ricardo. Although it is always possible to get the names wrong and still get the analysis right, Krugman likens this criticism of economics to a critique of psychoanalysis that confuses Freud and Jung. More substantively, Krugman chides Kennedy and other overconfident critics of economics for their "ingenious arguments [that] are familiar fallacies covered in an undergraduate textbook"[3] (like confusing comparative and absolute advantage), and concludes that public debate over international trade has often simply ignored the discipline of economics.

In fact, compared with those regarding agriculture or the environment, disputes over the impact of international trade on jobs tend to be hotter and more typically characterized by mutual accusations of erroneous theorizing. Thus, we examine here the main theoretical issues and then turn to some empirical findings about the interaction of trade and jobs.

THEORY: TRADE AND EMPLOYMENT

In order to examine differences in theoretical presumptions about the interaction of trade and employment, it is helpful to identify three separate issues: international competition among workers, international capital movements, and the relation of labor productivity to the notion of Third World "development."

International Competition Among Workers

As we have seen, one of the fundamental criticisms of increased international trade is that it threatens the welfare of workers in the industrialized world because it allows multinational firms to produce goods at low wages in developing nations and sell them to consumers in the industrialized world. For simplicity, we might refer to this as the "Level 1" jobs argument against trade: First World workers will inevitably suffer because the vast number of low-wage workers of the developing world will produce more and more of the world's goods, putting many First World workers out of work entirely and severely suppressing the wages and benefits of those fortunate enough to stay employed.[4]

The problem with this Level 1 argument is that it presumes that all workers are "roughly the same," and it also obscures a critically important difference among types of goods traded internationally.[5] In fact, what happens in international trade is that goods from one nation are sold in another and ultimately "paid for" by a movement of other goods in the opposite direction. International sales are transacted, of course, in one currency or another, and only occasionally is there explicit barter. However, the primary reason for accepting another country's currency is to exchange that money eventually for goods.

Thus, with an increase in international trade, the demand for some goods in the industrialized world will fall (those now imported from Third World manufacturers) while the demand for others will increase (those now exported in greater quantity to the developing world). As a result, it simply cannot be the case that *all* workers in the industrialized world will be harmed by greater trade with low-income nations. Only those could be worse off who make products that will, because of trade, be made elsewhere and imported. Workers who make products to be exported to the developing world will face an increased demand for their services, and thus they will benefit more than before.

Which workers will benefit and which will face rising unemployment? To answer this question we must recall the fundamental economic difference between "wealthy" nations and "poor" nations. A nation becomes wealthier when it produces more goods and services: when the average factory, farm, and worker become more

197

productive. Thus, in general, developing countries are poor because productivity levels (output per hour) are lower than in the industrialized world. Saying this is no insult to developing nations; nor does it attribute a moral superiority to industrialized nations. The availability of education, training, and capital goods explains the vast majority of the difference.

So what sorts of goods will be exported from the developing to the industrialized worlds? The theory of international trade (recall the discussion of absolute and comparative advantage in chapter 2) as well as common sense leads us to expect that developing nations will produce for export those goods whose production requires resources these nations have in abundance relative to industrialized countries. Developing countries will tend to export goods requiring low-skilled labor. Similarly, industrialized nations will tend to export "high-tech," or more properly "high-skilled," products because of the relative abundance of high-skilled labor there. As a result, low-skilled workers in the industrialized nations will tend to be hurt by trade, and high-skilled workers there will, in general, be helped.

Recognizing this, we can now frame a more refined accusation against trade, which we might call the "Level 2" jobs critique: Because of trade, workers in the First World will "on average" be harmed, because the loss of jobs for lower-skilled workers will outweigh the increase in welfare experienced by higher-skilled workers.

Interestingly, the core of this argument was presented in theoretical detail more than fifty years ago and has come to be known as the Stolper-Samuelson theorem.[6] It is based on a simple two-country model, where each country has only two types of labor (skilled and unskilled), with country A having an abundance of low-skilled, low-wage labor, and country B having an abundance of high-skilled, high-wage labor. Without trade, each nation produces two types of commodities: labor-intensive (requiring mostly unskilled labor) and capital-intensive (requiring mostly high-skilled labor). If trade commences between the two nations, country A will become the manufacturing site for labor-intensive commodities, while country B will focus on capital-intensive commodities. The key is that by algebraic necessity unskilled labor in country B will be in less demand and will see its wages fall.[7] This is the substance of the jobs argument made by Daly and Cobb and most critics of trade.[8] Ironically, this reliance on economic theory to predict the future leaves these critics open to the charge that they themselves resort to the same kind of misplaced concreteness they attribute to the economists they criticize.

The problem with this Level 2 critique is that, like the Level 1 argument, it still oversimplifies the complexity of "labor" in treating only two types: low-skilled and high-skilled. Many an international trade textbook *begins* with such simplified models but later rejects them as a basis for policy because a more realistic model is needed.[9] Suppose, a bit more realistically, that these two countries produce not just two commodities but three, ranging from highly labor-intensive to highly capital-intensive, with the "middle" good being produced with a nearly equal mix of skilled and unskilled labor. Initiating trade in this case would still cause highly labor-intensive production to move to country A, with its product now being imported into nation B. However, this says nothing about how large will be the increase in the export from nation B of the two more-capital-intensive goods, and there simply is no algebraic reason against supposing that the demand for the "middle" good will rise most and that the overall demand for labor in country B will rise as well. This is an empirical question. Recognizing especially the dynamic gains from trade, the answer depends largely on the changes in relative labor productivity in the three sectors in each of the two nations and the increased level of consumption of the workers in the lower-wage nation (who are now more able to pay for imported goods from country B).[10]

International Capital Movements

One of the most consistent elements in the jobs-based critique of trade is the concern that capital will move out of the industrialized world toward the developing world because of the lower wages available there. In its broadest sense, "capital" would include any investment today that will increase productivity tomorrow. The classic examples would be tools, machines, and factories, though economists today generally include "human capital" (investment in education and various forms of training and skill-building). From the perspective of Christian social ethics, we should also include national "investments" in political democracy and other institutions necessary for a humane society, which bring about stability and predictability, assets for production often overlooked. However, the "capital mobility" referred to in the critique of trade usually refers to the choices of multinational firms to move production facilities from the high-wage areas of the industrialized world to the low-wage areas of the developing world. This concern is often combined with an awareness of the advances in communications that have dramatically "shrunk" the world.

Thus, we might formulate a somewhat more refined "Level 3" jobs critique of trade that points the finger at the movement of capital: Because capital now moves more quickly than ever before, multinational firms can take even greater advantage of low-wage labor in the developing world, further harming workers—on average—in the industrialized world.

It is true that "capital" now flows almost instantaneously from one continent to another at the prospect of small percentage gains. This pertains largely to various forms of financial capital—transactions involving stocks, bonds, currencies, futures contracts, and so on. Financial capital has significant impact on the capital resources with which laborers work. When savers' assets are invested in the developing world, they create jobs there, not at home. When they move back, the reverse occurs. The rapid flight of financial capital out of Mexico in late 1994 and early 1995 had harsh consequences for ordinary Mexicans.

However this greater mobility of financial capital is really something of a red herring in discussions about "direct investment abroad," the choice by a domestic firm to construct and operate production facilities in another nation.[11] When a corporation decides between a domestic investment and one abroad, the central issue is and always has been the long-run rate of return over the life of the investment. The fact that a deal can now be consummated more quickly than was possible a century ago is not a strong determinant. Far more important is the political stability and economic predictability of developing nations. This doesn't increase capital's *ability* to move, but it surely increases its likelihood. Christians concerned about First World job loss, however, can hardly root for instability and unpredictability for the developing world.

The most important question is not how fast capital can move but what are the incentives for the movement? Consider the debate that occurred within the United States and Canada over the North American Free Trade Agreement (NAFTA). The reduction of U.S. tariffs on goods imported from Mexico does indeed make investment in Mexico more attractive to U.S. investors, but we must ask *how much* more. Much of the fear of NAFTA was and still remains based on the argument that Mexican low-skilled labor can be hired for about one-fifth the wage of U.S. labor. On the surface, that sounds like a dire threat to United States and Canadian workers: an 80 percent advantage. However, the average pre-NAFTA tariff on manufactured goods entering the United States from Mexico was (a relatively small) 4 percent. Thus one must ask a further question: Would U.S. capital, which before NAFTA had not yet flowed out to Mexico in response to an available 80 percent drop in wage costs, move to Mexico after NAFTA removed a 4 percent price disadvantage which Mexican products previously experienced due to U.S. tariffs?[12] Most economists answered "No."

The reality is that prior to NAFTA there was a kind of equilibrium between the two nations, with lower average productivity per hour being the fundamental reason for lower Mexican wages. This is the reason that most U.S. firms did not find lower Mexican wages a sufficient reason to move either before *or after* NAFTA. Eliminating the 4 percent tariff could be anticipated to lead *some* firms to move (those already on the "margin"), but it was wrongheaded and in some cases disingenuous of opponents of increased trade to focus on the 5 to 1 differential in wages as the driving force. Some U.S. firms who not long ago moved their operation to Mexico have since moved back, admitting their naivete about the wage differential.[13]

International capital mobility stands, then, as a potential threat to low-skilled workers in the industrialized world. We will return to the empirical question of how influential such capital movements have been, but it will be helpful first to reflect on one critically important effect of capital transfers to developing nations: the increase in labor productivity for workers there.

Labor Productivity and the Meaning of Economic "Development"

Some critics of trade focus on the poverty of the Third World and blame it primarily on the greed of multinational firms and local elites. Injustices by firms and individuals do indeed play a large role in preventing many of the poor of the world from increasing their economic well-being. This insight and the prophetic critique which flows from it are critically important, but they do not address the fundamental question about the character of poverty and wealth. Why is the average carpenter or baker or homemaker or farmer or factory worker in the industrialized world wealthier than someone in the same occupation in the developing world? The fundamental answer is that each of them produces more each day than the counterpart worker in the Third World.

Consider simply a Canadian or United States carpenter building a typical house. Because of electric saws, pneumatic nailers, and forklifts for raising building materials to the upper floors (to name just a few), this carpenter simply accomplishes more in a day's work than counterparts in, say, rural Africa, who must rely on hand tools and a strong back to accomplish everything. Economies of scale and other systemwide advantages also help: the availability of prefabricated rafters, windows, and doors; a generally efficient system of just-on-time delivery of building materials from the local wholesaler; a predictable housing market that keeps carpenters working even when there is no particular house-buyer standing by; as well as a network of postsecondary trade schools that reduces the cost of acquiring the skills necessary for modern carpentry. The reason that First World workers are wealthier is that they are more productive due to greater skill, a richer deposit of capital goods, and a highly differentiated and generally efficient political economy.

We should be clear that this implies no moral or cultural indictment of workers elsewhere. They face immense obstacles—from the absence of schools and medical clinics, to daily hours of toil securing fuelwood and potable water, to the self-interested excesses of local and multinational firms. There is no doubt that if the typical carpenter from rural Africa were given the tools and know-how, productivity there would rise dramatically. In fact, this is the essence of economic development: Skills, techniques, and tools are improved, allowing individuals to produce more per day, raising their daily wage. Political institutions are extremely influential in this process—in particular, public policies that prevent abuses that the otherwise unregulated assertions of self-interest by the wealthy and powerful would cause. Such policies need to be strengthened in the industrialized world and are woefully lacking in many developing nations. Nonetheless, increasing the daily economic productivity is essential for the future of the world's poor.

When employing arguments about capital mobility, Christians of the industrialized world need to recognize the positive advantage for workers in the developing world that derives both from an increase in the demand for their labor and from an increase in the capital endowments with which they work. This is sometimes dismissed as inconsequential due to the large number of unemployed there,[14] but it takes strong background commitments for Christians to devalue the creation of jobs in poorer nations, *especially* in the midst of large-scale unemployment.

The economic essence of a better life for the impoverished of the world is not financial transfers from the wealthy to the poor but the capacity of the poor to produce more in their daily work. As their productivity grows through better education, greater economic security, stronger institutions of economic organization, and a better capital endowment with which to work, those currently impoverished will be more and more on an economic par with workers in the industrialized world.

Christians must be committed to such change for the poor of the world. This change is not ensured, but if it does occur, even if it occurs in accord with principles of justice and sustainability, the workers of the developing world will indeed "compete" with workers of similar education and skill in the industrialized world even more directly than they do today. We need to be realistic about this.

At the same time, however, any adequate theoretical analysis of the impact of international trade on employment must include the welfare losses that will inevitably occur for low-skilled workers in the industrialized world. Although these losses are in general less severe than critics of trade portray, they are more severe than proponents of trade often imply. Critics of trade overestimate the problem because they tend vastly to overestimate the loss of jobs and deterioration of wages and benefits which trade effects, as we will see in the next section reviewing empirical findings. Proponents of trade often overlook the hardship caused for low-income workers when they simply report net gains for the industrialized world on average. We return to this issue later in this chapter after identifying an even more important influence that tends to dim the prospects for low-skilled workers in the industrialized world.

EMPIRICAL FINDINGS: TRADE AND EMPLOYMENT

Theoretical presumptions about how the world works are essential to any assessment of the effects of international trade. Nonetheless, differences between contrasting theoretical assumptions can rarely be sorted out without comparing them with what has actually been occurring. We should, of course, hold no illusions that "the facts speak for themselves"; there are always theoretical presumptions implicit, even in presentations that lay claim to objectivity. Still, a review of empirical findings is often quite helpful.

It is remarkably difficult to track accurately the causal factors in the creation or loss of particular jobs. While critics of increased trade can point to vivid instances of individual plants closing in the same year that the firm opens a similar plant in the developing world, proponents of trade point to equally clear instances of firms expanding their production and employment to meet the increased export demand for their products. Such anecdotal instances, however, inevitably add up to a minuscule proportion of national employment, and thus both sides ought to turn to broader changes in employment patterns to make their case.

Losing Manufacturing Jobs

Crucial to most jobs-based arguments against trade is the (accurate) observation that the United States and Canada have been losing manufacturing jobs. Although this loss of "good" jobs is critically important in any moral assessment of our economic situation today, its usual interpretation within arguments against trade is deeply flawed.

It is a commonplace of public discussion in the United States that, due to increased international trade, U.S. industrial jobs have flowed to Japan and Germany, and that this is directly attributable to a fall in manufacturing productivity in the United States. A similar explanation is offered for the drop in Canadian manufacturing jobs since 1989. But, as Paul Krugman has argued, this view is almost completely wrong.[15] Consider the claim that manufacturing jobs are flowing out of Canada or the United States to our leading industrial competitors. Figures 8.1 and 8.2 indicate the overall number of manufacturing jobs and the proportion of manufacturing jobs in the economy for Canada, the United States, Japan, and Germany for the twenty years from 1972 to 1992.

Millions of Manufacturing Jobs

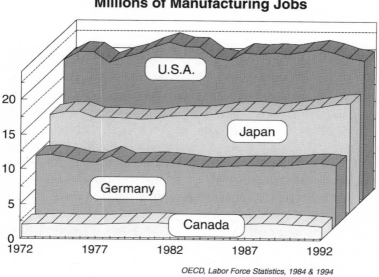

OECD, Labor Force Statistics, 1984 & 1994

Figure 8.1

Over this period Japan gained more than two million manufacturing jobs, Germany lost about a million, and the United States and Canada finished the period with about the same number of manufacturing jobs as at the beginning (though they have both lost jobs since 1980). However, it is clear from figure 8.2 that manufacturing employment is becoming less important for the economies of all four

205

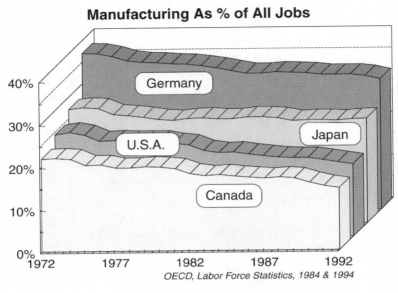

Manufacturing As % of All Jobs

OECD, Labor Force Statistics, 1984 & 1994

Figure 8.2

of these nations. Even Japan, with a remarkable record of large merchandise trade surpluses, saw manufacturing jobs drop from more than 27 percent of all jobs in 1972 to slightly more than 24 percent twenty years later. Isn't international trade a strong determining factor in the fate of manufacturing jobs? If so, how is it that the proportion of manufacturing jobs is dropping even in the "industrial success stories" of Germany and Japan, which have traditionally shown substantial merchandise trade balances? To answer these questions we must first retreat to a more general question: What is it that brings about changes in the number of jobs in the economy?

Explaining Total Job Growth

Several reciprocally interactive forces influence the number and kind of jobs that are generated in any national economy. Helpful in sorting through this complexity is a comprehensive 1994 study of employment completed by the Organisation for Economic Co-operation and Development, which aimed, among other things, to explain the

206

growth in the number of jobs in each of the leading industrialized nations of the world.[16] The authors isolated the five most important economic variables that influence job growth, analyzed the changes in each of these five factors from the first to the last year of the study, and estimated the number of jobs gained or lost because of changes in those five factors over that period. Figure 8.3 summarizes the study's explanation of the growth in jobs—over 23 million, shown by the bar on the left—in the United States from 1972 to 1985.[17]

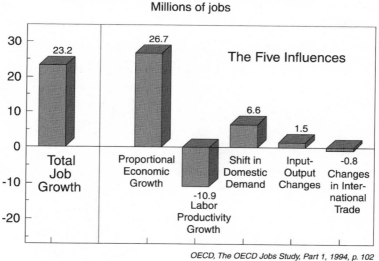

Causes of U.S. Job Growth: 1972-85

Millions of jobs

OECD, The OECD Jobs Study, Part 1, 1994, p. 102

Figure 8.3

The single most significant factor in explaining job growth is simply the proportional economic growth of the nation's economy. The United States population grew by nearly 14 percent during that period, and the GDP rose nearly 40 percent. The first bar on the right-hand side of the chart shows what would have happened to job growth had every sector of the economy grown in proportion to the overall GDP. By itself this would have led to more than 26 million new jobs.

As the second bar indicates, a growth in labor productivity over the period actually cut the nation's job growth by more than 10 million jobs. How improvements in labor productivity cost jobs may not seem obvious at first, but consider a factory where 100 workers in 1972 produce 1,000 units per week. If an increase in labor productivity by 1985 allows those same 1,000 units to be produced by, say, 90 workers, that's a loss of 10 jobs. (Of course, the demand for these products may also rise, because of the growth of the population and the economy, but that increased demand for the products—and implicitly for the workers who make them—has already been accounted for in the 26 million new jobs from proportional growth.)

The next two bars in the chart are more technical. When consumers make changes in how they spend their dollars, they may shift that purchasing power away from industries which generate less than the average number of jobs per dollar toward industries that generate more than the average, a theme to which we return presently in examining service sector employment. Over this period such shifts in domestic demand led to an increase of more than 6 million new jobs. The fourth factor is even more technically complicated but simply represents the employment effects of changes in other technical patterns of production.

Most important for our purposes is the last element: changes in total job growth due to shifts in international trade during the period covered by the study. As the chart indicates, changes in the international trade position of the United States between 1972 and 1985 cut into total job growth: a loss of nearly 800,000 jobs, about seven-tenths of 1 percent of all U.S. jobs in 1985, largely through a sharp increase in the gap between imports and exports that occurred during this period.[18]

By coincidence the beginning and ending years of the *OECD Jobs Study* spanned a dramatic change in the U.S. trade balance. As figures 8.4 and 8.5 indicate, in 1972 U.S. merchandise trade with the rest of the world was almost balanced, showing a $6 billion deficit. By 1985 the U.S. was nearly at the bottom of the trough of the huge merchandise trade deficits that occurred in the 1980s: The 1985 deficit (imports minus exports) was more than $129 billion, meaning it worsened by $123 billion during the period covered by the *Jobs Study*. Thus it was not simply increased trade (lots of exports *and* lots of imports) that brought about the job losses. The trade deficit (far faster growth of imports than exports) was the critical change.

208

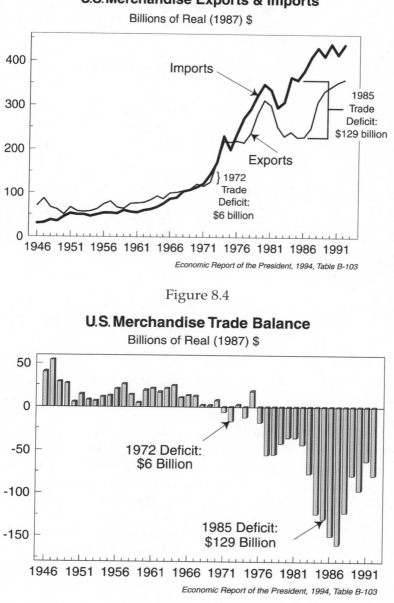

U.S. Merchandise Exports & Imports
Billions of Real (1987) $

Imports

1985 Trade Deficit: $129 billion

Exports

} 1972 Trade Deficit: $6 billion

Economic Report of the President, 1994, Table B-103

Figure 8.4

U.S. Merchandise Trade Balance
Billions of Real (1987) $

1972 Deficit: $6 Billion

1985 Deficit: $129 Billion

Economic Report of the President, 1994, Table B-103

Figure 8.5

209

In order to view more carefully the disaggregated causes within this trade effect, the *OECD Jobs Study* goes on to distinguish between sources of imports and destination of exports for manufactured goods, as figure 8.6 indicates.

Employment Effects of Changes in Trade
U.S.A.: 1972-85

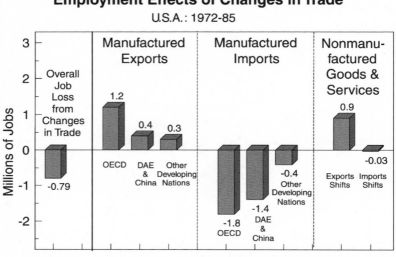

OECD, The OECD Jobs Study, Part 1, 1994, p. 102

Figure 8.6

The effect of the huge growth in the merchandise trade deficit from $6 billion to $129 billion by 1985 is apparent in the difference between manufactured exports and manufactured imports. The gross merchandise trade figures in the previous charts included nonmanufactured goods but excluded services, and thus the charts do not correspond completely. Nonetheless, the sizable imbalance between manufactured trade in the U.S. and that of both the other industrialized nations (the OECD) and that of the rapidly growing Asian nations (China and the "dynamic Asian economies" [DAE]) accounts for the job losses due to changes in trade over this period.

On the far right of the chart are the job effects of trade in services and in nonmanufactured goods. Here the United States experienced a sizable increase in jobs, largely due to increases in the export of professional services (typically purchased by foreign firms) and of subsidized agricultural products over this fifteen-year period.[19]

The *OECD Jobs Study* of the creation of jobs in Canada shows a simpler picture than for the United States, largely because Canada's trade has consistently been nearly balanced in recent decades. As figure 8.7 indicates, the two biggest influences in job growth are again proportional economic growth and labor productivity growth. Figure 8.8 gives a breakdown of the trade effects, explaining the small (26,000) but real growth in jobs attributable to changes in Canada's trade position over the period.

The economic success stories of Germany and Japan also gained jobs due to changes in trade.[20] The United States is the only one of the four nations for which changes in trade over the life of the study cost domestic jobs. The large merchandise trade imbalances are the fundamental difference between the U.S. experience and that of the other OECD nations. We must, however, distinguish this imbalance in trade from the overall volume of trade. That is, the volume of trade can be quite large, with both high exports and high imports, even though the balance of trade is generally even. This is the situation of Canada, Japan, and Germany.

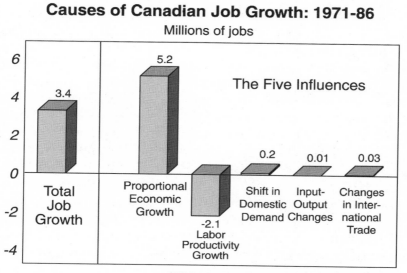

Causes of Canadian Job Growth: 1971-86

Millions of jobs

OECD, The OECD Jobs Study, Part 1, 1994, p. 102

Figure 8.7

Employment Effects of Changes in Trade
Canada: 1971-86

OECD, The OECD Jobs Study, Part 1, 1994, p. 102

Figure 8.8

How is it that the United States is able to incur sizable imbalances in trade for a decade running? Other countries don't export goods without payment, and the United States has only two ways to make "payments": exports of goods and services or inflows of capital from abroad (in effect, the "export" of financial claims on U.S. assets). Both the federal deficit (funded in part by loans from abroad) and increasing foreign investments in the United States help explain how the United States has been able to sustain this trade imbalance for so long. While the mechanisms for adjustment are complicated (and to some extent controverted), nearly everyone agrees that the rising federal budget deficits, creating the need to borrow more than $200 billion per year by 1985, had a critically large impact. Thus nearly everyone agrees that reducing the federal budget deficit will improve the balance of trade, and everyone accepts that closing the gap between imports and exports would increase the demand for United States labor.

Closing this gap is needed, but we should keep in mind that this is quite different from simply reducing international trade.

International Capital Mobility

As we have seen, one of the most forceful arguments among critics of international trade has been that capital will flow out of the industrialized world in response to lower wages in the developing world, leaving more and more workers of the industrialized world without adequate employment. As evidence of that move, critics often point to the sizable increases in manufacturing exports from the developing world to the industrialized nations, as figure 8.9 illustrates.

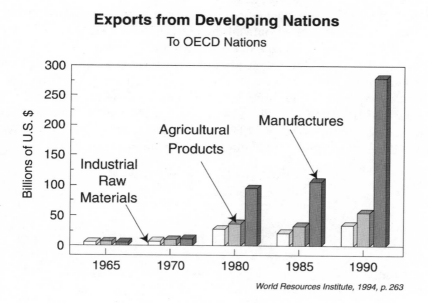

Exports from Developing Nations

To OECD Nations

World Resources Institute, 1994, p. 263

Figure 8.9

Those exports have indeed been immensely helpful to developing nations. However, from the point of view of the industrialized world, this change is at most a minor one for two reasons. The first is that this trade is roughly balanced. Although the United States has sustained a sizable deficit beginning in the early 1980s, the industrialized nations taken as a whole have roughly balanced trade with the developing world. Exports from the industrialized to the developing world have increased apace. Second, important though a $300

213

billion export of manufactured goods was for developing nations as a whole (especially since the jobs in manufacturing tend to be among the best-paying in the economy), that amount represented only about 1.5 percent of the $19 trillion gross domestic product of the industrialized world in 1990.

The primary concern expressed by critics of trade who worry about its employment effects has been directed at the incentives for multinational firms to close down plants in the United States, Canada, and other industrialized nations and reopen them in the Third World. The focus here, then, is on "foreign direct investment," the purchase abroad of land and buildings, usually the decision to build a factory from scratch, on the part of multinational firms. There are other forms of investment—financial investments—where persons buy "portfolio" assets such as stocks or bonds in a foreign country, but these are not central to the argument of most critics of trade. Rather, the focus is on the location where large multinational firms manufacture the goods they will ultimately sell in the industrialized world.

As figures 8.10 and 8.11 show, this hypothetical possibility that lower wages in the Third World would lead to massive capital outflows from the United States and Canada has simply not occurred.

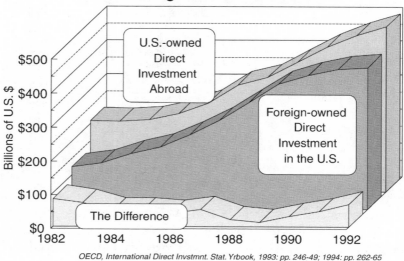

OECD, International Direct Invstmnt. Stat. Yrbook, 1993: pp. 246-49; 1994: pp. 262-65

Figure 8.10

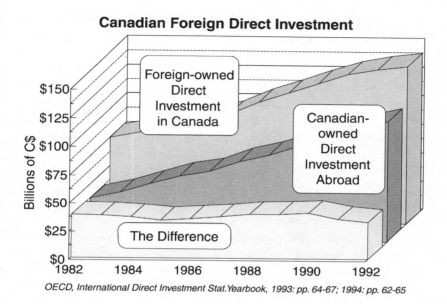

Canadian Foreign Direct Investment

OECD, *International Direct Investment Stat.Yearbook, 1993: pp. 64-67; 1994: pp. 62-65*

Figure 8.11

There has been a continued increase in U.S.-owned direct investment abroad, but there has simultaneously been an increase in foreign-owned direct investment in the U.S., with the two capital flows more or less offsetting each other. As figure 8.11 indicates, the Canadian experience is similar, though as is true for most smaller economies located adjacent much larger ones, foreign-owned direct investment in Canada has historically been larger than Canadian-owned direct investment abroad.

In addition, most of the direct investment abroad (the outflow of capital) by domestic firms in both countries has primarily gone to other industrialized nations. For the United States, more than two-thirds is in other industrialized nations, a proportion that has remained remarkably consistent even during recent years of sizable imbalances in trade. An even larger portion of Canadian direct investment abroad (more than 80 percent) is in other industrialized nations, primarily the United States.[21]

Inflows of capital have been influential in the Third World because they are sizable in relation to the total capital stock there, but

215

they represent only a small portion of OECD investment overall. Even the $100 billion of total movement of capital (both foreign direct investment and purely financial investments) to newly industrialized nations in the record year of 1993 represented only 2.5 percent of the $4 trillion of total domestic investment of the industrialized world each year. In most years the capital flow is far smaller.[22] This is hardly strong evidence that cheap labor in the south will drain capital away from the north.

There is no claim here that capital, including the critically important foreign direct investment, would not flow south if there were sufficient financial incentives to do so. The question, rather, is whether capital flow and international trade are sufficient to explain the employment problems of the north. As we have seen, even within the United States, which has run a uniquely large imbalance of trade for years, the multi-year employment effect of trade has been the loss of fewer than a million jobs, and this is because of the size of the trade deficit, not the amount of trade. In nearly all the other nations of the OECD, each having roughly balanced trade or trade surpluses, the employment effects have been positive. The loss of almost 800,000 jobs is no small matter from a moral point of view, but in a nation of 115 million jobs, this loss represents only seven-tenths of 1 percent and international trade simply cannot be understood as the main force behind 6 percent unemployment and stagnated wages.

In the industrialized world as a whole, nearly 8 percent of all workers were unemployed in 1994.[23] The problem is an immense one and enormously important from the point of view of Christian ethics. However, the very enormity of the problem means that international trade with—and capital flows to—the developing world are far too small to be responsible for more than a small slice of the problem.

Becoming a Service Economy

Having seen that most industrialized countries have indeed lost manufacturing jobs but, at the same time, trade effects and the capital flows from the industrialized to the developing world are too small

216

to explain this change, we are left with a question: What has happened to those "good" jobs in the industrialized world?

The answer, it turns out, is a combination of manufacturing productivity and consumer demand. Figure 8.12 illustrates the growth of manufacturing productivity for the industrialized nations of North America and the European Community from 1957 to 1988.

Figure 8.12

Sizable increases in manufacturing productivity have been a central part of the story of the drop in overall manufacturing employment. We had a glimpse of this earlier. If an increase in labor productivity allows 90 workers to produce the 1,000 units per week for which 100 workers used to be required, then all 100 workers can keep their jobs only if output rises in proportion. This may sound very abstract, but figure 8.13 depicts concrete examples: three manufacturing industries—cooking equipment, hosiery, and tires—that had roughly the same increases in labor productivity (3.5 to 4.5 percent) over the decade from 1973 to 1983. Employment in any industry (represented in the chart by total hours worked) can only rise if the industry's output rises faster than labor productivity

217

(output per hour). This was the situation for U.S. manufacturers of cooking equipment between 1973 and 1983.

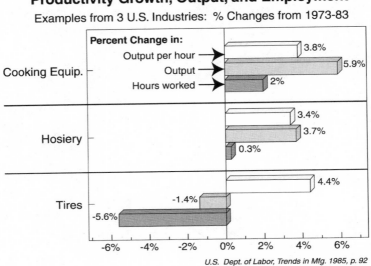

Productivity Growth, Output, and Employment
Examples from 3 U.S. Industries: % Changes from 1973-83

Figure 8.13

Because output in the hosiery industry rose about as fast as labor productivity, total employment remained about constant, rising 3/10 of 1 percent. As the example of tires shows, when output per hour rises while overall output falls, employment in the industry will fall. The reason behind the drop in employment in the production of tires is that factories do not for long produce output that will not be sold.

We need not investigate here the particular reasons for the increase in the demand for cooking equipment or the decrease in demand for tires over that ten-year period. The point of the three examples is that what is true for each industry individually is true more generally for manufacturing taken as a whole: When the overall growth in manufacturing productivity exceeds the overall growth in demand for manufactured products, manufacturing employment has to fall.

The question at hand in the face of rising labor productivity in manufacturing is, What has occurred to the overall demand for

218

manufactured products? Figure 8.14 gives an insight based on the Canadian experience, a good place to start because, unlike the United States, Canada has quite consistently exported more goods than it has imported.

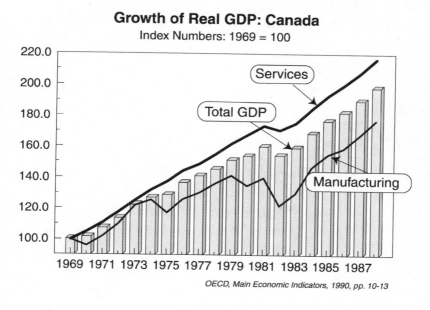

Growth of Real GDP: Canada
Index Numbers: 1969 = 100

OECD, Main Economic Indicators, 1990, pp. 10-13

Figure 8.14

The vertical bars are an index (1969 = 100) of the overall gross domestic product for Canada, and the two lines show the growth of manufacturing and services. The lower line indicates the growth in production of manufactured goods: a fairly rapid growth, but not as rapid as overall GDP. The upper line indicates that the service sector has been growing faster than the rest of the Canadian economy. What does this mean?

Because international Canadian trade in goods has been more or less balanced over this twenty-year period, with a modest surplus of exports over imports, manufacturing output has not been harmed by shifts in international merchandise trade (as we have seen, it has been helped slightly). The explanation we are then left with is that Canadians themselves have been spending a higher and higher portion of their incomes on services and a lower portion of their incomes on manufactured goods. In analyzing the structural changes brought about by consumption patterns that vary with income, we are back again to the notion of the income elasticity of demand for various products, a topic that standard textbooks on economic development treat in some detail.[24]

The experience in the United States is remarkably similar in the movement of consumption (and employment) away from goods and toward services. Because the U.S. has been running a significant merchandise trade deficit for much of the last thirty years, many have argued that the fall in manufacturing employment in relation to service employment has its primary source in growing imports. Although there is no doubt that some manufacturing jobs have "moved" abroad, this phenomenon has been badly overemphasized by opponents of trade. A completely unrelated change in consumption patterns seems to explain most losses, as figure 8.15 indicates.

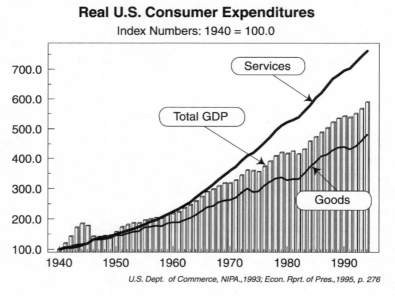

Real U.S. Consumer Expenditures

Index Numbers: 1940 = 100.0

U.S. Dept. of Commerce, NIPA.,1993; Econ. Rprt. of Pres.,1995, p. 276

Figure 8.15

The chart displays the consumption expenditures of U.S. citizens for goods (both "durable" goods like automobiles and refrigerators, and "nondurable" goods like clothing and gasoline). People have been spending more on both goods and services as incomes rise, but the increases in expenditures for services have been significantly higher.

In addition, as we just saw, rates of productivity growth in the production of goods have been substantial. Precise measures of productivity in the service sector are notoriously difficult to develop,[25] but most economists judge that productivity increases come more easily in the production of goods than in the production of services. Figure 8.16 illustrates the growth rate of labor productivity in five different sectors of the economy since World War II.

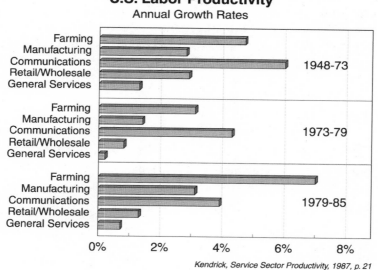

Kendrick, Service Sector Productivity, 1987, p. 21

Figure 8.16

Labor productivity (i.e., output per hour) can and does grow when workers gain knowledge and skills that allow them to produce more in the same time. However, this force is available in all sectors of the economy, and thus the main explanation for the *differences* in rates of labor productivity growth over different sectors of the economy is the role of capital: machines, tools, and logistical support. The primary difference is that in most goods-producing sectors and in some service sectors (such as communications, transporta-

221

tion, and public utilities) there are, given the current state of technology, more opportunities for capital investments to increase productivity than exist for the more "ordinary" service industries such as wholesale and retail trade, and the cluster of "general" services, including such diverse sectors as restaurants, entertainment, repair, education, health, social services, and a number of others. One can easily imagine how an autoworker or a farmer can produce more and more per hour, but it is much harder to improve the hourly productivity of restaurant workers, police officers, retail clerks, or teachers. These lower rates of labor productivity growth in most services mean that the large increase in the national demand for services is only slightly offset by productivity growth rates, and thus the demand for employment rises significantly.

Figure 8.17 shows the issue in yet another way. Over the fifty years from 1940 to 1990, U.S. consumers increased their expenditures for both goods and services, but, with large advances in the technology of goods production, the increase in the labor force required to provide the increase in goods demanded was far less than the increase in the labor force required to provide the additional services.

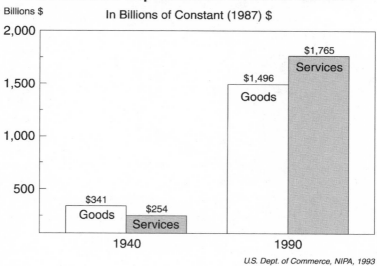

U.S. Consumer Expenditures: Goods & Services

Figure 8.17

Figures 8.18 and 8.19 illustrate the trends: The number of service-producing jobs in Canada and the United States has risen dramatically, while the number of goods-producing jobs has risen less than 50 percent. The United States and Canada have become "service economies," but not because of international trade.

The United States and Canada have a higher proportion of service jobs than do most other industrialized nations, but as figure 8.20 shows, this is changing rapidly as other nations experience rates of growth in service jobs even greater than that in North America.

The loss of "good" manufacturing jobs in the industrialized world has clearly contributed to the stagnation and in many cases losses in economic welfare experienced by working-class citizens in recent years. This moral problem has become even more intractable in a time when the political will to address it seems weaker than ever. There is no doubt that international trade creates a tendency toward lower wages for low-skilled workers in industrialized nations, but the difficulty here is that some opponents of trade attribute all or

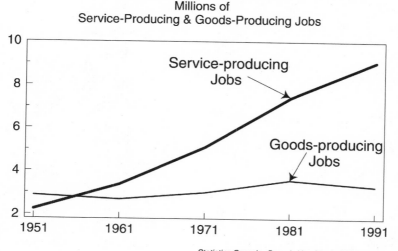

Canadian Employment

Millions of
Service-Producing & Goods-Producing Jobs

Statistics Canada, Canada Year Book: 1994, p. 208

Figure 8.18

U.S. Employment

Millions of
Service-Producing & Goods-Producing Jobs

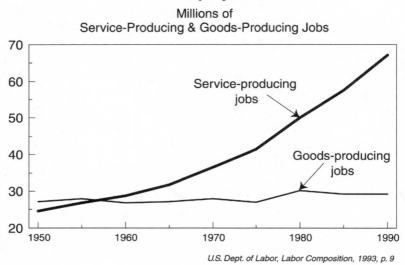

U.S. Dept. of Labor, Labor Composition, 1993, p. 9

Figure 8.19

Service Jobs as % of All Jobs

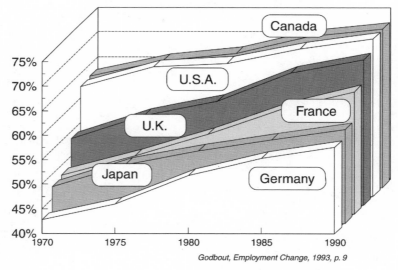
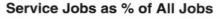

Godbout, Employment Change, 1993, p. 9

Figure 8.20

nearly all of the loss of "good" jobs to trade itself. In fact, trade has been a minor influence.

The sense of inevitability of such developments in consumer expenditures presents particular problems for Christian social ethics. There is no "correct" proportion of jobs in the nation that "should" be in manufacturing, or in agriculture for that matter. The difficulty, however, arises when economic change hurts middle-income or low-income groups, when it hurts most those who are most vulnerable and least able to recover. Indeed this is largely why we call them vulnerable. There are critically important policy changes that must be made to increase the accountability of more powerful economic agents, such as multinational firms, toward their employees and the communities in which they operate. The point here, however, is that these immensely important moral debates are only hindered when the economic causes of underlying problems are misidentified, in this case, by a faulty accusation against international trade as the sole or even primary source of events actually effected by deeper patterns in the economy.

A MORAL ASSESSMENT

Critics of increased trade who worry about the job prospects for the workers of the industrialized world begin with a fully appropriate moral concern. The Christian doctrine of creation, viewing God's gift to humanity as directed toward all and not simply toward the wealthy, recognizes that the ordinary way that people lay claim to a portion of that gift of creation is through daily employment and the income it brings. For those who are unable to support themselves—for example, the very young and very old—a different sort of claim on creation's gifts is quite appropriate. However, the ordinary way that most of us participate in God's gift to us is through our work.

As we have seen, while international competition among workers might, in theory, bring about sizable problems for the workers of industrialized nations, the data indicate that other causes currently lie behind the trend of widening gaps between those prosperous and those struggling economically. In the United States, this trend has been demonstrated primarily as a widening gap between the in-

225

comes of those with "good" jobs and the majority. In Europe, the trend is better described by the high and steady unemployment rates experienced in the 1990s but unheard of in earlier decades. The Canadian experience seems to be a mixture of these two problems: stagnant incomes and rising unemployment.

A number of thoughtful commentators have argued that these two apparently different problems are really not so different as they seem.[26] By historical tradition, the United States has chosen to expose its working class to the harsh realities of the market to a far greater degree than have European nations. This trend was exacerbated during the 1980s with the weakening of unions and shifts in tax policy brought about by the Reagan and Bush administrations. Europe, and to a large extent Canada, have had a longer and stronger history of softening the harsh "discipline" of the market by encouraging stronger unions and providing better unemployment insurance and stronger forms of social security for citizens of all ages. As a result, the same institutional shifts that have caused a stagnation and in many cases worsening of the economic status of U.S. workers have instead brought about high and persistent levels of unemployment in Europe and Canada.

There are lively debates about the underlying causes of this state of affairs, and we are once again at background convictions that heavily influence people's opinions in other areas. Some assume they have explained the cause of these problems by attributing all this to "late-twentieth-century capitalism," but this is far more persuasive to those already committed to a socialist economic structure than to others. Whether one approves of or condemns current forms of capitalism, the question remains why these particular problems have arisen more acutely now than they did, say, twenty years ago. Once it is clear that international trade has played but a small role in this process, the two interacting forces—shifts in consumer demand toward services, and productivity increases in manufacturing that outpace those in services—we are still left with a moral problem but have no easy moral scapegoat.

Presuming that the trend toward a service economy continues, we face a future where more and more people will experience slow productivity growth, and thus only slowly growing incomes at best. The fact that international trade has some effect, though one far less important than critics assert, only makes the problem worse. The solution from the point of view of Christian ethics must include a more concerted effort to increase the employment and productivity of lower-skilled workers in the industrialized world and a more vigorous use of progressivity in taxation. Although this takes us far afield from the focus on international trade, it is clear that a Christian commitment would require the provision of more assistance to those hurt by this long-term trend, including better educational systems— elementary, secondary, and trade schools—as well as more productive efforts at retraining workers and upgrading skills. There have been a multitude of criticisms against federal, provincial, and state efforts at job training and skill development, and in fact these programs have often been inefficient. The solution, however, is not to end these efforts but rather to improve them. In addition, with the growing importance of service jobs, research and development should be channeled toward increasing productivity there, and not so predominantly toward goods production.

We face serious employment problems in the industrialized world, but trade has played a minor role in them.

CHAPTER 9

IMPROVING THE RULES OF TRADE

All human interaction requires rules of some sort—whether explicitly agreed upon or simply internalized unconsciously. Trade is no exception. Thus, the task of setting rules for international trade is exceedingly important, but it is remarkably difficult. The immense scale of trade is part of the problem—it affects so much of daily life around the globe. An equally important impediment, however, arises because each nation begins with the conviction that many of its trading partners don't "play the game" by the same rules. The diversity of cultures is a key feature here.

The moral and economic health of any nation depends both on the character of its people and the quality of its institutions. These two—character and institutions—are reciprocally reinforcing. The behaviors and attitudes structured into organizations and social rules arise out of the moral character of persons. At the same time, those organizations and rules shape people's character traits through the institutional definition of success and "acceptable behavior."[1]

Within any one homogeneous group of people—for example, an ethnic group in a particular location—this interplay of personal character and institutional expectation is so subtle that people tend to be unaware of its power in shaping their lives until they have contact with other groups who live differently. The same act that in one culture is understood as an immoral bribe, in another is interpreted as a gift of appreciation. The same work schedule and intensity that in one culture indicates a commitment to excellence in one's work is seen in another as a somewhat irrational and nearly manic compulsion.

Different nations take for granted different rules by which daily life and commerce should ordinarily occur. Thus, it is quite common that a nation believes it is disadvantaged because its international trading partners "play the game" by rules that provide them with an unfair advantage. United States firms point to the economic advantages of the Japanese "keiretsu" system of closely integrated industrial firms, a monopolistic advantage forbidden in the U.S. under antitrust laws. Canadian firms point to the economic advantage of their American competitors due to weaker (and less costly) protections for workers and the unemployed in the U.S. The list of examples could be extended, but the principle is the same: We take for granted most of the ordinary ways of doing things at home (even if that puts outsiders at a disadvantage), and we are vividly aware of the advantages that others abroad enjoy, particularly those which we ourselves have eliminated at home due to moral conviction. As a result, an international agreement on "fair" rules of trade is critically important.

In fact, existing international agreements on a host of issues far beyond trade stand as a truly significant moral accomplishment of the modern world. Though limited and flawed in many ways, international agreements concerning arms reduction, environmental standards, human rights, and a long list of other important moral issues mark a real moral progress.

MORALITY, SELF-INTEREST, AND THE "RULES OF THE GAME"

Christians throughout history have had to cope with the moral ambiguities of political and economic institutions. The problem, of course, is that the ethic of love and self-denial which Jesus preached and Christians endorse cannot easily be translated into political and economic rules, even in a nation comprising only Christians. It is far more complicated in a pluralistic society where religious appeals have limited effect in public discourse. Although a full-blown investigation of the complexities of neighbor-love and self-interest lies beyond the scope of this volume, two insights are critical for Christians thinking about the rules of trade. First, those who would "play hardball" in trade negotiations and feel justified in asserting national self-interest in all settings misunderstand the necessary limits on self-interest. Second, those who would propose purely altruistic principles for international economic relations underestimate the complexities of political and economic organization.

An adequate Christian response to modern economic life understands the assertion of self-interest in a nuanced way. Although there are indeed times when looking out for one's own interests is morally justifiable, the centrality for the Christian of love of neighbor means that any moral endorsement of self-interest must be limited and context-dependent. Consider two examples.

When applying for a job, most Christians will make a sincere effort, despite their awareness that others will not have the job if they themselves get it. Similarly, few Christians will take home from the grocery the most badly bruised cantaloupe, even though that would leave a better choice for shoppers who come later in the day. Self-denial and love of neighbor must remain critically important for Christian faith. Still, most Christians realize that in assessing our effects on the neighbor we consider not only the short-term, immediate effects of our actions but also the long-term, institutionally mediated results.

This is particularly true in institutional life, and especially so in political or economic activity. Thus, when hiring for jobs occurs in a system that is generally fair, the social advantages from a mutual assertion of self-interest—applicants seeking the job most in their interests and employers hiring the best available employees—means that neither side needs to feel guilty about "taking away" a job from someone. In fact, the current debate over affirmative action can be understood as a debate about whether the system for the distribution of jobs in society is and has been "generally fair" enough to warrant an endorsement of this mutual assertion of self-interest. Laws forbidding discrimination based on race, religion, and a variety of other factors are efforts to make the system fairer so that the normal assertion of self-interest in applying and hiring might subsequently be morally justified.

Similarly, choosing the best cantaloupe does indeed limit the options for later shoppers, but within a food distribution system with adequate supplies and broad availability, the cumulative institutional effect is a positive one. The grocer sees that bruised fruit does not sell and has an incentive to train employees to exercise more careful stewardship, or perhaps to change to a different food wholesaler who will do the same. National efforts to provide food subsidies to the poor (whether through cash transfers such as food "stamps" or through outright gifts of food itself) are an attempt to render the food distribution in society "fair enough" that we can then trust the distribution of the vast majority of food in the economy to the self-interested interaction of buyers and sellers. The general fairness of the context and the social good produced by the process justifies our acting in a self-interested manner.

The key principle here is that the assertion of self-interest is in some contexts justifiable but only conditionally so. Only within a framework of rules (whether laws or internalized standards of behavior) is self-interest justifiable. Without such restrictions, self-interest might include thuggery, fraud, and a host of other evils. Most people on the right and the left—once they stop to think about it—agree on this in principle; their disagreements focus on the length of the list of immoral actions that ought to be eliminated by the "rules of the game."

A consequence of this insight is the realization that, from a moral point of view, there is a tremendous difference between asserting one's self-interest "within the game" (where a set of good rules covering this context can render this morally justifiable) and asserting self-interest in *constructing* the rules of the game (where self-interested action has no such "systemic" moral justification). From a moral point of view, then, the task of devising internationally agreed-upon rules for trade must begin not simply with the self-interest of the participants to the conversation but with moral values which they want to protect by agreeing to rules that prevent those assertions of self-interest which cause the most harm.

This is the moral logic behind allowing individuals to interact self-interestedly in any social situation. Strong believers in the "free market" often talk as if self-interested behavior is always morally justified and thus often presume that their nation may act in a purely self-interested manner in negotiating international rules of trade. Christian social ethics, however, would argue that this is far too self-serving a view of the process.

Of course, we should not be naive about the possibilities. In his classic text, *Moral Man and Immoral Society*, Reinhold Niebuhr prudently cautioned Christians not to expect from nations the same level of morality that we hope for from individuals. The dynamics of institutional life, whether of the nation or smaller organizations, render self-sacrifice an impossibility and the restraint of self-interest the highest feasible moral goal.[2]

Each nation involved in the negotiation of international rules of trade can come to two critical insights that can lead it to restrain its self-interest. First, different cultural traditions begin with different assessments of what is fair economically: Our own nation has both moral convictions to insist upon and moral blind-spots that others can help us recognize. Second, noncooperation internationally is far more costly than compromise. These two insights hold out the possibility of a moral foundation for the rules of trade. It will not be guaranteed, but if morally conscientious citizens of nations around the world press for it, it is a real possibility.

MORAL VALUES AND THE RULES OF TRADE

In accord with this understanding of the relation of self-interest and the "rules of the game," the rules of trade should be crafted to prevent abuses which the exertion of self-interest in trade would otherwise inevitably cause. The current restrictions on the destructive effects of trade embodied in international agreements today are inadequate. Although particular formulations can only be hammered out in actual international negotiations, an authentically Christian view of trade would require that the following moral concerns be integrated into the rules of trade.

1. The Economic Welfare of the World's Poor

Christian commitment requires an option for the poor. As we have seen, the hope of increasing the daily economic productivity of the world's poor is a fundamental moral argument in favor of international trade. Thus it is no surprise that an explicit concern for the welfare of the world's poor should be integrated into the rules of trade.

In fact, existing international trade agreements already include the "generalized system of preferences" (GSP), which is designed to assist developing nations in the face of the greater economic power of the industrialized world. The GSP was developed in the 1970s to grant preferential access to the markets of industrialized countries for the exports of the developing world. More than twenty industrialized nations currently operate GSP schemes, benefiting producers (both owners and workers) in more than 140 developing nations.[3] In 1994, about 3 percent of total U.S. imports, $18.4 billion, entered duty-free under the GSP.[4] Although such preferential treatment will predictably be less and less helpful as average tariffs facing all nations are reduced over time, the GSP remains a morally important force within the rules of trade.

It is an unfortunate fact of life that the United States and many other developed countries have "voluntarily negotiated" many exceptions to the GSP regime in response to pressures from domestic producers of textiles, footwear, clothing, and other products exported from the Third World.[5] Because of such exceptions, analysts estimate that the GSP raises exports of developing countries by only 1 or 2 percent. A complete removal of developed nations' trade restrictions (including tariffs and nontariff barriers) facing Third World exports would raise those exports by approximately 10 percent, resulting in about a 3 percent increase in the GDP of developing nations, a sizable annual benefit.[6] Although this is small in comparison with the long-run productivity increases developing nations need, it is a sizable increase in annual economic welfare and would allow Third World nations significantly greater flexibility in reaching their development goals.[7] Other "exceptions" for the poorest of the developing nations—such as an exemption from the prohibition on export subsidies—have been built into the World Trade Organization, as they were in the earlier GATT agreements.[8] Further and more substantial recognition of the importance of such systematic exemption to trade rules is needed.

Equally important is the more substantial inclusion of representatives of Third World nations in the administrative mechanisms for world trade. The councils overseeing global and regional trade agreements as well as the dispute resolution committees established to adjudicate concrete allegations of trade rule violations should include sizable representation from Third World nations. The World Trade Organization, like its predecessor the GATT, is overseen by a Council comprising its 120 member nations, each casting a single, unweighted vote.[9] As a result, there is clearly the potential for developing nations to have a greater influence over the WTO than over many other international economic institutions.

2. Sustainability

A Christian commitment to the integrity of creation requires strong action in response to environmental dangers. The rules of international trade must reflect this global concern. Even secular policy analysis requires the inclusion of environmental goals within the rules of trade. Besides this most general objection to the reigning philosophy of current trade rules, the most critical problem is that current rules forbid one of the most critically important methods for curbing environmental destruction: "process standards."

International trade agreements have traditionally *allowed* for one important kind of restriction on trade for environmental reasons: the banning of particular products by any nation or group of nations, as long as both domestic and foreign products fall under the same ban. Thus, for example, any nation concerned about ozone depletion could, if it wished, ban all sale of ozone-depleting chlorofluorocarbons without violating the standards of international trade rules. (In fact, the Montreal Protocol and related agreements have scheduled a phase-out of numerous ozone-depleting substances.)

An outright prohibition of some products is appropriate—for example, some particularly destructive chemicals. Far more important in reducing environmental damage, however, are restrictions on manufacturing processes themselves, penalizing in one way or another processes that generate disproportionate environmental

235

damage. Thus, for example, efforts to reduce the amount of sulfur coming from the smokestacks of power plants or to reduce the toxicity of wastes flowing into sewers and rivers have been fundamentally important methods of restricting environmental damage within any one nation.

The problem in international trade arises, however, because the rules of trade have traditionally rejected "process standards." Nations aren't free to discriminate among identical products, allowing the import of some but restricting the import of others based on *how* they were produced. Thus, while a nation is free to ban trade in CFCs, it is not free under international trade agreements to restrict trade in products simply because they were made with technologies that produce CFCs as a waste product. The original motive behind this policy was the concern that individual nations would, in a protectionist manner, simply assert that the dominant production processes used domestically were environmentally (or by some other standard) superior to those used abroad, thus protecting domestic producers by prohibiting the import of that product unless foreign producers switched technologies (a change that would increase costs, at least in the short run).

Today it is simply too obvious that a multitude of environmental problems can be addressed only by process restrictions. Every industrialized nation has used process restrictions domestically to reduce the polluting effects of production. This is true whether the nation chooses to mandate particular "clean" technologies or establishes a system of tradable pollution permits to reduce overall pollution levels. A blanket rejection of process restrictions in international trade rules is today simply indefensible. With such an "environmental legitimacy" added to the agreements of the World Trade Organization and with further efforts by the WTO to incorporate the trade-related sections of international environmental agreements, the rules of international trade could be shaped to encourage sustainability rather than ignore it.[10]

During the Uruguay round of GATT negotiations, the signatory nations agreed to the establishment of a new "Committee on Trade and the Environment" within the World Trade Organization. It is charged with examining and eventually proposing WTO policies concerning the transparency of trade rules, the relation of the WTO to various international environmental agreements, and more concrete issues such as process standards and the export of goods prohibited from domestic sale.[11]

3. Labor Standards

Christians recognize that every human being has a dignity based on creation in the "image of God" and that this sets standards for all human interaction, whether domestic or international. International agreements should recognize the right of workers to organize, the importance of child labor laws, and need for fundamental workplace health and safety regulation. As a corollary, rules of trade should allow individual nations to discriminate against imports from other nations where such fundamental labor standards are disregarded. A number of large international retailers have begun to set labor standards for their Third World suppliers because of consumer pressures, and while this effort is far from completely successful, it indicates a potential for stronger international agreements in this area that did not exist a decade or two ago.[12]

The United States, during the Uruguay round of GATT negotiations, pressed for an agreement to establish within the World Trade Organization a committee on workers' rights. The nations of Europe were mildly supportive, but the proposal was strenuously opposed by many developing countries, which feared that producers in the industrialized world would employ allegations of abuse of workers' rights as an excuse for further protectionism.[13]

We should recognize, of course, that even concerning such basic issues, the moral judgment is a difficult one once the debate moves beyond some fundamental level of guaranteed labor standards. Different nations have taken different approaches to the powers and opportunities given to unions, the age and conditions under which children may work (particularly in developing nations without an adequate school system), and the degree of health and safety risks which are allowed. These issues are hotly debated within each nation, and though Christian ethics has much to contribute here, a single unified standard for all nations is inappropriate. Differences in both cultural meanings and political possibilities are too large. Employing trade restrictions to move beyond minimum guarantees of labor standards would be debatable. That, however, is a problem which has not arisen, since even those minimum standards have not yet been recognized as grounds for discrimination in trade.

4. Cultural Identity

Different cultures and ethnic groups have devised over the centuries innumerably different ways to experience and express human fulfillment. One of the characteristics of the modern world is the more frequent interaction between people of diverse cultural identities, and this has had both good and bad effects.

In learning more about the stranger from another culture, humans have allayed the fear and hatred of others, reduced the disparagement of others' points of view, and made ethnic wars less likely. The viciousness and inhumanity apparent in the struggles in Bosnia in the 1990s stand as an example of some of the worst kinds of inter-ethnic hatred. Still, the fact that so many people around the world find such hatred not only morally repulsive but almost incredible stands as a tribute to a real, though limited, moral development in world history. International commerce has meant greater frequency of contact between peoples and a growing interdependence. Thus, as Montesquieu observed two hundred fifty years ago, economic interaction between cultures has indeed played a positive role in this growing tolerance for difference in the world.

At the same time, economic forces have also had morally destructive effects on cultural identity. Consider simply the entertainment industry. Many openly lament the poor quality of the offerings on commercial television. TV networks are in the business of selling advertising time, and thus are lured by the "bottom line" to broadcast not the best entertainment but that which will draw the most viewers. Similar commercial forces press the movie industry toward the sensationalism of sex and violence.

It is morally discouraging when this process occurs within your own nation: Domestic entertainment firms act as a sort of pander, appealing to the baser elements of our culture. The process is far more objectionable when such entertainment is available primarily through international trade. Particularly for "small" nations facing an onslaught of sophisticated entertainment products from "large"

238

nations abroad, a simplistic "free trade" answer to such objections is morally inadequate. Economists in particular tend to underestimate the importance of institutional and cultural factors in national life and as a result tend to see "the culture industry"—like the appliances or financial services industry—as simply another part of the economy. In the Uruguay round of the GATT, for example, France insisted on the right to restrict the importation of (largely American) movies and television shows out of a combined concern for the future of French firms producing materials for the cinema and television and for French culture itself.

At the same time, however, no absolute ban on imports affecting national cultural identity is morally defensible. The fundamental human rights of individuals require access to different points of view from which governments and national elites might at times wish to isolate their population. Thus any agreement on the rules of trade concerning culturally important products and services will have to be a careful compromise, one that will necessarily be a rough approximation rather than a precise definition of a just trading policy.

5. .Human Rights

Although a number of the preceding elements include particular sorts of human rights, there are other more general and more generally recognized human rights that each nation should recognize for its own people. Rights of free speech, assembly, a free press, universal suffrage, and a variety of other more concrete political guarantees are morally critical for responsible public life.

Although these need to be recognized in international agreements, including trade agreements, it remains a debatable prudential judgment whether and to what extent they should be endorsed as grounds for trade discrimination.

On the one hand, a moral argument can be made that if a nation violates the rights of its citizens it should be open to restrictions if importing nations so wish. Thus, many critics of human rights violations in China have argued that the other industrialized nations of the world should reduce their international trade with China to penalize the Chinese government for its actions. On the other hand, however, there are moral arguments against such a policy. The first is that a moral humility causes a responsible observer to recognize that there is likely no single nation perfectly responsible in all matters of human rights. The second is that the improvement of the human rights records of the industrial democracies has come not simply from moral conviction but also from a rise in the economic welfare of the citizenry, something which has yet to occur in many parts of the world. Thus other critics of Chinese human rights policy argue that the most likely cause of a transformation in that policy will be the domestic pressure arising from citizens whose economic welfare has increased, in part through international trade.

Thus, while the internal logic of trade negotiations would call for the inclusion of work-related human rights standards within the rules of trade, well-meaning people will likely continue to disagree about the use of trade policy to further more specifically political human rights. Strong efforts need to be made to further human rights throughout the globe, and these may include sanctions as strong as those implemented by the United Nations against South Africa. However, the temptation of protected industries to appeal to human rights arguments is so strong that relying on trade policy to further a human rights agenda is inappropriate.

6. Moral Responsibility for the Dislocations from Trade

The moral argument in favor of international trade is that, within the proper "rules of the game," trade does more good than harm. A large portion of the harm done consists of dislocations caused by long-term trends in industries affected by trade. Similar to dislocations caused by purely domestic changes in technology, dislocations caused by the movement of production facilities from one nation to another is both personally painful and economically costly to the workers harmed. A number of studies of worker dislocation have attempted to assess empirically the cost imposed on dislocated workers. One typical study of workers displaced from 1980 to 1986 from jobs they had held for many years indicated that the financial losses to those workers were largest during the first year after displacement, averaging as much as 40 percent of their predisplacement earnings. With time for adjustments and the seeking of better jobs, average losses dropped, with the average earner's income being only 25 percent lower during the fifth year after separation.[14] We should note that those on the left who seem to assume people will remain unemployed are as wrong as those on the right who tend to assume that workers will find jobs equivalent to the ones they lost.

As a result, any morally founded national trade policy must anticipate such dislocations and assist affected workers in the transition to another job. Unemployment payments, retraining and relocation stipends, and employment counseling are critical to the process, even though they cannot guarantee an income as great as that prior to dislocation. In fact, if a group of workers is currently working at the highest-paid job available to them, any dislocation will leave them with only lower-income alternatives. Put more simply, although international trade will bring consumers lower prices and increase the demand for workers in export industries, those producing products that are now competing more directly with imports will be harmed. As a result, "trade adjustment assistance," as it is called in the literature, is critically important and must be seen not as an optional element of national largesse but as a morally integral part of a nation's trade policy.

DEMOCRATIZING THE RULES OF TRADE

Critics of trade are rightly frustrated by the neglect of critical moral values in current international trade agreements. In response, many call for the "democratizing" of the process that creates and enforces the rules of trade. In particular, critics argue that the World Trade Organization, as successor to the GATT, was not only drawn up with insufficient consultation but is overseen by a General Council made up of representatives of the economically powerful, who will ultimately opt for corporate interests over workers' rights, global sustainability, or other "noneconomic" values.[15]

On the one hand, such a call to democratize the rulemaking is morally preferable to asserting national sovereignty against the authority of international rules of trade. Nations are increasingly interdependent in the modern world, and a whole host of problems in addition to those of trade can be solved only through international agreements that limit traditional claims of national sovereignty. Encouraging sovereignty claims against international rules of trade can only weaken such efforts.

On the other hand, this call for democratizing must be understood carefully. Although it correctly insists that values other than narrowly economic ones be included in the rules of trade, "democratizing" all procedures involving international rules of trade would likely lead to results which many critics of trade would themselves condemn.

Critical here are the insights of "public choice" theory, a subdiscipline within both economics and political science.[16] Public choice analysis attempts to understand and predict the forces influencing decision making in a democracy. By itself, of course, public choice theory is an inadequate view of the world. It presumes that legislators and other government officials care only about their self-interest (i.e., re-election or re-appointment) and shape their policy decisions to improve their chances for staying in office. This overlooks the moral principles that must be part of any well-functioning democracy. Nonetheless, this view is helpful in a moral analysis of policy because it so starkly identifies the predictable political forces with which government officials must deal.

Essential to the public choice view of government (including, in this setting, the World Trade Organization and other "voluntary" frameworks) is the awareness that the "correct" outcomes do not automatically occur simply because those who set up the governmental structure intended them. One important example, particularly relevant to the rules of trade, is "regulatory capture." This is the tendency for a governing body, whether your town's local planning commission or the General Council of the WTO, eventually to become dominated by the very interests it was originally designed to hold in check. How does this happen?

Any rule-making body has the power to make rules that favor one group or another. There are inevitably some individuals who have much to gain from particular rule changes, and thus they would be willing to expend considerable resources (money, time, and energy) to have those changes made.

Those sizable advantages will come at someone's expense, of course, but often the expense amounts to very little for each of a very

242

large number of people. Thus, for example, a particular industry might desire a tax break from the national government, which could be quite sizable for the firms involved while only costing the average citizen a few dollars per year. We all hope, of course, that our national representatives will judge such proposed policies on their merits and only vote for them if they really are best for the nation. However, public choice analysis points out that if the total cost to the average citizen were only a few dollars per year, it really would not be in any individual citizen's interest to try to stop the proposed tax break for firms, since organizing like-minded citizens or even writing several successive letters to one's representative would end up costing more in time and money than could be saved even if such efforts were successful.

On the other hand, the firms slated to reap large financial benefits would be willing to spend part of that windfall to hire lobbyists to press hard for this legislation. Public choice theory goes on to observe that the number of regulatory agencies is so large and the financial impact on any one citizen so small that most citizens quite understandably don't expend the time and resources required even to *find out about* the many proposals for bad policies in the first place. This incentive on the part of a few who are in a position to reap large rewards leads often, the theory predicts, to the capture of the regulatory body by these vested interests. In large part such "regulatory capture" occurs because nearly all those people who are most qualified to sit on a regulatory body are those whose careers have been lived out within the corporations the agency is to regulate. Can this bias toward industry-based experts be overcome by democratizing the process?

The hope for democratization, of course, is not that there will be a sizable letter-writing campaign on every particular issue but that representatives of the public will be named to these regulatory agencies and boards. This is clearly a step in the right direction, but some proponents overestimate its ultimate worth. The persons serving on regulatory bodies are inevitably appointed to their positions within a democratic political process that by nature is similarly vulnerable to the influence of special interests. It is a fact of life that many citizens cannot even name their elected representatives at various levels of government. Very few can name anyone on a national regulatory body or even on their local planning or zoning board. Although we may wish that people were politically more active and aware, those seeking greater justice should strive to be realistic about the capacities of the political process.

Such presumptions about the character and efficacy of democratic decision making compose yet another set of background convictions affecting the trade debate. For most proponents of trade, a mistrust of government increases their confidence in markets. Opponents of trade tend to take a more ambiguous stand here. While they criticize the influence of multinational firms in government, they look to law and government regulation as the solution. For example, although Daly and Cobb propose a severe reduction in international trade (because they doubt it can be rendered benign), they would allow some limited trade when that is in the national community's interest.[17] This would require a government agency to decide when to allow trade, and such an agency would need to resist regulatory capture.

Public choice theory makes clear another dynamic of the national political process that is relevant to the debate over trade. Every elected official is subject to political pressures from his or her district, while the person elected president or prime minister represents in a quite real way citizens from all across the nation. Although the special-interest effect influences all elected officials, it is felt more strongly by regional representatives than by the national leader. This is particularly true in international trade discussions. Why is this?

The costs of trade—for the workers and owners of firms affected by increased imports—are felt intensely in the areas where such firms are located. As a result, the representatives from those particular areas hear quite vividly about the costs and are most motivated to enact trade restrictions in response. The advantages of increased trade are two: Lower product prices help all consumers across the nation, and increased demand from abroad brightens the economic prospects of workers and firms. Increased employment is expected but those jobs do not yet exist; somebody will get the jobs, but those workers are in no position to lobby their representatives for increased trade (and it may not even be clear in advance which representatives' districts stand to gain the new jobs).

244

In this situation, then, public choice theory predicts that a number of, though not all, individual legislators would tend to advocate protection from the dislocations of trade, while the president or prime minister would tend to press for the advantages to come from increased trade. We should not be so simplistic as to think that the prior political convictions about trade held by a president or prime minister become immaterial when he or she takes office, but practice in Canada and the United States indicates that prime ministers and presidents—even those from parties critical of increased trade—have been more favorable toward increasing international trade than have most others in their party. An additional influence, of course, is the fact that presidents and prime ministers are the ones who meet face-to-face with officials from other nations and hear firsthand the rationales of other nations wanting to export products.

From the perspective of Christian ethics, the democratic process in modern industrialized nations is critically important for a thoughtful shaping of economic processes in accord with fundamental human values held by Christians and others. While public choice analysis provides a sobering view of the dangers of the democratic process, its fundamental cynicism about the capacity of humans to rise above narrow self-interest renders it far too thin a theory to be a morally adequate foundational view of public life. For all their dangers, regulatory bodies are necessary because rules of trade must be constructed and enforced and disputes about those rules must be adjudicated. Without this, self-interest could not be trusted. In fact, regulatory bodies are effective to a greater degree than public choice theory itself can account for. It is the "nonrational" (i.e., nonselfish), principled conviction of both citizens and legislators that prevents such processes from deteriorating into nothing but special-interest politics.

The rules of trade do indeed need to be democratized to the extent that appointments to the relevant boards and councils should come from a diverse group of persons and not only trade "experts," and the rules of trade must include not only economic productivity but a full range of values to which the signatory nations are committed.

REGULATING UNFAIR TRADE

In recent decades, the several "rounds" of talks under the aegis of the GATT have slowly reduced tariffs: the fees which national governments charge on goods coming into their nation. Figure 9.1 depicts the reduction of average tariffs on goods entering the United States that occurred due to each of these rounds of GATT negotiation. Tariff levels are shown as percentage reductions from levels prior to 1945. Similar changes have occurred in Canada.

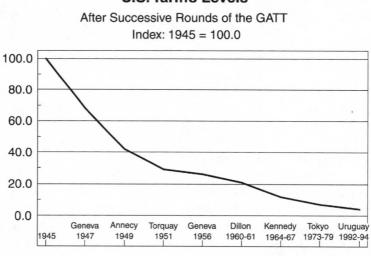

U.S. Tariffs Levels

After Successive Rounds of the GATT

Index: 1945 = 100.0

Bhagwati, 1988, p. 4, and Schott, 1994, p. 152

Figure 9.1

As these tariffs have fallen, there has been a simultaneous rise in the significance in nontariff barriers on trade for two reasons. The first is that even if the nontariff barriers remain unchanged, they become relatively more important when significant tariff barriers have been reduced. This is something like the role of arthritis in the life of a heart attack victim. At the time of the heart problem, the arthritis is a minor issue. If the far more threatening problems with the heart are resolved, the less important effects of arthritis become more visible. The second reason is that the international pressure to cut tariffs has pressed nations wishing to protect their domestic industries to use less visible, nontariff techniques. Included here are national subsidies to particular industries, underenforcement of antitrust laws, national product standards or government procurement standards that discriminate in favor of domestic firms, and a variety of other administrative procedures. Also included are activities that foreign firms can undertake without the support of their governments at home, for example, "dumping" products abroad.

Because the North American economies of the United States and Canada have on average been less protected by high tariffs than those of their competitor nations, there has been rising concern that too much may have been conceded in focusing so much on reducing tariffs across the globe and that "unfair" trade is occurring through this panoply of nontariff barriers erected by "competitor" nations. This more recent sense of needing to combat unfair, nontariff barriers of other nations has added equity to the list of arguments proposed by threatened firms to support national policies aimed at protecting domestic industry. The difficulty in sorting through such claims is that although there can indeed be truth to assertions about unfair trade, such assertions can easily mask more self-interested, protectionist proposals that will in fact not benefit the nation as a whole. When appeals for governmental relief in the face of "unfair trade" are teamed with concerns about, for example, the family farm, the environment, or the loss of manufacturing jobs, which we have reviewed in the foregoing three chapters, the moral difficulty becomes even greater.

Thus, though space is insufficient for an exhaustive analysis, it may be helpful to review two of the most important elements in the debate over unfair trade: dumping and subsidies.

Dumping

Nearly everyone would prefer to pay lower prices for goods and services. Thus, it would seem that most people would be quite happy if a large manufacturing firm wanted to cut its prices by reducing its profits or perhaps even selling at a loss. The difficulty, of course, is that a very large firm might do this to drive smaller competitors out of business, to be left free to raise prices after attaining a monopoly.

247

For this reason nations have antitrust laws preventing such "predatory pricing" practices.

The international equivalent of such destructive pricing is called dumping. The most direct definition of this practice is the sale abroad of goods priced below the prices of comparable goods sold in the country of origin. The danger with dumping is that a large multinational firm with a strong hold on its domestic market could use large profits at home to subsidize predatory pricing abroad in order to drive competitors from that foreign market. In fact, most economists don't worry much about predatory pricing through dumping since the process is remarkably risky. It is not only very costly, but even if it successfully drives domestic producers into bankruptcy, those producers' factories remain in existence, and if the foreign competitor eventually raises prices to take advantage of the monopoly, some other large domestic firm eventually buys up the factories and begins production again.

In response to the threat of dumping, many nations have established laws that prohibit and penalize it, with Canada enacting the first such law in 1904 due to the cut-rate sale of steel by the US Steel Corporation.[18] The difficulty in enforcing both the domestic predatory pricing laws and the international dumping laws is that periodic discounting of prices is quite normal for firms that face a fluctuating demand and yet have high fixed costs. A prime example here is that of automobile companies, who face high demand for their product during a boom time but find consumer demand dropping off severely as average consumer income falls during a recession. Such firms do adjust their production schedules by laying off workers, but the high fixed costs of existing plant and machinery lead them to be willing to produce automobiles and sell them below cost if necessary during recessions so that they will have adequate plant and machinery available during the next boom.

The obvious problem here is that business cycles in different nations are not identical. The United States or Canada might be experiencing a recession when, say, Japan is still at a "boom" stage prior to a slow-down. In such a situation it is quite problematic to use the standard that dumping occurs when a firm sells its product at lower prices abroad than at home. As a result of complications such as this and because of the pressure of domestic firms for protection, the operating definition of dumping has shifted, beginning with the Trade Act of 1974 passed by the United States Congress. In that statute a foreign company was considered to be dumping if the selling price abroad was equal to the selling price at home but both were below the production costs for the item. This and a number of more technical changes made it more likely that allegations of dumping in the United States would be upheld and that penalties would be enacted in response.

The classic case in recent decades that has fueled the fear of dumping was the success in the 1980s of leading Japanese manufacturers of computer memory chips to undercut and drive out of business most U.S. chip makers. From the perspective of U.S. producers, the Japanese were "dumping" their chips in the United States because of deep discounts they were offering. From the point of view of the Japanese, however, these large companies—Toshiba, Fujitsu, NEC, Mitsubishi, and others—were competing vigorously in every nation with one another as well as with their U.S. counterparts. The dispute was a complicated one, and in 1986 the U.S. government reached a voluntary agreement with the government of Japan—the Semiconductor Trade Arrangement—to limit the number of chips entering the United States each year. Such "voluntary export quotas" have become a more frequently employed technique in international trade negotiations, particularly by the United States as a powerful trade negotiator. Similar agreements limit the number of automobiles that Japan exports to the U.S. each year and the amount of textiles and other goods many Third World nations export as well.

Any ethical assessment of the economic issues underlying disputes over dumping must share the same concerns that are raised by domestic predatory pricing concerning monopoly and antitrust. There is the additional concern that in the case of some products national security interests could conceivably be at stake. At the same time, recent allegations of dumping within the leading industrialized nations, and particularly within the United States, often seem to mask a more self-interested protectionism on the part of large firms. Adjudicating such claims and counterclaims is morally important, but it is very complex and requires a case-by-case analysis. It

249

may prove helpful here to note two dangers usually accompanying this process.

The first is that the strategy most frequently used to combat dumping—"voluntary" export quotas—requires the exporting nation to organize a producer cartel. Thus, in order to comply with the Semiconductor Trade Agreement, Japan's Ministry of International Trade and Industry (MITI) explicitly gathered the computer companies into a group, coordinated cutbacks, and made pricing suggestions. The economic effect of this was to reduce competition among the various Japanese firms in their attempts to gain larger markets, allowing them to charge higher prices on a smaller quantity of chips sold in the United States. A similar outcome has occurred with automobiles. Rather than antitrust laws forbidding Japanese automakers to set common policies, the voluntary export agreement with the United States actually requires firms to do so, reducing interfirm competition. Restricted to a lower number of automobile exports to the U.S., the Japanese firms have concentrated exports in luxury automobiles, where profits are highest.

The second problem with the usual approach to allegations of dumping is that attention is focused almost exclusively on the domestic producers who claim they have been damaged by the dumping, the "frontline" competitors. From the point of view of a truly national moral assessment of economic welfare, the appropriate authorities should also take into consideration any negative effects which remedies for alleged dumping might have. In our computer chip example, it is clear that U.S. producers of computer chips were harmed by lower-priced Japanese chips: U.S. workers lost jobs and firms earnings. However, there is in the United States an even larger industry with more jobs and earnings at stake in the production of computers themselves, *buying* computer chips in the process. If these firms must purchase chips at higher prices due to such voluntary export agreement, their products become correspondingly more expensive and less able to compete with computers imported from elsewhere in the world where computer chips are available at the lower world price.

The technicalities involved in assessing such claims and counterclaims are immense. Here we may content ourselves with the moral standard that any damage done by the unfair pricing of foreign goods should be assessed not simply for the costs imposed on domestic producers of similar goods; the benefits or damages caused to all domestic producers and consumers should also be assessed. Any administrative process designed to assess dumping complaints should recognize that the special-interest effect will leave frontline competitors more inclined to lodge and lobby for their complaints than other producers and consumers will be to present evidence against them.

Subsidies

If the problems surrounding the definition and assessment of dumping are difficult, those same issues concerning subsidies are even more complicated.

At one level it would seem that every nation has the moral right to collect and spend the citizens' taxes in accord with citizens' wishes. For example, if the government of Canada chooses to spend tax dollars to further the nation's forests or farms or any other business enterprise, it would ordinarily have the right to do so. At the same time, however, nations have entered into trade agreements which have attempted to reduce the subsidies national governments otherwise grant to domestic industries. Such limitations on the fiscal options open to national governments do indeed limit national sovereignty. We should begin our consideration of trade subsidies with the two central reasons why nations agree to trade rules that prohibit them.

The first reason is that nations are in a sort of "prisoner's dilemma" situation concerning the subsidy of exports. If only one nation chooses to subsidize its export industries, it can quite conceivably enhance them and reap some of the dynamic gains from trade outlined in chapter 2. This is often called "strategic trade policy." However, once one nation has begun the process, most other nations feel driven to effect similar subsidies. Once this occurs, the aggregate expense of all national governments on subsidies is far greater than the aggregate benefits accruing to them. This amounts to a simple transfer of funds from taxpayers to owners and workers in those subsidized industries. This line of reasoning is quite similar to the well-founded argument against a system of tax breaks granted by

251

local units of government to entice relocating firms from other parts of the nation to establish factories locally. If only one municipality does it, it can gain jobs and tax base because it offers the relocating firm lower costs than are available elsewhere. However, such policies predictably force nearly all other municipalities to do the same. The result is simply a system that transfers money from local taxpayers—both individuals and corporations—to relocating firms and has almost no effect on the overall number of jobs available in the economy.

The second reason nations agree to trade rules that limit subsidies is rooted in the "special-interest effect," something we have already seen. Small producer groups—including both owners and employees—will often exert disproportionate pressure on national legislatures to fund subsidies even if these may cost the nation more than they are worth. We might refer to such arguments in favor of subsidies as "national priority" arguments, where those advocating the subsidy argue that the nation's interests require this expenditure. Included here are arguments for strengthening the industrial base ("If war were to come we wouldn't want to be dependent upon our enemies for x"), or for cultivating "infant industries" ("We will never get industry x started in the face of international competition unless we subsidize it"), or for pursuing environmental priorities ("If we want a healthier environment we should not let free-trade agreements prevent us from investing in it"), or a series of similar concerns.

Both kinds of subsidies—the national priority subsidy and the strategic trade subsidy—may violate trade agreements designed to prevent the waste involved in replicating export-subsidy industries throughout the world. From a moral perspective, the two kinds of subsidies need to be treated differently.

National priority subsidies need to be defended in principle even though in practice, among special interest groups, they often amount to an excuse rather than a principled stand. The complaints of United States lumber interests against the expenditure of Canadian tax dollars to subsidize Canadian reforestation is a case in point. From the U.S. perspective this allows Canadian timber companies to lower their costs of production. At the same time, many Canadians defend the subsidy as an effort to invest in long-term environmental development. Without getting into the specifics of this case and others,

252

the point here is that those who assert a national priority argument need to give evidence that it is not simply a fig leaf for protectionism. Thus in the Canadian forestry case one would have to ask whether the subsidy leads toward a long-term net increase in forested acreage or simply a higher rate of annual timber harvesting or lower exploitation fees for timber companies cutting from public lands.

Any moral assessment of strategic trade subsidies depends heavily on an empirical assessment of their effectiveness. The classic case here is the leadership provided by Japan's Ministry of International Trade and Industry (MITI) since World War II. The prevailing perception in North America is that MITI's subsidies and protection of key high-tech industries explains Japan's remarkable economic success over the past half century. This perception has led many in the United States and Canada to argue strongly for an analogous "industrial policy" or "strategic trade policy" that might promise similar economic success. Careful economic analyses of various episodes in this history, however, have shown a mixed record. MITI's Very Large-Scale Integrated Circuit Program was indeed remarkably successful, leading to the Japanese dominance in computer memory chips in the 1980s. Less often heard about are a number of notorious blunders, as when MITI tried to consolidate automobile production in Japan, attempting to eliminate Honda Motors, and discouraged Sony after World War II from investing in transistor technologies.[19] At stake here are critically important empirical presumptions about the effectiveness of subsidies and broader national strategic trade policies, but investigations of those lie beyond the scope of this study.

Most important, this very brief view of debates over regulating "unfair" trade has illustrated the recurring complexity of the issue. On the one hand, morally appropriate concerns about foreign firms dumping products or foreign governments unfairly subsidizing their own industries need to be dealt with both in the fundamental international rules of trade and in national laws designed to cope with violations of those international rules. On the other hand, domestic producers will predictably accuse foreign competitors of dumping and their governments of unfair subsidies even in situations where a more broadly based moral assessment might find their claims completely self-interested and the remedies they propose actually harmful to national welfare as a whole. Such assessments need to occur on a case-by-case basis.

CONCLUSION

From a moral perspective, the rules impinging on international trade are as important as the rules of purely domestic trade. In fact, of course, international economic exchange must follow nearly all the domestic rules for commerce in both nations. Because this fact is so elementary it is often overlooked in discussions about trade; advocates of increased trade are tempted to speak of "free" trade, by which they mean there would be no limitations on international trade which would not exist on domestic interaction. The problem caused by this oversight is that they then often come to think of such economic exchanges as simply not requiring a moral analysis to decide what aspects of these exchanges need to be regulated or even forbidden.

Once we recognize that a long list of restrictions on economic exchange, both domestic and international, must exist due to moral conviction, it becomes easier to see that the question is not whether trade can be "free" or not but rather what sort of framework of limitations or restrictions is needed in order to legitimate morally the assertion of self-interest on the part of individuals and firms in international trade.

As we have seen, a moral assessment of trade from the perspective of Christian faith requires that the framework within which trade occurs must attend to several fundamental moral concerns: the welfare of the world's poor, sustainability, labor standards, cultural identity, and human rights more generally. Such concerns will influence the rules of trade in diverse ways. Concerns about labor standards would give signatory nations to trade agreements the right to discriminate against foreign imports produced under conditions that violate the fundamental human rights of workers. Concerns about cultural identity would give "small" nations the right to restrict the import of mass media entertainment products from "large" nations. Concerns about sustainability will require that international rules of trade incorporate not only product-based discriminations but process-based discriminations as well in order to

254

discourage the environmentally irresponsible but cheaper production processes to which foreign competitors might otherwise resort. Concerns about the economic welfare of the world's poor endorse the generalized system of preferences already in place and call upon nations to develop more effective biases in favor of the exports from the world's developing nations, particularly the poorest in that group. Critically important here is the removal of tariffs and nontariff barriers in the industrialized world, which currently discourage imports of agricultural products and textiles from the developing world.

The move to "democratize" the rules of trade is an important one, but its significance has been overestimated by many of its advocates. Broadening the membership on the councils overseeing trade agreements beyond narrowly focused "trade specialists" is essential. Because values other than increased trade and rising productivity are critically important for every nation, those values must be represented vividly in such councils. Nonetheless, the more that the particular rules of trade are subject to adjustment by usual democratic processes, the greater will be the temptation on the part of special interests to press their local and regional representatives for changes that may not be in the best interest of their nation as a whole. An important example of this phenomenon is the effort to regulate "unfair trade." Although unfair trade occurs and needs to be dealt with, governmental responses to special-interest appeals for protection against dumping and foreign subsidies often cover a protectionist self-interest. The moral values involved and the costs and benefits to both immediately affected "frontline" groups as well as less directly affected groups such as other producers and consumers must be carefully discerned.

A moral trade policy will be, then, a complicated matter. It must begin with a list of core moral values to which nations are committed and out of which general rules for a framework of trade flow. Because the rules of trade are an international compromise, they will usually not meet the standards of the most morally responsible nations which are parties to the agreement. They can, however, increase global responsibility and, when well crafted, will substantively assist in the accomplishment of the moral values on which they are founded.

CHAPTER 10

CONCLUSION

This book has attempted to sort through the cacophony of voices expounding international trade and ask what difference Christian faith makes in assessing these disagreements. The debate is a complicated one.

LOOKING BACK

We saw in chapter 2 the arguments for and against increased international trade. The fundamental argument in favor of trade is that it is simply an extension of the welfare-enhancing exchange in domestic markets that has been responsible for much of the increase in prosperity wealthy citizens of the globe currently enjoy. Traditional economic analysis has appealed to the "static" gains from trade as identified by David Ricardo early in the nineteenth century. These are analyzed by the understanding of "comparative advantage," a counterintuitive notion that a nation can gain from trading with other nations even if all other nations are less efficient in the production of all products. The "new" international trade theory carefully examines a number of "dynamic" benefits of trade. These arise largely from the economies of scale, positive externalities, and intensified producer rivalries that trade engenders.

At the same time critics of increased trade argue that trade leads to unemployment in First World nations because of the movement of capital to Third World nations with lower wages. Such economic forces create additional political pressures on local and national governments to reduce "costly" regulations originally designed to provide protections for workers and the environment. Critics of trade argue that the authority invested in international trade agreements entails a loss of democratic control within even large nations such as the United States. More important, trade undermines community because the economic forces unleashed by trade press people to leave their communities out of economic necessity and render communities unable to control their own common life.

There are both normative and empirical elements in the differences between these two sides. Chapters 3 through 9 have been an investigation of these two elements.

Any normative Christian assessment of these issues must be rooted in the biblical sources, examined briefly in chapter 3. Implications for ownership and stewardship arise out of the creation of the material world by a loving God. Our understanding of human personhood is rooted in the Christian conviction that humans are created in "the image of God" and live in covenant with one another and the Lord. The reality of sin, grace, and redemption entails an understanding of all human life living under the judgment of God. Chapter 2 also included a brief review of the role of international trade in the Bible itself. Although such accounts provide no simple advice for us today, they do indicate that the advantages and problems which international trade ordinarily causes are by no means recent developments in Judeo-Christian history.

In order to make such biblical insights more concrete, chapter 4 briefly outlined a number of ethical concerns that Christians bring to any understanding of economic life today. These included the priority of God's reign over both individual decisions and institutional forms; the love of neighbor and its implications in a preferential option for the poor; a commitment to environmental sustainability; a concern for both fellow citizens and foreigners; and a nuanced understanding of the interrelation of science and ethics. Christians face a complicated task in attempting to affect public policy in these matters. On the one hand, Christian ethics holds love of neighbor to be central and provides a fundamental critique of self-interest in our lives. On the other hand, public economic and political institutions must be designed not only to recognize self-interested activity but to structure human interaction to prevent the worst abuses of self-interested activity while allowing citizens to press their interests. This perspective stands as a critique of both those who would advocate only altruistic activity in economic life and of those who would endorse the interaction of self-interest with little concern for restrictions to prevent the injustices it will otherwise inevitably cause.

This analysis of international trade is at best partial and incomplete. As is clear in the arguments of many participants to the debate, there are a number of "background commitments" often held with great vigor, which heavily affect debates about trade. These include notions about markets and multinational firms, national identity and interests, equity, employment, economic growth and the welfare of the poor, the promise and risk of technology, a spiritual assessment of economic consumption, and models of change in history. None of these issues is addressed in adequate detail in this volume, and yet these issues, more fundamental than trade, quite rightly have their effects on the debate over trade. Thus people who differ on one or more of these background issues need to spend time investigating those disparities before there can be any hope of ultimately resolving differences concerning trade.

Nonetheless, many disagreements over trade are of a more limited sort and involve disputes about concrete issues where a more focused attention can indeed provide help. Because much energy in the debate over trade focuses on the effects of trade on three policy areas—agriculture, environment, and employment—chapters 6, 7, and 8 addressed each of these in some detail.

Long-term economic developments in agriculture were examined closely in chapter 6. Rising agricultural productivity (due to technological change) and the shrinking of agricultural production as a slice of the national economic pie (due to the character of consumers' demand for food) together imply that as general economic well-being rises, the proportion of citizens who are farmers is destined to fall. Out of a concern for the fate of "family farms" and at the political insistence of agricultural interests, industrialized nations of the world have established large subsidy programs and trade restrictions to aid farmers within their borders. The chapter went on to identify the ineffectiveness of domestic agricultural subsidies intended to help struggling farm families—they go predominantly to large farms that have little need for them—and the negative effect on farmers in the Third World, who are unable to sell their products in the industrialized world because of such subsidies and trade restrictions.

A Christian commitment to sustainability and the integrity of God's creation requires a view of trade that holds environmental values central. The chapter investigated five separate issues concerning trade and the environment. The first, resource depletion, is a critical concern, though less central for many nonrenewable mineral resources (where substitutions are more likely when prices rise) than for several other critical resources such as water and forests. Biodiversity is also threatened by the growth that trade encourages, and tighter international agreements are required to ensure a respect for the integrity of creation. The second important issue is pollution. A relatively small amount arises in the transport of products in international trade, but the most serious problems arise from the ordinary industrial processes of the modern world, with or without trade. As a result, steps taken to reduce such pollution (for example, a carbon tax to address global warming) are far more effective than attempts to curtail trade.

The third sustainability issue entails arguments that weak environmental laws in the Third World lead to capital flows that hurt the environment. Here an accurate theoretical insight indicates that firms in "dirty" industries have an incentive to move to take advantage of lower pollution abatement costs in Third World nations. However, empirical analysis shows that very little such movement has occurred, apparently indicating that the differentials in pollution abatement costs are small relative to other concerns firms have in the decision to relocate. At the same time, of course, strong and well-enforced pollution laws are needed in every nation because firms located there will tend to ignore the social costs of the pollution they cause. The last two issues concern the loss of national sovereignty and the use of unilateral trade restrictions to force better environmental policies in other nations. In both cases, a morally preferable and politically more effective approach is to increase the environmental accountability of international trade agreements themselves.

The most divisive issue concerning trade focuses on its employment effects. Chapter 8 reviewed both theory and data concerning the tendency of jobs to move to Third World nations because of lower labor costs there. Lower-skilled jobs do tend to "move" toward developing nations, while higher-skilled jobs are created in the industrialized world. This effect is real and needs to be offset by national policies aimed at reducing the costs of dislocation of workers. However, the data indicate that this tendency has not been a strong one. Instead, the loss of "good" manufacturing jobs seems far more attributable to a long-term shift of consumer expenditures within industrialized nations toward the service sector as incomes rise. The problem is twofold. Many service industry jobs have lower pay than goods-producing jobs, but even more important they tend to have lower rates of productivity growth and thus lesser prospects for economic improvement. Overdrawn accusations against trade and endorsements of excessive trade distract public attention from these morally critical situations for workers in the industrialized world.

Chapter 9 reviewed several issues concerning the rules of trade, beginning with an examination of moral values that need to be applied in developing international trade agreements. The call for the democratization of trade rules is a helpful one but needs to be balanced by the insights of public choice theory that recognize many limitations in this process. The chapter concluded with a brief review of the complexities of regulating "unfair trade," such as dumping and export subsidies.

At each point along this journey through the issues related to trade, moral assessments need to be made. A number of these have been articulated from my own point of view throughout the text, but ultimately each reader needs to come to conclusions based on an assessment of the situation and his or her own position on the several background commitments identified earlier.

MORALITY AND SCIENCE

Perhaps the most difficult single conceptual issue complicating the continuing debate about trade is the relation of morality and science. All participants, of course, recognize that good policy must be based on both good human values and an accurate understanding of causality in the world. Nonetheless, looking back on debates concerning increased trade one is struck with excesses on the right and the left concerning the interplay of science and morality.

Taking Causality Seriously

Although all participants to the debate over trade value science, people with very strong background commitments concerning moral values often are less attentive to causal connections than they should be. Those on the right, who tend to endorse increases in international trade, tend to value empirical analysis but at times are overdependent on the theoretical presumptions of mainstream economics. This, of course, was a critique articulated by Daly and Cobb. When most careful, mainstream economists identify in some detail the limitations implicit in their theoretical assumptions; thus international economics textbooks do indeed analyze the issues of capital mobility and the effects of trade on different groups of workers. However, in less careful public discourse, economists and other advocates of increased trade always endorse the gains "for the nation" and often do not advert to the tradeoffs between winners and losers that give rise to resistance to trade in the first place.

Those on the left, who tend to oppose greater international trade, are also quite interested in causality, but are more frequently susceptible to making easy, unfalsifiable causal attributions. These would be assertions that one event causes a second, which are practically impossible to prove or disprove.[1] One version of this is the "after-the-fact explanation." For a common example unrelated to trade, recall the "expert" stockbroker interviewed for the evening stock market report. If the market has fallen, the expert will identify some event that occurred that day as the "explanation." Because this event *tends* to bring about lower prices for stocks, people are inclined to accept this explanation, even though a host of other events—some pushing prices up, some pushing them down—also occurred that day. In a similar way, critics of trade exhibit an unfortunate tendency to cite trade agreements as "the explanation" for a variety of economic problems. The mistake is that, while those problems may be exacerbated by trade, they may actually be caused by other economic forces altogether.

A second version of the misuse of causality attributes particular effects to "the system" as a whole. Thus in debates on trade, many on the left explain most economic problems—rising income inequality, environmental problems, the loss of manufacturing jobs—as caused by "the world capitalist system." For those already disposed toward a strong critique of capitalist markets, such assertions are reassuring. However, attributing causes to "the system" does not explain why the system didn't make these things happen in an earlier era and thus doesn't explain why they appeared more recently. Nor does it explain how things might be different ten or twenty years from now. We should note, of course, that those on the right at times make this same mistake: Many have argued that it was "the system" of socialism that led to the collapse of the Soviet Union. As heartening as this may be to critics of an active governmental presence in economic life, there were far too many forces at work in the U.S.S.R. to justify the claim about socialism in all its forms.

A third version of the easy, unfalsifiable attribution of causality occurs when one's position is "proved" true, regardless of the outcome of events. Thus some critics of the Canada-U.S. Free Trade Agreement argued that Canada would be harmed because capital (and jobs) would flow out of Canada to the rest of the world, in particular the United States. Of course, capital actually flowed in both directions, but when Canada experienced a net inflow of capital, some of these same critics of trade then criticized the Free Trade Agreement for harming Canada because some Canadian businesses were being bought by outsiders. Mysteriously, that a net increase in capital investment would create jobs in Canada seemed to have been overlooked.

Of course, there is always some truth behind these misuses of causality. Later events can only be explained by earlier events, and "the system" taken as a whole can indeed be said to cause events within the system. The problem arises when participants to the debate too quickly assume causal connections rather than attend to the careful empirical and theoretical work that would need to occur to establish a credible case for them. Participants to the debates about trade would be well served by greater care and theoretical humility on both sides.

Taking Morality Seriously

Everyone involved in the debate over trade acknowledges that human values are an essential part of the public policy process. There are, however, discernible differences that typify the two sides.

Critics of trade on the left, particularly Christians, speak frequently of the values of community and fairness in public discourse. Justice within and among nations is essential for public life. At the same time, critics of trade tend to spend far more time in prophetic denunciation of continuing evils than in an ethical analysis of the institutions necessary to correct them. Given the immense injustices done over the centuries to poor people around the world, prosperous Christians must remain open to such critique. Prophecy alone, however, does not beget solutions and is eventually met by frustration even on the part of those open to making the needed changes.

Simultaneously, many on the right exhibit a parallel tendency to misunderstand the role of morality in public policy. Many advocates of increased trade seem oblivious to the real harm done to lower-skilled workers as imports to the industrialized world increase. Similarly, many refuse to recognize the tyranny of cultural products exported from economically "large" countries to "smaller" ones. More broadly, many on the right are so convinced of the excesses of government that they fail to acknowledge a basic moral fact of institutional life: It is only the elimination of the abuses of self-interest through the rule-making power of governments—and international agreements—that can engender the provisional moral endorsement which markets can at their best enjoy. In recent decades, Christians on the right have quite rightly stressed the importance of individual moral character in economic life: on the part of both the poor and the powerful. This, however, can act as a barrier to responsible economic life if it weakens our appreciation for the hard-headed, morally founded rules necessary to prevent the abuses self-interest would otherwise cause.

Recognizing the Interpenetration of Problems

Public policy is complicated because life is complicated. Participants to policy debates need to recognize that the solution to one difficulty often brings about other problems that may not have been anticipated. A few examples will help.

Thirty years ago, those most concerned with the plight of the poor in the developing world regularly lamented the deteriorating "terms of trade" at which Third World nations exchanged primary products—largely minerals and basic foods—for the manufactured goods of the First World. Year after year, a ton of raw sugar or of mineral ore sold in world trade for fewer and fewer of the manufactured goods that developing nations imported. Many viewed these deteriorating terms of trade as a sign of the fundamental injustice of the world trading system. In truth, this fact of life for Third World producers mirrors quite closely the situation of First World farmers in relation to other First World producers that we reviewed in chapter 6: Primary products shrink as a proportion of global production as economic welfare rises. The obvious solution to this problem is to "process" those raw materials within the developing world and to export finished products to the developed world. As we saw in chapter 8, this has indeed been happening. The export of manufactured goods from the developing world to the industrialized world has risen dramatically over the past twenty-five years. This dramatic change has meant significantly higher incomes for many formerly poor citizens in the Third World. It has by no means helped all nations equally nor all persons within any one nation. Nonetheless, increasing manufactured exports from the developing world will be a critical part of increasing human welfare there.

The problem, of course, is that it is these very manufactured goods that have reduced the economic well-being of low-skilled workers in the developed world. Significant steps must be taken to assist those people. The point here, however, is that advocates of greater justice for low-skilled workers in the developed world need to recognize that the decline in their well-being is one result of a solution to an even larger problem, the plight of the poor in the rest of the world.

A similar example of the complex interpenetration of problems can be seen in the shifting focus of consumer expenditures from goods toward services in the modern world. Many have for decades lamented the "consumerism" of the First World, where buying more and more goods seemed to be an end in itself. A shift toward services is more benign to the environment and will create more jobs. However, as we have also seen in chapter 8, those jobs tend to have lower wages and, even more important, lower wage-growth over time. Forces that alleviate one problem often exacerbate another.

One final example of this interaction of possibilities and problems involves the growth in the size of organizations in the modern world. A sizable portion of modern prosperity is attributable to the "economies of scale" available when larger organizations can produce goods at lower costs because of lower administrative expenses per unit of output. At the same time, the growth of firms to transcontinental dimensions requires not only strong national restrictions but increased international regulation as well, something which advocates of increased trade on the right often overlook.

LOOKING AHEAD

At the end of this investigation into debates about the morality of international trade, there is something ironic to be noted about the unfortunately high level of moral energy characterizing the dispute. Trade helps and trade hurts, but neither the benefits it produces nor the costs it imposes warrant the moral passions it seems to inspire.

In part, the focus on trade is overdrawn because of "other agendas" being played out in the debate over trade. In part, other forces are at work causing most of the problems and most of the advantages, which the current set of trade agreements is often alleged to effect. Perhaps most important, the focus on trade is overdrawn because other "solutions"—unrelated to trade—show far more promise in correcting the multiplicity of obvious problems we face. Thus, for example, in the critical matter of just and sustainable improvements in the economic welfare of the poor of the world, even vastly improved structures of trade (by whatever definition one might use) pale in importance when compared with properly structured and restricted economic institutions at the national level.

Consider a question: Why is the economic welfare of the average citizen in Canada or the United States higher today than it was a century ago? Changes in the distribution of power and available income between social classes have been part of the answer. National legislation has been enacted in taxation, social welfare policy, workers' safety, trade unions, and a host of other areas. Social assurances are absolutely critical to the increase in economic welfare. More recently, a deterioration in those assurances and a shift in the distribution of income between social classes over the last fifteen years has indeed been responsible for a portion of the losses in economic welfare experienced by middle-income and lower-income people.

However, such changes in distribution explain only a small part of the change in economic welfare of the average United States or Canadian citizen over the past century. By far the largest part of the increase experienced by average working people has not come from a transfer of assets from the wealthy. The wealthy a century ago had not nearly enough wealth, even had it all been taken and divided among the workers. To account for the rise in the standard of living, one has to point to productivity growth: The average worker today simply produces far more per hour than the average worker a century ago. This is primarily due to the increasing productivity of the tools and machines with which people work and to the growth in the skill and educational level of the average worker.

Consider a similar question: What is the best prospect for raising the economic welfare of currently impoverished citizens in the United States or Canada or, even more important, in the Third World? Here too, debates about trade or about redistributing income between social classes are helpful but are only a small portion of an ultimate answer. The key will need to be an increase in the daily productivity of ordinary people. This is a daunting task but not a complete mystery. Fundamental here are increases in the quality of education available and in the access to better tools with which to work. For those debating trade from the left, this requires a shift in focus from prophetic critique of current problems to include constructive proposals to help ordinary people become more productive. For those debating trade on the right, it requires a shift of focus from the generic national benefits of trade to include the obligation to improve the access to education and tools for ordinary people and to limit the abuses of powerful economic actors.

It remains true that carefully constructed laws and regulations are necessary to prevent abuses and injustice, which would otherwise occur in an unregulated market, whether domestic or international. In this, critics from the left are correct. It also remains true that the best hope for the poor today is helping them to improve their own productivity and, as a result, their economic welfare. In this, critics on the right are correct. None of this is easy, but toning down the rhetoric over trade and attending more carefully to the empirical realities of trade will make attention to these critically important issues more likely and can increase our realistic hope for a more just and sustainable world economy.

CHAPTER 1: TRADE TALK: A CACOPHONY OF VOICES

1. The chart gives data for exports only. Since all exports are imported by some *other* nation on the planet, exports and imports are in principle identical. Due to statistical discrepancies in gathering information, the data show that world exports exceed imports by about 4 percent each year. This is caused, presumably, by the difference in incentives to report: Businesses importing goods from abroad face charges (tariffs) and quotas far more often than firms exporting goods to other countries.

2. For greater detail on international trade in services within the industrialized world, see OECD, *Services: Statistics on International Transactions, 1970–1992* (Paris: OECD, 1995).

3. World GDP in 1992 was almost $28 trillion, while the value of merchandise exports that year was about $3.8 trillion (in 1990 US$). See Angus Maddison, *Monitoring the World Economy: 1820–1992* (Paris: OECD, 1995), p. 19.

4. Paul Hawken, *The Ecology of Commerce: A Declaration of Sustainability* (New York: HarperCollins Publishers, 1993), p. 97.

5. Llewellyn H. Rockwell, Jr., " 'Free Trade' as Interventionism," *The Free Market* (Newsletter of the Ludwig von Mises Institute) 9, no. 8 (August 1991): 2.

6. Mark Ritchie, "Free Trade versus Sustainable Agriculture," in John Cavanagh, John Gershman, Karen Baker, and Gretchen Helmke, eds., *Trading Freedom: How Free Trade Affects Our Lives, Work, and Environment* (San Francisco: Institute for Food and Development Policy, 1992), p. 76.

7. Mark Ritchie, "Free Trade versus Sustainable Agriculture: The Implications of NAFTA," *The Ecologist* 22, no. 5 (September-October 1992): 222.

8. Mark Ritchie, "GATT, Agriculture, and the Environment: The U.S. Double Zero Plan," *The Ecologist* 20, no. 6 (November-December 1990): 214.

9. See, e.g., Sanford J. Lewis, Marco Kaltofen, and Gregory Ormsby, "Border Rivers in Peril," in Cavanagh, et al., eds., *Trading Freedom*, pp. 68-70.

10. Hawken, *Ecology of Commerce*, p. 99.

11. George Crowell, "Free Trade: Canada's Morning After," *Christianity and Crisis* 29, no. 2 (February 20, 1989): 34-35.

12. Sandra Sorensen, "Developing Healthy Economies: An Interview with Sandra Sorensen," in Cavanagh, et al., eds., *Trading Freedom*, p. 102.

13. For the debate between Krugman and historian Paul Kennedy, see Paul Krugman, "The Illusion of Conflict in International Trade," *Peace Economics, Peace Science, and Public Policy* 2, no. 2 (Winter 1995): 9-18; and Paul Kennedy "Too Serious a Business: A Reply to Professor Krugman," *Peace Economics, Peace Science, and Public Policy* 2, no. 4 (Summer 1995): 16-30. For the interchange between Krugman and a number of well-known economists including Lester Thurow, see Paul Krugman, "Competitiveness: A Dangerous Obsession," *Foreign Affairs* 73, no. 2 (March-April 1994): 28ff.; and Lester C. Thurow, "Microchips, Not Potato Chips," *Foreign Affairs* 73, no. 4 (July-August 1994): 186-204.

CHAPTER 2: THE ARGUMENTS FOR AND AGAINST TRADE

1. It is, of course, true that many economic goods purchased by the developed nations of the world are primarily "defensive," and represent expenditures made to obviate problems which have themselves been generated by economic growth. For a broader discussion of the difficulties of estimating economic welfare, and in particular the shortcomings of using gross national product as a measure of welfare, see Herman E. Daly and John B. Cobb, Jr., *For the Common Good: Redirecting the Economy Toward Community, the Environment, and a Sustainable Future* (Boston: Beacon Press, 1989), chap. 3. This index has been taken over and renamed the "Genuine Progress Index" by the group Redefining Progress, 116 New Montgomery, San Francisco, CA 94105.

2. Adam Smith, *An Inquiry into the Nature and Causes of the Wealth of Nations* (London: W. Strahan and T. Cadell, 1776; repr., ed. Edwin Cannan, New York: Modern Library, 1937), pp. 398ff.

3. Ibid., p. 5.

4. Ibid., p. 17.

5. Ibid., p. 461. We might recall that in Smith's day workers could neither vote nor form unions, so he had little reason to label them protectionist.

6. Paul R. Krugman, "The Narrow and Broad Arguments for Free Trade," *American Economic Review*, Papers and Proceedings of Annual Meeting January 5-7, 1993, 83, no. 2 (May 1993): 362.

7. David Ricardo, *The Principles of Political Economy and Taxation* (1821, 3rd ed., repr., London: J. M. Dent & Sons, 1911), pp. 77-93.

8. Ricardo's example presumes that the international rate of exchange of cloth and wine will be one bolt of cloth for one barrel of wine. In fact, the exchange can be made within a range of prices. The Portuguese would never pay more than 1.1 barrels of wine for a bolt of cloth (because they can produce it at home for that price). The British would never accept less than 10/12 (that is .833 barrels of wine for a bolt of cloth) since they can "exchange" cloth for wine domestically at that price. The actual international price is indeterminate in Ricardo's system; it will fall somewhere between .83 and 1.1 barrels of wine for a bolt of cloth. It

was not until demand analysis was later added by John Stuart Mill and others that economists explained how the actual price is set in the market.

9. Ricardo, *Principles*, p. 83.
10. See, e.g., Rachel McCulloch, "The Optimality of Free Trade: Science or Religion?" *American Economic Review* 83, no. 2 (May 1993): 367-71.
11. Krugman, "Narrow and Broad Arguments," 363.
12. Paul R. Krugman, *The Age of Diminished Expectations: U.S. Economic Policies in the 1990s* (Cambridge, Mass.: MIT Press, 1992), p. 131.
13. Daly and Cobb, *For the Common Good*, pp. 35ff.
14. The authors include a lengthy appendix outlining a promising proposal for an "index of sustainable economic welfare." They incorporate earlier attempts within mainstream economics to adjust GNP for defensive expenditures and go on to adjust further for factors such as resource depletion (treated as the inverse of net capital investment) and income inequality (Daly and Cobb, *For the Common Good*, pp. 401-55).
15. Daly and Cobb, *For the Common Good*, pp. 211ff.
16. Ricardo, *Principles*, p. 83.
17. Daly and Cobb, *For the Common Good*, p. 214.
18. Ibid., p. 215.
19. Ibid., p. 218.
20. Ibid., p. 220.
21. Ibid., p. 231.
22. Herman E. Daly, ed., *Economics, Ecology, Ethics: Essays Toward a Steady-State Economy* (New York: W. H. Freeman & Co., 1980), p. 20.
23. Lawrence Summers, "Internal Memo," in *The Economist* 322, no. 7745 (February 8, 1992): 66.
24. See, e.g., John Cavanagh, John Gershman, Karen Baker, and Gretchen Helmke, eds., *Trading Freedom: How Free Trade Affects Our Lives, Work, and Environment* (San Francisco: Institute for Food and Development Policy, 1992).
25. Herman E. Daly, "Problems with Free Trade: Neoclassical and Steady-state Perspectives," in Durwood Zaelke, Paul Orbuch, and Robert F. Housman, eds., *Trade and the Environment: Law, Economics, and Policy* (Washington, D.C.: Island Press, 1993), p. 147.
26. Herman E. Daly, "From Empty-World Economics to Full-World Economics: Recognizing an Historical Turning Point in Economic Development," in Robert Goodland, Herman E. Daly, and Salah El Serafy, eds., *Population, Technology, and Lifestyle: The Transition to Sustainability* (Washington, D.C.: Island Press, 1992), pp. 23-37.
27. Clifford W. Cobb and John B. Cobb, Jr., "The Cost of Free Trade," *Christian Century* 108l, no. 30 (October 23, 1991): 968.
28. Daly, "Problems with Free Trade," pp. 148-49.
29. Daly and Cobb, *For the Common Good*, pp. 85-96.
30. Ibid., p. 215.

CHAPTER 3: BIBLICAL AND THEOLOGICAL THEMES RELEVANT TO THE DEBATE

1. *Rule of Benedict*, Ch 31, 35.
2. See, e.g., Lynn White, Jr., "The Historical Roots of Our Ecologic Crisis," *Science* 155, no. 3767 (March 10, 1967): 1203-7.

3. James A. Nash, *Loving Nature: Ecological Integrity and Christian Responsibility* (Nashville: Abingdon Press, 1991), p. 106.

4. *In acta Apostolorum* 11.3, PG 60:98.

5. Gösta W. Ahlström, *The History of Ancient Palestine,* ed. Diana Edelman (Minneapolis: Fortress Press, 1993), p. 334.

6. Ibid., pp. 432-54, 480-501.

7. Ibid., p. 518.

8. Ibid., pp. 555-56.

9. Ernest Samhaber, *Merchants Make History: How Trade Has Influenced the Course of History Throughout the West* (New York: Day, 1964), p. 132. Cited in Morris Silver, *Prophets and Markets: The Political Economy of Ancient Israel* (Boston: Kluwer-Nijhoff Publishing, 1983), p. 49.

10. Ahlström, *Ancient Palestine,* p. 516. There is even some archaeological evidence of Israelite oil being exported from Phoenicia. See Silver, *Prophets and Markets,* p. 17.

11. Douglas Edwards, "The Socio-economic and Cultural Ethos of the Lower Galilee in the First Century: Implications for the Nascent Jesus Movement," in Lee I. Levine, ed., *The Galilee in Late Antiquity* (New York: Jewish Theological Seminary of America, 1992), pp. 60-61.

12. Ibid., p. 61.

CHAPTER 4: ETHICAL RESOURCES RELEVANT TO THE DEBATE

1. For a classic treatment of alternative Christian understandings of the relation of faith and human accomplishment, see H. Richard Niebuhr, *Christ and Culture* (New York: Harper, 1975).

2. Thomas Aquinas, *On Kingship,* trans. Phelan and I. Th. Eschmann (Toronto: Pontifical Institute of Mediaeval Studies, 1949).

3. Manfred Marquardt, *John Wesley's Social Ethics: Praxis and Principles,* trans. John E. Steely and W. Stephen Gunter (Nashville: Abingdon Press, 1992), pp. 23-135.

4. See, e.g., Lee Cormie, "Vantage Points of the Historically Marginalized in North America: A Response to Gustavo Gutiérrez," *Proceedings of the Forty-seventh Annual Convention,* vol. 47 (Santa Clara, Calif.: Catholic Theological Society of America, 1992), pp. 35-38.

5. See, e.g., Larry Rasmussen, "The Integrity of Creation: What Can It Mean for Christian Ethics," *Annual of the Society of Christian Ethics* (1995), pp. 161-75.

6. For a more complete description of this presumption, see Robert Solow, "The Economics of Resources or the Resources of Economics," *American Economic Review* 64, no. 2 (May 1974): 1-14.

7. See, e.g., Gene Outka, *Agape: An Ethical Analysis* (New Haven: Yale University Press, 1972), pp. 268ff.

8. For an enlightening interdisciplinary treatment of special relationships and sociobiological analysis of a genetic predisposition to selfishness, see Stephen J. Pope, *The Evolution of Altruism and the Ordering of Love* (Washington, D.C.: Georgetown University Press, 1994).

9. Readers interested in the broadest of these issues might seek out any of a multitude of introductory textbooks in the philosophy of science or the philosophy of social science. Those interested in related methodological issues in economics might turn to Bruce J. Caldwell, ed., *The Philosophy and Methodology of Economics* (Brookfield, Vt.: E. Elgar, 1993); or Daniel M. Hausman, *The Inexact*

and Separate Science of Economics (Cambridge: Cambridge University Press, 1992).

10. Michael Walzer, *Spheres of Justice: A Defense of Pluralism and Equality* (New York: Basic Books, 1983), chap. 4.
11. *De officiis ministrorum* 1.28 *Patrologia Latina* (hereafter *PL*) 16:62.
12. *Psalmum* 147 12, *PL* 37:1922.
13. *Sermon* 50 1.2, *PL* 38:326.
14. Thomas Aquinas, *Summa theologiae,* trans. Fathers of the English Dominican Province (New York: Benziger Bros, 1948), II-II, Q66, a. 2.
15. Ibid., II-II, Q66.
16. Ernst Troeltsch, *The Social Teaching of the Christian Churches*. 2 vols. Trans. Olive Wyon. Introduction by H. Richard Niebuhr (Chicago: University of Chicago Press, 1981), vol. 2, p. 555.
17. David Little, "Economic Justice and the Grounds for a Theory of Progressive Taxation in Calvin's Thought," in *Reformed Faith and Economics,* ed. Robert L. Stivers (Lanham, Md.: University Press of America, 1989), p. 64.
18. John Wesley, *The Works of John Wesley,* 3rd ed., T. Jackson, ed., 14 vols. (London, 1872, repr. Grand Rapids: Zondervan Publishing House, 1958), 7:286, quoted in Marquardt, *John Wesley's Social Ethics,* p. 37.
19. James M. Gustafson, "An Analysis of Church and Society Social Ethical Writings," *The Ecumenical Review* 40, no. 2 (April 1987): 267-78.
20. Ibid., 269.
21. Ibid., 270.

CHAPTER 5: BACKGROUND COMMITMENTS

1. Ralph B. Potter, "The Logic of Moral Argument," in Paul Deats, Jr., ed., *Toward a Discipline of Social Ethics: Essays in Honor of Walter George Muelder* (Boston: Boston University Press, 1972), pp. 108-9.
2. Bruce W. Wilkinson, "Trade Liberalization, the Market Ideology, and Morality: Have We a Sustainable System?" in *The Political Economy of North American Free Trade,* Ricardo Grinspun and Maxwell A. Cameron, eds. (New York: St. Martin's Press, 1993), p. 28.
3. See, e.g., Steve Charnovitz, "GATT and the Environment: Examining Issues," *International Environmental Affairs* 4, no. 3 (Summer 1992): 208ff.
4. Stephen Shrybman, "Selling the Environment Short," in John Cavanagh, John Gershman, Karen Baker, and Gretchen Helmke, eds., *Trading Freedom* (San Francisco: Institute for Food and Development Policy, 1992), p. 40.
5. Donald B. Conroy, "The Church Awakens to the Global Environmental Crisis," *America* 162, no. 6 (February 17, 1990): 152.
6. Ibid.
7. Ben Bolch and Harold Lyons, *Apocalypse Not: Science, Economics, and Environmentalism* (Washington, D.C.: Cato Institute, 1993), p. 7.
8. See, e.g., Ronald Bailey, ed., *The True State of the Planet* (New York: Free Press, 1995); Joseph L. Bast, Peter J. Hill, Richard C. Rue, *Eco-Sanity: A Common Sense Guide to Environmentalism* (Lanham, Md.: Madison Books, 1994).
9. James M. Buchanan, "Economics and Its Scientific Neighbors," in *What Should Economists Do?* (Indianapolis: Liberty Press, 1979). Originally published in Sherman Roy Krupp, ed., *The Structure of Economic Science: Essays on Methodology* (Engelwood Cliffs, N.J.: Prentice-Hall Publishers, 1966), p. 212.

273

10. Milton Friedman dubbed this the "natural rate of unemployment." Less ideologically driven economists have eschewed such claims to "nature" and have instead adopted the awkward but more neutral NAIRU.

11. See, e.g., Mark Ritchie, "Free Trade versus Sustainable Agriculture: The Implications of NAFTA," *The Ecologist* 22, no. 5 (September-October 1992); John B. Cobb, Jr., "Against Free Trade," *Theology and Public Policy* 4, no. 2 (Fall 1992).

12. Herman E. Daly and John B. Cobb, Jr., *For the Common Good: Redirecting the Economy Toward Community, the Environment, and a Sustainable Future* (Boston: Beacon Press, 1989), p. 280.

13. Roger Hutchinson, "Study and Action in Politically Diverse Churches," in Cranford Pratt and Roger Hutchinson, eds., *Christian Faith and Economic Justice: Toward a Canadian Perspective* (Burlington, Ontario, Canada: Trinity Press, 1988), p. 181.

CHAPTER 6: TRADE AND AGRICULTURE

1. In the U.S., it is 2.6 percent (*Statistical Abstract of the United States: 1994* [Washington, D.C.: U.S. Bureau of the Census, 1994], p. 412), and in Canada the number is 3.6 percent (Statistics Canada, *Canada Year Book 1994* [Ottawa: Communications Division, 1993], p. 208).

2. Herman E. Daly and John B. Cobb, Jr., *For the Common Good: Redirecting the Economy Toward Community, the Environment, and a Sustainable Future* (Boston: Beacon Press, 1989), p. 275.

3. Walter R. Goldschmidt, *As You Sow: Three Studies in the Social Consequences of Agribusiness* (Montclair, N.J.: Allanheld Osmun Publishers, 1978).

4. Daly and Cobb, *For the Common Good*, p. 272.

5. Alternative Women-In-Development, *Breaking Boundaries: Women, Free Trade, and Economic Integration* (Washington, D.C.: Alternative Women-In-Development, 1993), p. 5.

6. Quoted in Frederic D. Schwarz, "O Pioneers," *Invention and Technology* 10, no. 1 (Summer 1994): 20.

7. Percy Wells Bidwell and John I. Falconer, *History of Agriculture in the Northern United States: 1620 to 1860* (New York: Peter Smith, 1941), pp. 268-69.

8. Leo Rogin, *The Introduction of Farm Machinery in Its Relations to the Productivity of Labor in the Agriculture of the United States During the Nineteenth Century* (Berkeley: University of California Press, 1931), pp. 31-35.

9. Robert Leslie Jones, *History of Agriculture in Ontario: 1613–1880* (Toronto: University of Toronto Press, 1946), pp. 198-202.

10. Bidwell and Falconer, *History of Agriculture*, p. 269.

11. See, e.g., Tony Ward, "The Origins of the Canadian Wheat Boom, 1880–1910," *Canadian Journal of Economics* 27, no. 4 (November 1994): 865-83.

12. Jones, *History of Agriculture*, pp. 89-90.

13. Ibid., pp. 212-15.

14. Statistics Canada, *Canada Year Book 1990* (Ottawa: Communications Division, 1989), Charts 9.30 and 9.31.

15. *Statistical Abstract of the United States: 1991* (Washington, D.C.: U.S. Bureau of the Census, 1991), p. 647.

16. F. H. Leacy, ed., *Historical Statistics of Canada*, second edition (Ottawa: Statistics Canada, 1993), series F33.

17. *Historical Statistics of the United States: Colonial Times to 1970*, part 1 (Washington, D.C.: U.S. Bureau of the Census, 1975), p. 490.
18. *Statistical Abstract of the United States: 1994*, p. 665.
19. For simplicity this analysis presumes that there is no change in the proportion of farm revenues—of total sales—that go to farmers as income, either as wages, profits, or capital gains on farmland. In fact, the proportion of purchased nonfarm inputs in total agricultural expenses tends to rise over time (as farmers economize on their labor), so this simplification tends to overstate the growth in average farm income in a growing national economy. The proportion of the value of farm products made up of "value-added" in farming (rather than arising from the value of purchased inputs) is only about half as large—as a percentage—in industrialized nations as in the developing world (or in the industrialized nations a century ago). Similarly, the proportion of value-added in farming arising from labor is also about half as large in advanced economies as in the developing nations. See, e.g., Rod Tyers and Kym Anderson, *Disarray in World Food Markets: A Quantitative Assessment* (Cambridge/New York: Cambridge University Press, 1992), p. 87.
20. Organisation for Economic Co-operation and Development (OECD), *Agricultural Policies, Markets, and Trade: Monitoring and Outlook 1994* (Paris: OECD Publications, 1994), pp. 279, 327.
21. The consumer subsidy equivalent of the OECD is actually a bit more complicated than just explained. The base number, which results from multiplying the difference in price between domestic and world markets times the number of bushels purchased in the nation, is further adjusted by subtracting certain subsidies to consumers which result directly from agricultural policies. Thus in the United States, for example, the periodic distribution of cheese and powdered milk to low-income citizens by the U.S. Dept. of Agriculture is considered a subsidy to consumers and thus reduces the overall subsidy granted from consumers to food producers. Of course, in this case, such subsidies to consumers come from all taxpayers and not from farmers themselves. For a more complete description of the consumer subsidy equivalent, see Organisation for Economic Co-operation and Development (OECD), *Agricultural Policies, Markets, and Trade: Monitoring and Outlook 1992* (Paris: OECD Publications, 1992), pp. 243-52.
22. Actually, the producer subsidy equivalent is a bit more complicated. It also includes any additional government financial support for agriculture more generally, and entails the subtraction of any levies or assessments on agricultural production and the additional subtraction, in the case of livestock products, of an adjustment for the cost of subsidized feed grains. For a more complete description, see OECD, *Agricultural Policies, Markets, and Trade 1992*, pp. 243-52.
23. While the United States has at least minor subsidies for each of these products, we should note that Canada does not provide subsidies for rice, pork, mutton, or wool. OECD, *Agricultural Policies, Markets, and Trade: Monitoring and Outlook 1994*, pp. 280-81, 326-27.
24. A contrasting example would be the market for new automobiles, where consumer demand is quite "elastic." Here a small change in price brings about a large change in consumer behavior, with a 10 percent change in price bringing about perhaps a 20 percent change in the quantity of automobiles consumers are willing to buy that year. In this sort of market, there is greater stability of

prices but more volatility in the quantity sold. The result here is seen in the large fluctuations in employment and corporate profits in the automobile industry from year to year.

25. This example presumes a large "consumer subsidy equivalent," as is the case for most farm support programs. It is conceivable that all subsidies could occur through direct government payments to farmers, but this is politically more difficult because higher prices tend to be less visible than higher taxes. The second reason this is not the ordinary practice is that consumers would wish to import agricultural products in years with low international prices, and governments would either have to ban or highly tax such imports or face mounting payments to domestic farmers.

26. This section depends heavily on the analysis of Tyers and Anderson, *World Food Markets*, chap. 2. See also W. L. Peterson, "International Farm Prices and the Social Cost of Cheap Food Policies," *American Journal of Agricultural Economics* 61, no. 1 (February 1979): 12-21.

27. For example, one estimate for the extent of this "taxation" of agriculture for the years between 1975 and 1983 finds farmers in Argentina facing an effective 25 percent penalty, with the average of all of Latin America a 10 percent penalty. E. Saxon, K. Anderson, and R. Tyers, "Historical Trends in Grain, Livestock Products, and Sugar Markets: The Price Data"; Annex B to "Distortions in World Food Markets: A Quantitative Assessment," in R. Tyers and K. Anderson, background paper prepared for the World Bank's *World Development Report 1986* (Washington, D.C.: January 1986), cited in Tyers and Anderson, *World Food Markets*, p. 60. For another series of estimates—somewhat higher and covering a long period—see David Turnham, *Employment and Development: A New Review of the Evidence* (Paris: OECD Publications, 1993), p. 194.

28. Andrew Schmitz and Douglas Christian, "The Economics and Politics of U.S. Sugar Policy" in Stephen V. Marks and Keith E. Maskus, eds., *The Economics and Politics of World Sugar Policies* (Ann Arbor: University of Michigan Press, 1993), p. 50.

29. Ibid., pp. 66-69.

30. Brent Borrell and Ronald C. Duncan, "A Survey of World Sugar Policies," in Marks and Maskus, eds., *Economics and Politics*, pp. 19-20.

31. *Wall Street Journal*, June 26, 1990, p. A1.

32. OECD, *Agricultural Policies, Markets, and Trade: Monitoring and Outlook 1994*, p. 167.

33. Simon A. Harris and Stefan Tangermann, "A Review of the EC Sugar Regime," in Marks and Maskus, eds., *Economics and Politics*, p. 110.

34. Part of the complication comes from defining three separate categories of sugar production: the A quota (receiving the highest price support), the B quota (receiving a lower support), and C sugar, which is sold on the international market with no price support at all. Although farmers are the intended beneficiaries, the EU price supports actually apply to processed sugar (both crystal sugar and molasses) because sugar beets cannot be stored for very long and the "backstop" for any commodity price support is the willingness of governments to purchase surpluses at above-market prices. Supporting processed sugar means the EU would warehouse a commodity which does not deteriorate, and not the beets themselves.

35. Harris and Tangermann, "Review of the EC," p. 121.

36. Joachim Zeitz and Alberto Valdés, "The Potential Benefit to LDCs of Trade Liberalization in Beef and Sugar by Industrialized Countries," *Weltwirtschaftliches Archiv* 122, no. 1 (1986): 93-111.

37. Vernon O. Roningen and Praveen M. Dixit, "Economic Implications of Agricultural Policy Reforms in Industrial Market Economies," U.S. Department of Agriculture, Economic Research Service, 1989, Staff Report no. AGES 89-36.

38. Rod Tyers and Kym Anderson, *Liberalizing OECD Policies in the Uruguay Round: Effects on Trade and Welfare* (Australian National University, 1987), Working Papers in Trade and Development no. 87/10.

39. James G. Brown, *The International Sugar Industry: Developments and Prospects* (World Bank, 1987), Staff Commodity Working Paper no. 18.

40. Tyers and Anderson, *Disarray in World Food Markets*, 1992, pp. 206-7.

41. Statistics Canada, Agriculture Division, *Agricultural Profile of Canada*, part 2, no. 93-351 (Ottawa: Industry, Science, and Technology Canada, 1992), table 24, pp. 28-29.

42. *Statistical Abstract of the United States: 1994*, p. 670.

43. Borrell and Duncan, "World Sugar Policies," p. 20. Such estimates are admittedly tricky. The extent of the subsidy depends heavily on the gap between domestic and international prices and thus will shift substantially from year to year depending on the international price in any year.

44. Attempts at "set aside" programs counteract such incentives by inducing or requiring farmers to leave a certain proportion of their land fallow to offset the production incentives the subsidy creates.

45. See, e.g., John Whalley and Randall Wigle, "Terms of Trade Effects, Agricultural Trade Liberalization and Developing Countries" in Ian Goldin and Odin Knudsen, eds., *Agricultural Trade Liberalization: Implications for Developing Countries* (Washington, D.C.: World Bank, 1990), pp. 371-86.

46. For a helpful analysis of this effect within U.S. agricultural policy, see David W. Skully, "The Governance of Agricultural Trade: Perspectives from the 1940s," in Mathew D. Shane and Harald von Witzke, eds., *The Environment, Government Policies, and International Trade: A Proceedings* (Agriculture and Trade Analysis Division, Economic Research Service, U.S. Department of Agriculture, Staff Report no. AGES 9314, September 1993), pp. 165-88.

47. *Statistical Abstract of the United States: 1994*, p. 411.

48. For a brief discussion of the relation of economic justice and the problem of isolation, see John Rawls, *A Theory of Justice* (Cambridge: Harvard University Press, 1971), pp. 269-72.

49. See, e.g., Paul Faeth, et al., *Paying the Farm Bill: U.S. Agricultural Policy and the Transition to Sustainable Agriculture* (Washington, D.C.: World Resources Institute, 1991).

50. Data for 1992, *Statistical Abstract of the United States: 1994*, p. 670.

51. Data for 1991, Statistics Canada, *Canada Year Book 1994*, p. 475.

52. This process of tariffication is meant to make price supports more visible to the average citizen. It has been, as a result, resisted by many farm groups.

CHAPTER 7: TRADE AND THE ENVIRONMENT

1. James A. Nash, *Loving Nature: Ecological Integrity and Christian Responsibility* (Nashville: Abingdon Press, 1991), pp. 173ff.

2. John B. Cobb, Jr., *Sustainability: Economics, Ecology, and Justice* (Maryknoll, N.Y.: Orbis Books, 1992), p. 15.

3. Herman E. Daly, "Problems with Free Trade: Neoclassical and Steady-State Perspectives," in *Trade and the Environment: Law, Economics, and Policy*, Durwood Zaelke, Paul Orbuch, and Robert F. Housman, eds. (Washington, D.C.: Island Press, 1993), p. 155.

4. See, e.g., Ben Bolch and Harold Lyons, *Apocalypse Not: Science, Economics, and Environmentalism* (Washington, D.C.: Cato Institute, 1993). See also Ronald Bailey, *Eco-scam: The False Prophets of Ecological Apocalypse* (New York: St. Martin's Press, 1993).

5. Food and Agriculture Organization of the United Nations, *FAO Yearbook: Trade, 1991*, FAO Statistics Series, no. 109, vol. 45 (Rome: FAO of the UN, Economic and Social Policy Department, Statistics Division, 1992), p. 39.

6. Donella H. Meadows, Dennis L. Meadows, Jürgen Randers, and William W. Behrens, *The Limits to Growth: A Report for the Club of Rome's Project on the Predicament of Mankind* (New York: Universe Books, 1972), p. 67.

7. Ibid., p. 66.

8. Price changes for the period 1975–92. World Resources Institute, *World Resources: 1994–95* (New York: Oxford University Press, 1994), p. 262.

9. See John Tierney, "Betting the Planet," *New York Times Magazine*, December 2, 1990, pp. 52-81.

10. Ronald Bailey, *Eco-Scam: The False Prophets Of Ecological Apocalypse* (New York: St. Martin's Press, 1993), p. 78.

11. Herman E. Daly, "From Empty-World Economics to Full-World Economics: Recognizing An Historical Turning Point in Economic Development," in Robert Goodland, Herman E. Daly, and Salah El Serafy, eds., *Population, Technology, and Life Style: The Transition to Sustainability* (Washington, D.C.: Island Press, 1992), pp. 23-37.

12. Ibid., p. 26.

13. World Resources Institute, *World Resources: 1994–95*, p. 5.

14. Ibid., pp. 91-92.

15. See, e.g., *Worldwatch Magazine* 8, no. 3 (May-June 1995), pp. 34-35.

16. See Christopher Flavin, "Harnessing the Sun and the Wind," in Lester R. Brown, et al., *State of the World 1995: A Worldwatch Institute Report on Progress Toward a Sustainable Society* (New York: W. W. Norton & Co., 1995), pp. 58-75. See also Christopher Flavin and Nicholas Lenssen, *Powering the Future: Blueprint for a Sustainable Electricity Industry*, Worldwatch Paper 119 (Washington, D.C.: Worldwatch Institute, 1994).

17. Data presented for the seven leading importing nations are for net imports (total imports minus total exports), and for the leading exporting nations are net exports (total exports minus total imports). Data in the table refer to "roundwood," all wood harvested for any purpose, whether for industrial use or for fuel. Although a small amount of fuelwood and charcoal is traded internationally, the bulk of traded woods comprises sawlogs, veneer logs, pulpwood, wood chips, particles, and other wood residues used industrially. Each is reported in its roundwood equivalent.

18. World Resources Institute, *World Resources: 1994–95*, p. 135.

19. For a more thorough discussion of the illegal timber trade, see Clare Barden, "Combatting the Illegal Timber Trade—Is There a Role for ITTO?" in Helge Ole Bergesen and Georg Parmann, eds., *Green Globe Yearbook of International*

Cooperation on Environment and Development: 1994 (Oxford: Oxford University Press, 1994), pp. 55-65.

20. For further details, see Bergesen and Parmann, *Green Globe Yearbook*, pp. 232-33.
21. E.g., see Alan Thein Durning's otherwise very helpful *Saving the Forests: What Will It Take?* Worldwatch Paper 117 (Washington, D.C.: Worldwatch Institute, December 1993). In the same paragraph where he reports that "half the world's wood is burned as fuel, mostly in developing countries," Durning observes that "the gathering of fuelwood . . . rarely threatens closed-canopy forests, however, and is therefore omitted from this paper." Focusing on only part of the problem is quite respectable, but Durning makes it sound as if the burning of wood for fuel plays a negligible role in the current unsustainable use of the world's forests, an unfortunate way to explain his focus.
22. World Resources Institute, *World Resources: 1994–95*, pp. 308-9.
23. Food and Agriculture Organization of the United Nations, *FAO Yearbook: Forest Products, 1992*, FAO Forestry Series no. 27, FAO Statistics Series no. 116 (Rome: Food and Agriculture Organization of the United Nations, 1994), pp. 2, 18.
24. World Resources Institute, *World Resources: 1994–95*, p. 132.
25. J. M. O. Scurlock and D. O. Hall, "The Contributions of Biomass to Global Energy Use," *Biomass* 21, no. 1 (1989): 75-81, quoted in Douglas F. Barnes, Keith Openshaw, Kirk R. Smith, and Robert van der Plas, *What Makes People Cook with Improved Biomass Stoves? A Comparative International Review of Stove Programs*, World Bank Technical Paper no. 242, Energy Series (Washington, D.C.: World Bank, 1994), p. 1.
26. For the relative efficiencies of alternative stoves and the complete energy systems powering them, see World Resources Institute, *World Resources: 1994–95*, p. 173.
27. Related efforts concern the introduction of cleaner-burning cooking fuels. For one important example—sun-dried roots in arid regions—see J. Raloff, "Digging up Cleaner-Burning Cooking Fuels," *Science News* 144, no. 20 (November 13, 1993): 309.
28. Barnes, et al., *Stove Programs*, p. 22. For a more general discussion of energy efficiency in developing nations, see World Resources Institute, *World Resources: 1994–95*, pp. 172-73.
29. For a description of the complexities, see Barnes, et al., *Stove Programs*, 1994.
30. See, e.g., John C. Ryan, *Life Support: Conserving Biological Diversity*, in Worldwatch Paper 108 (Washington, D.C.: Worldwatch Institute, April 1992), p. 46.
31. See, e.g., *Global Biodiversity Strategy: Guideline for Action to Save, Study, and Use Earth's Biotic Wealth Sustainably and Equitably*, World Resources Institute, The World Conservation Union, and United Nations Environment Programme, (Washington, D.C.: World Resources Institute, 1992), pp. 63-64.
32. For a discussion, see Bergesen and Parmann, *Green Globe Yearbook*, pp. 226-27.
33. For an outside evaluation of the Global Environmental Facility's work in biodiversity, see *Global Environment Facility: Independent Evaluation of the Pilot Phase*, United Nations Development Programme (UNDP), United Nations Environment Programme (UNEP), and The World Bank (Washington, D.C.: World Bank, 1994), pp. 49-57.
34. See, e.g., Mohan Munasinghe and Walter Sherer, eds., *Defining and Measuring Sustainability: The Biogeophysical Foundations* (Washington, D.C.: World Bank, 1995).

35. For a broader discussion of the dangers of the waste trade, particularly for developing nations, see D. Kofi Asante-Duah, F. Frank Saccomanno, and John H. Shortreed, "The Hazardous Waste Trade: Can It Be Controlled?" in *Environmental Science and Technology* 26, no. 9 (1992): 1684-93.

36. For a more detailed description, see Bergesen and Parmann, *Green Globe Yearbook*, pp. 170-71.

37. Marian Radetzki, "Economic Growth and Environment," in *International Trade and the Environment*, Patrick Low, ed., World Bank Discussion Papers, no. 159 (Washington, D.C.: World Bank, 1992), p. 127.

38. The graph is adapted from Radetzki, "Economic Growth," Figure 8-4, pp. 130-31, and is reproduced with permission of The World Bank.

39. See, e.g., Gene M. Grossman and Alan B. Krueger, *Environmental Impacts of a North American Free Trade Agreement*, Discussion Papers in Economics no. 158 (Princeton, N.J.: Woodrow Wilson School, Princeton University Press, 1992).

40. Indur M. Goklany, "Richer Is Cleaner: Long-term Trends in Global Air Quality," in Ronald Bailey, ed., *The True State of the Planet* (New York: Free Press, 1995), p. 341. One egregious example appeared as an op-ed piece in the *Wall Street Journal*. Bruce Bartlett argued incredibly that, because economic growth correlated with lower local pollution problems, the U.S. government could improve the environment by eliminating various pollution control laws, since these add to the cost of doing business, which lowers annual growth in GDP. See Bruce Bartlett, "The High Cost of Turning Green," *Wall Street Journal*, September 14, 1994.

41. Ibid., p. 345.

42. Estimating what proportion of new production technologies is attributable to pollution abatement requirements and what proportion to simple technological change is a daunting task. The estimate given here comes from the U.S. Environmental Protection Agency (*Environmental Investments: The Cost of a Clean Environment*, Office of Planning and Evaluation, EPA 230-12-90-084, Washington, D.C.: Government Printing Office, December 1990). That pollution abatement costs amount to "well over 2% of the gross domestic product of the United States" is an interpretation provided by Ronald Bailey, ed., in his *True State of the Planet* (pp. 396-97), a volume generally critical of many fundamental presumptions of environmentalists.

43. For a summary, see World Resources Institute, *World Resources: 1994–95*, pp. 198-99.

44. Gerard Peet, "International Cooperation to Prevent Oil Spills at Sea: Not Quite the Success It Should Be," in Bergesen and Parmann, eds., *Green Globe Yearbook*, p. 41.

45. For details on MARPOL, see Bergesen and Parmann, *Green Globe Yearbook*, pp. 180-81.

46. Peet, "Oil Spills," p. 41.

47. UNDP, UNEP, and The World Bank, *Global Environment Facility*, p. 69.

48. For a review of these issues, see Florentin Krause, Wilfrid Bach, and Jonathan Koomey, *Energy Policy in the Greenhouse* (New York: John Wiley & Sons, 1992), pp. 100-186; and World Resources Institute, *World Resources: 1994–95*, pp. 203-10.

49. The World Resources Institute data for 1991 does not exist for South America or the former U.S.S.R. The estimate of bunker fuel emissions of the other regions of the world (Africa, Asia, North America, Europe, and Oceania) is 257 million

metric tons, 1.47 percent of the total industrial CO_2 emissions of those regions, about 17.5 billion metric tons. See World Resources Institute, *World Resources: 1994–95*, pp. 362-63. Data on bunker fuels originates from the Carbon Dioxide Information Analysis Center (CDIAC), Oak Ridge National Laboratory, which does not produce statistics for bunker fuels for international *air* transport.

50. The data on methane and on CO_2 from land clearing and industry come from World Resources Institute, *World Resources: 1994–95*, pp. 199-210, 362-72. To simplify the chart, estimates of CFC-11 and CFC-12 (minuscule in proportion to CO_2 emissions) and a number of even less important greenhouse gases are not shown. Data on CO_2 from the burning of biomass fuels is not included in the WRI dataset, but because of its significance, the author has included estimates in the chart. In Krause, et al., *Energy Policy*, p. 119, the authors estimate that biomass fuel releases 1.6 billion tons of carbon in the form of CO_2, meaning about 5.8 billion tons of carbon dioxide itself. This has been allocated in the chart based on each region's proportionate use of total world fuelwood (FAO 1992, pp. 2-39), an imperfect procedure because nonwood biomass fuels are included with fuelwood in the global emissions estimate. The data in the chart follows the World Resources Institute custom of reporting the full mass of carbon dioxide, whereas a number of other organizations, in particular, the Carbon Dioxide Information Analysis Center (CDIAC) reports only the mass of the carbon contained in carbon dioxide. The appropriate weight of actual carbon released into the atmosphere can be obtained by dividing the weight of carbon dioxide by 3.664 (carbon making up about 27 percent of the weight of carbon dioxide). See World Resources Institute, *World Resources: 1994–95*, p. 368.

51. The World Resources Institute data for CO_2 from land clearing is not available for Europe and the former U.S.S.R. The chart includes the author's estimates for these two regions, projected from the North American data. This probably represents an overstatement for Europe and an understatement for the former U.S.S.R., but in any case, land clearing is a minor source of CO_2 in industrialized regions.

52. This chart ignores international trade in services, but these are far less energy-intensive than the production and transport of goods and are less relevant to the question of global warming.

53. See chapter 3, "Environmental Implications and Alternative Scenarios," of *World Energy Outlook: 1994 Edition* (Paris: OECD/International Energy Agency [IEA], 1994).

54. For an explanation of the study, see OECD/International Energy Agency, *World Energy Outlook: 1994 Edition*, pp. 110ff.

55. For a review of a number of more sophisticated studies, most of which include the availability of backstop technologies, see OECD, *The Costs of Cutting Carbon Emissions: Results from Global Models* (Paris: OECD, 1993). Uncertainties abound, of course. Chief here are assumptions about the eventual availability of back-stop technologies at various prices, and presumptions about the ordinary annual increase in energy efficiency in the economy. No one knows what will be the growth rate of this "autonomous energy efficiency" over the next century, but choosing a 1 percent growth rate rather than a .5 percent rate means that world carbon emissions by the end of the next century would be 20 billion tons greater annually! Obviously, when half a percentage point of difference

in one variable brings about a nearly 50 percent change in overall world CO_2 emissions, predicting the future is a tricky business.

56. See Flavin, "Harnessing the Sun," in Brown, et al., *State of the World*, pp. 59-75.
57. See Jeff Bailey, "Carter-Era Law Keeps Price of Electricity up in Spite of a Surplus," *Wall Street Journal*, May 17, 1995, pp. A1, A12.
58. U.S. per capita commercial energy consumption was 320 gigajoules in 1991, while the figure for Japan was 140, about 44 percent of the U.S. average. Total U.S. commercial energy consumption for 1991 was 80,839 petajoules, implying that U.S. consumption would drop by more than 45,000 petajoules. The combined commercial energy consumption of South America and Africa is about 17,000 petajoules, almost exactly equal to the total energy consumption in Japan. For data, see World Resources Institute, *World Resources: 1994–95*, pp. 334-35.
59. For details, see Bergesen and Parmann, *Green Globe Yearbook*, pp. 160-64.
60. The following treatment of CFC reductions relies heavily on World Resources Institute, *World Resources: 1992–93* (New York: Oxford University Press, 1992), pp. 152-53.
61. OECD/International Energy Agency, *World Energy Outlook: 1994 Edition* (Paris: OECD, 1994), p. 179.
62. Paul Hawken, *The Ecology of Commerce: A Declaration of Sustainability* (New York: HarperCollins Publishers, 1993), p. 99.
63. Rodney E. Leonard and Eric Christensen, "Lax Enforcement of Environmental Laws in Mexico," in John Cavanagh, John Gershman, Karen Baker, and Gretchen Helmke, eds., *Trading Freedom: How Free Trade Affects Our Lives, Work, and Environment* (San Francisco: Institute for Food and Development Policy, 1992), pp. 73ff.; and Ricardo Grinspun, "The Economics of Free Trade in Canada," in Ricardo Grinspun and Maxwell A. Cameron, eds., *The Political Economy of North American Free Trade* (New York: St. Martin's Press, 1993), p. 114.
64. Patrick Low, "Trade Measures and Environmental Quality: The Implications for Mexico's Exports," in Patrick Low, ed., *International Trade and the Environment*, World Bank Discussion Paper no. 159 (Washington, D.C.: World Bank, 1992), pp. 113-14.
65. Ibid.; and Hilary French, "Reconciling Trade and the Environment," in Brown, et al., *State of the World*, p. 166.
66. Patrick Low and Alexander Yates, "Do 'Dirty' Industries Migrate?" in Low, ed., *International Trade and the Environment*, pp. 89-103.
67. Nancy Birdsall and David Wheeler, "Trade Policy and Industrial Pollution in Latin America: Where Are the Pollution Havens?" in Low, ed., *International Trade and the Environment*, pp. 159-67.
68. Adam B. Jaffe, Steven R. Peterson, Paul R. Portney, and Robert N. Stavins, "Environmental Regulation and the Competitiveness of U.S. Manufacturing: What Does the Evidence Tell Us?" *Journal of Economic Literature* 33, no. 1 (March 1995): 147-48. For another study (with a remarkably similar result) not reviewed in the Jaffe article, see Ingo Walter, "Environmentally Induced Industrial Relocation to Developing Countries," in Seymour J. Rubin, and Thomas R. Graham, eds., *Environment and Trade: The Relation of International Trade and Environmental Policy* (Totowa, N.J.: Allanheld, Osmun & Co., 1982), pp. 67-101. See also Charles S. Pearson and Robert Repetto, "Reconciling Trade and Environment: The Next Steps," Appendix A: "Empirical Studies of Trade

Effects and Industry Relocation Due to National Differences and Environmental Control Costs," in Jan C. McAlpine and Patricia LeDonne, eds., *The Greening of World Trade,* A Report to EPA from the Trade and Environment Committee of the National Advisory Council for Environmental Policy and Technology, EPA 100-R93-002 (Washington, D.C.: U.S. Environmental Protection Agency, 1993), pp. 101-4; or Judith Dean, "Trade and Environment: A Survey of the Literature," in Low, ed., *International Trade and the Environment,* p. 27.

69. For a more detailed discussion, see Eric Christensen and Samantha Geffin, "GATT Sets Its Net on Environmental Regulation: The GATT Panel Ruling on Mexican Yellowfin Tuna Imports and the Need for Reform of the International Trading System," *Inter American Law Review* 23.2 (Winter 1991–92): 569-612; Steve Charnovitz, "GATT and the Environment: Examining Issues," *International Environmental Affairs* 4.3 (Summer 1992): 203-33; and Jan Adams, "Life-Cycle Management and Trade Rules," in OECD, *Life-Cycle Management and Trade* (Paris: OECD, 1994), pp. 170-85.

70. There were, of course, other issues, including two aspects of the U.S. law that put foreign tuna producers at a distinct disadvantage, amounting to the sort of "discrimination" against imports that the GATT was constructed to reduce. Though not widely published in the United States, part of the GATT panel's decision seems to have been related to two dimensions of the law. The first was that U.S. fishing boats were dealt with through a permit system while foreign boats faced only the possibility of an import embargo. The second was that the standard in the U.S. law for the degree of safety of fishing nets was that "the average incidental dolphin take rate must not exceed 1.25 times the average take rate of U.S. vessels in the same period." Even Mexican fishers who might *want* to live up to the new standard would have to first survey U.S. tuna fishers to find out their dolphin take rate. In addition, this standard would be a moving target because, presumably, the average take rate of U.S. fishing vessels would improve as time went on. While the secrecy of GATT panels leaves most of the rationale behind their decisions unspoken, such differential treatment of foreign and domestic producers has historically been grounds for GATT action. See Adams, "Life-Cycle Management," pp. 170-75.

71. Daniel Esty, *Greening the GATT: Trade, Environment, and the Future* (Washington, D.C.: Institute for International Economics, 1994), p. 51. In fact, informed opinion in public policy circles seems to be moving in this direction as well. See, e.g., Stewart Hudson, "Trade, Environment, and the Pursuit of Sustainable Development," in McAlpine and LeDonne, *Greening of World Trade,* p. 36. See also Esty, *Greening the GATT,* pp. 73-98.

72. Charnovitz, "GATT and the Environment." This is, however, a controversial proposal. See, e.g., Jagdish Bhagwati, "Trade and the Environment: The False Conflict," in *Trade and the Environment,* Zaelke, et al., eds., pp. 175ff.

73. Christensen and Geffin, "GATT Sets Its Net."

74. See, e.g., Esty, *Greening the GATT,* chap. 4, "GATTing the Greens," pp. 73ff. See also Hilary French, "Forging a New Global Partnership," in Lester R. Brown, et al., *State of the World 1995: A Worldwatch Institute Report on Progress Toward a Sustainable Society* (New York: W. W. Norton & Co., 1995), pp. 170-89.

75. See, e.g., Jagdish Bhagwati, "Aggressive Unilateralism: An Overview," in Jagdish Bhagwati and Hugh T. Patrick, eds., *Aggressive Unilateralism: America's*

301 *Trade Policy and the World Trading System* (Ann Arbor: University of Michigan Press, 1990), pp. 3-38.

76. "Free Trade's Green Hurdle," *The Economist,* June 15, 1991.
77. For further details, see John Clark and Scott Barrett, *The Danish Bottles Case* (Washington, D.C.: Management Institute for Environment and Business, 1991); and Pascale Kromarek, "Environmental Protection and the Free Movement of Goods: The Danish Bottles Case," *Journal of Environmental Law* 2, no. 1 (1990): 89-107; and Adams, "Life-Cycle Management," pp. 183-84.
78. For a brief discussion, see Esty, *Greening the GATT,* p. 274.
79. Cf. Gerald Helleiner, "Canada's Economic Relations with Developing Countries," in Cranford Pratt and Roger Hutchinson, eds., *Christian Faith and Economic Justice: Toward a Canadian Perspective* (Burlington, Ontario, Canada: Trinity Press, 1988), pp. 96-98.
80. Robert Repetto, "Note on Complementarities Between Trade and Environment Policies," in McAlpine and LeDonne, eds., *Greening of World Trade,* p. 79.
81. Daly, "Problems with Free Trade," p. 156.
82. French, "Reconciling Trade," p. 159.

CHAPTER 8: TRADE AND JOBS

1. Paul Krugman, "The Illusion of Conflict in International Trade," *Peace Economics, Peace Science, and Public Policy* 2, no. 2 (Winter 1995): 9-18.
2. Kennedy is author of *The Rise and Fall of the Great Powers: Economic Change and Military Conflict from 1500–2000* (New York: Random House, 1987); and *Preparing for the Twenty-first Century* (New York: Random House, 1993).
3. Krugman, "Illusion of Conflict," 16.
4. See, e.g., John B. Cobb, Jr., "Against Free Trade," *Theology and Public Policy* 4, no. 2 (Fall 1992): 11.
5. For simplicity, this analysis will address only goods, and not services, in international trade. Many services are rarely "traded" internationally: People don't ordinarily buy auto repair or haircuts from other nations. Some services, however, are important in trade. For an overview, see OECD, *Services: Statistics on International Transactions, 1970–1992* (Paris: OECD, 1995).
6. Wolfgang F. Stolper and Paul A. Samuelson, "Protection and Real Wages," *Review of Economic Studies* 9, no. 1 (November 1941): 58-73.
7. The Stolper-Samuelson theorem goes farther to show that even if the low-skill group in nation B shifts its consumption toward the lower-priced, labor-intensive good now imported from country A, its economic welfare (that is, its real wage) will nonetheless unambiguously fall.
8. See Herman E. Daly and John B. Cobb, Jr., *For the Common Good: Redirecting the Economy Toward Community, the Environment, and a Sustainable Future* (Boston: Beacon Press, 1989), chap. 11.
9. See, e.g., I. F. Pearce, *International Trade* (New York: W. W. Norton and Co., 1970), pp. 389-410.
10. For a relatively simple explanation of the economic analysis here, see Paul Krugman, "Does Third World Growth Hurt First World Prosperity?" *Harvard Business Review* 72, no. 4 (July-August 1994): 113-21.
11. By international agreement, "direct investment abroad" also includes stock purchases amounting to more than 10 percent of the value of a foreign firm, on the presumption that a single owner of this large a share can influence the

management of a firm on a continuing basis. OECD, *International Direct Investment Statistics Yearbook 1993* (Paris: OECD Publications, 1993), pp. 260, 295.

12. It is true that there would be some nontariff effects of NAFTA, such as the likelihood of more stable Mexican trade rules (Robert Z. Lawrence, "Comment by Robert Z. Lawrence," in Lustig, et al., *North American Free Trade* [Washington, D.C.: Brookings Institute, 1992], pp. 64-65), but the question remains why a 4 percent disadvantage has prevented firms from taking advantage of an 80 percent drop in labor costs.

13. Analysts point out that decades of free trade with Puerto Rico, another low-wage Hispanic area, has led to a small increase (approximately 30,000) in manufacturing jobs over the past twenty years there but has entailed no great damage to the United States. A number of studies of Mexican labor have indicated that forces such as absenteeism, turnover, lower standards of education, inadequate transportation systems, and a host of other problems explain the differential in productivity. See, e.g., the *Wall Street Journal*, September 15, 1993, A1.

14. See Richard Rothstein, "Free Trade Scam," in Cavanagh, et al., eds., *Trading Freedom* (San Francisco: Institute for Food and Development Policy, 1992), p. 59; Daly and Cobb, *For the Common Good*, pp. 220-23.

15. Paul R. Krugman and Robert Z. Lawrence, "Trade, Jobs, and Wages," *Scientific American* 270, no. 4 (April 1994): 44-49; also Paul Krugman, "Europe Jobless, America Penniless?" *Foreign Policy*, no. 95 (Summer 1994): 19-34.

16. OECD, *The OECD Jobs Study: Evidence and Explanations*, Part 1: Labor Market Trends and Underlying Forces of Change (Paris: OECD, 1994).

17. Similar data are presented there for Canada (1971–86), Germany (1978–86), Japan (1972–85), and several other industrialized nations, little of which, for lack of space, can be reviewed here.

18. The precise number of jobs lost through changes in trade according to the *OECD Jobs Study* is 787,000. This represents 3.4 percent of the 23,175,000 jobs gained over the period (*OECD Jobs Study*, p. 102). It also represents sixty-eight one-hundredths of 1 percent of the 115,461,000 civilian jobs held in 1985 (*Statistical Abstract of the United States*, 1994, p. 396).

19. International Trade Administration, "U.S. Foreign Trade Highlights: U.S. Trade in Goods, 1970–1993," December 26, 1994, in *U.S. Dept. of Commerce, Economics and Statistics Administration, National Trade Databank*, January 1995.

20. Data on the other OECD countries indicate that changes in trade over the period of the study generated jobs in Denmark, France, Germany, Japan, and the Netherlands, with the only countries showing job losses from trade being the United States and the United Kingdom (*OECD Jobs Study*, p. 102).

21. OECD, *International Direct Investment Statistics Yearbook 1994*, pp. 62-65, 262-65.

22. Paul Krugman, "Technology's Revenge," *Wilson Quarterly* 18, no. 4 (Autumn 1994): 58.

23. Thirty-five million workers were without jobs in 1994 out of a total workforce of 425 million; see OECD, *Employment Outlook: July 1994* (Paris: OECD, 1994), p. 6.

24. See, e.g., Bruce Herrick and Charles P. Kindleberger, *Economic Development* (New York: McGraw Hill Book Company, 1983), chap. 4.

25. See Mark K. Sherwood, "Difficulties in the Measurement of Service Output," *Monthly Labor Review* 117, no. 3 (March 1994): 4-19. For several vivid examples of such difficulties, see Alfred L. Malabre, Jr., and Lindley H. Clark, Jr.,

"Dubious Figures: Productivity Statistics for the Service Sector May Understate Gains," *Wall Street Journal*, August 12, 1992.

26. See, e.g., Jürgen Elmeskov, "High and Persistent Unemployment: Assessment of the Problem and Its Causes," Economics Department Working Paper no. 132 (Paris: OECD, 1993); see also the *OECD Jobs Study, 1995*.

CHAPTER 9: IMPROVING THE RULES OF TRADE

1. For the classic sociological analysis of this interplay of human behavior and institutional patterns, see Peter Berger and Thomas Luckmann, *The Social Construction of Reality: A Treatise in the Sociology of Knowledge* (New York: Doubleday, 1966).

2. In addition, not all bad effects brought about by trade ought to be legislated out of existence. This limitation, of course, is not unique to trade. There are limits to legislating morality in any institution, whether political, economic, or even familial, as has been recognized throughout the history of Christianity. Thus, for example, relying on Augustine before him, Thomas Aquinas argued that "human law cannot punish or forbid all evil deeds, since, while aiming at doing away with all evils, it would do away with many good things and would hinder the advance of the common good, which is necessary for human intercourse" (Aquinas, *Summa theologiae*, Q91, a.4). We have laws against lying under oath, but would we want laws against lying in any situation? This would not only swamp the courts but could cripple casual conversation. Similarly, the only way to prevent all the bad effects of trade—or of technological change—would be to forbid the activity.

3. For a brief description, see Dominick Salvatore, ed., *National Trade Policies* (New York: Greenwood Press, 1992), p. 8.

4. Allan I. Mendelowitz, "International Trade: Reauthorization of the Generalized System of Preferences Program," Testimony before the House Sub-committee on Trade, Committee on Ways and Means, GAO/T-GGD-95-104 (Washington, D.C.: United States General Accounting Office, 1995), p. 1.

5. It should be noted that in spite of the preeminence of the United States in negotiating such exceptions to the GSP, the U.S. imports far more from developing nations than do Japan or the nations of Europe. This is true both in absolute terms and as a proportion of national production. See Salvatore, ed., *National Trade Policies*, p. 8.

6. See Michael J. Finger and P. A. Messerlin, *The Effects of Industrial Countries' Policies on Developing Countries* (Washington, D.C.: World Bank, 1989); and Salvatore, ed., *National Trade Policies*.

7. For further discussion, see The World Bank, *World Development Report 1990* (Oxford: Oxford University Press, 1990), p. 124.

8. Jeffrey J. Schott, *The Uruguay Round: An Assessment* (Washington, D.C.: Institute for International Economics, 1994), pp. 158-59.

9. Ibid., pp. 138-39.

10. For further discussion on these issues, see, e.g., Daniel C. Esty, *Greening the GATT: Trade, Environment, and the Future* (Washington, D.C.: Institute for International Economics, 1994), esp. chap. 9.

11. Schott, *Uruguay Round*, pp. 34-37.

12. For several examples of U.S. retailers' labor standards and enforcement problems, see Bob Ortega, "Broken Rules: Conduct Codes Garner Goodwill for Retailers, but Violations Go On," *Wall Street Journal*, July 3, 1995, pp. A1, A4.
13. Schott, *Uruguay Round*, p. 37.
14. Louis Jacobson, Robert LaLonde, and Daniel Sullivan, *The Cost of Worker Dislocation* (Kalamazoo, Mich.: W. E. Upjohn Institute for Employment Research, 1993).
15. See, e.g., Adolfo Aguilar Zinser, "Authoritarianism and North American Free Trade: The Debate in Mexico," in *The Political Economy of North American Free Trade*, ed. Ricardo Grinspun and Maxwell A. Cameron (New York: St. Martin's Press, 1993), pp. 205-16; Saskia Sassen, "Economic Globalization: A New Geography, Composition, and Institutional Framework," in *Global Visions: Beyond the New World Order*, ed. Jeremy Brecher, John Brown Childs, and Jill Cutler (Boston: South End Press, 1993), pp. 53-60.
16. For a general introduction to public choice theory, see James M. Buchanan and Robert D. Tollison, eds., *Theory of Public Choice: Political Applications of Economics* (Ann Arbor: University of Michigan Press, 1972). See also Macur Olson, *The Logic of Collective Action: Public Goods and the Theory of Groups* (Cambridge: Harvard University Press, 1965).
17. Herman E. Daly and John B. Cobb, Jr., *For the Common Good: Redirecting the Economy Toward Community, the Environment, and a Sustainable Future* (Boston: Beacon Press, 1989), pp. 232-33.
18. Pietro S. Nivola, *Regulating Unfair Trade* (Washington, D.C.: Brookings Institution, 1993), p. 31.
19. Ibid., pp. 160, 39-41.

CHAPTER 10: CONCLUSION

1. There is, of course, a sizable literature in the philosophy of science, the philosophy of social science, and the philosophy of economics about the role of "falsifiability" in good science. There are quite respectable schools of thought within the philosophy of science that reject the simple falsifiability criterion proposed by Carl Popper and adopted somewhat simplistically by many economists. Nonetheless, the weakness referred to in our discussion here is exactly the sort of uncritical approach to science that Popper felt impelled to critique. For a good description of "falsificationism," see David Oldroyd, *The Arch of Knowledge* (New York: Methuen, 1986), chap. 8.

BIBLIOGRAPHY

Adams, Jan. "Life-Cycle Management and Trade Rules." In *Life-Cycle Management and Trade*. OECD, 1994.

Ahlström, Gösta W. *The History of Ancient Palestine*. Diana Edelman, ed. Minneapolis: Fortress Press, 1993.

Ahmad, Yusuf J., Salah El Serafy, and Ernst Lutz, eds. *Environmental Accounting for Sustainable Development*. Washington, D.C.: World Bank, 1989.

Alternative Women-In-Development. *Breaking Boundaries: Women, Free Trade, and Economic Integration*. Washington, D.C.: Alternative Women-In-Development, 1993.

Aquinas, Thomas. *On Kingship*. Phelan and I. Th. Eschmann, trans. Toronto: Pontifical Institute of Mediaeval Studies, 1949.

————. *Summa Theologiae*. Fathers of the English Dominican Province, trans. New York: Benziger Bros., 1948.

Asante-Duah, D. Kofi, F. Frank Saccomanno, and John H. Shortreed. "The Hazardous Waste Trade: Can It Be Controlled?" *Environmental Science and Technology*, vol. 26, no. 9, 1992.

Bailey, Jeff. "Carter-Era Law Keeps Price of Electricity Up in Spite of a Surplus." *Wall Street Journal*, May 17, 1995.

Bailey, Ronald. *Eco-Scam: The False Prophets of Ecological Apocalypse*. New York: St. Martin's Press, 1993.

Bailey, Ronald, ed. *The True State of the Planet*. New York: Free Press, 1995.

Barden, Clare. "Combatting the Illegal Timber Trade—Is There a Role for ITTO?" In *Green Globe Yearbook of International Cooperation on Environment and Development: 1994*. Bergesen and Parmann, eds. Oxford: Oxford University Press, 1994.

Barnes, Douglas F., Keith Openshaw, Kirk R. Smith, and Robert van der Plas. *What Makes People Cook with Improved Biomass Stoves? A Comparative International*

Review of Stove Programs. World Bank Technical Paper No. 242, Energy Series. Washington, D.C.: World Bank, 1994.

Bartlett, Bruce. "The High Cost of Turning Green." *Wall Street Journal*, September 14, 1994.

Bast, Joseph L., Peter J. Hill, and Richard C. Rue. *Eco-Sanity: A Common Sense Guide to Environmentalism*. Lanham, Md.: Madison Books, 1994.

Berger, Peter, and Thomas Luckmann. *The Social Construction of Reality: A Treatise in the Sociology of Knowledge*. New York: Doubleday, 1966.

Bergesen, Helge Ole, and Georg Parmann, eds. *Green Globe Yearbook of International Cooperation on Environment and Development: 1994*. Oxford: Oxford University Press, 1994.

Bhagwati, Jagdish. "Aggressive Unilateralism: An Overview." In *Aggressive Unilateralism: America's 301 Trade Policy and the World Trading System*. Bhagwati and Patrick, eds. Ann Arbor: University of Michigan Press, 1990.

———. *Protectionism*. Cambridge, Mass.: MIT Press, 1988.

———. "Trade and the Environment: The False Conflict." In *Trade and the Environment: Law, Economics, and Policy*. Zaelke, et al., eds., 1993.

Bhagwati, Jagdish, and Hugh T. Patrick, eds. *Aggressive Unilateralism: America's 301 Trade Policy and the World Trading System*. Ann Arbor: University of Michigan Press, 1990.

Bidwell, Percy Wells, and John I. Falconer. *History of Agriculture in the Northern United States: 1620 to 1860*. New York: Peter Smith, 1941.

Birdsall, Nancy, and Andrew Steer. "Act Now on Global Warming—But Don't Cook the Books." *Finance and Development*, vol. 30, no. 1, March 1993.

Birdsall, Nancy, and David Wheeler. "Trade Policy and Industrial Pollution in Latin America: Where Are the Pollution Havens?" In *International Trade and the Environment*. Low, ed. 1992.

Bolch, Ben, and Harold Lyons. *Apocalypse Not: Science, Economics, and Environmentalism*. Washington, D.C.: Cato Institute, 1993.

Borrell, Brent, and Ronald C. Duncan. "A Survey of World Sugar Policies." In *The Economics and Politics of World Sugar Policies*. Marks and Maskus, eds., 1993.

Brecher, Jeremy, John Brown Childs, and Jill Cutler, eds. *Global Visions: Beyond the New World Order*. Boston: South End Press, 1993.

Brown, James G. *The International Sugar Industry: Developments and Prospects*. Staff Commodity Working Paper No. 18. World Bank, 1987.

Brown, Lester R., et al. *State of the World 1993: A Worldwatch Institute Report on Progress Toward a Sustainable Society*. New York: W. W. Norton & Co., 1993.

———. *State of the World 1995: A Worldwatch Institute Report on Progress Toward a Sustainable Society*. New York: W. W. Norton & Co., 1995.

Buchanan, James M. "Economics and Its Scientific Neighbors." In *What Should Economists Do?* Indianapolis: Liberty Press, 1979. Originally published in Sherman Roy Krupp, ed. *The Structure of Economic Science: Essays on Methodology*. Engelwood Cliffs, N.J.: Prentice-Hall Publishers, 1966.

Buchanan, James M., and Robert D. Tollison, eds. *Theory of Public Choice: Political Applications of Economics*. Ann Arbor: University of Michigan Press, 1972.

Caldwell, Bruce J., ed. *The Philosophy and Methodology of Economics*. Brookfield, Vt.: E. Elgar, 1993.

Cavanagh, John, John Gershman, Karen Baker, and Gretchen Helmke, eds. *Trading Freedom: How Free Trade Affects Our Lives, Work, and Environment*. San Francisco: Institute for Food and Development Policy, 1992.

Charnovitz, Steve. "GATT and the Environment: Examining Issues." *International Environmental Affairs*, vol. 4, no. 3, Summer 1992.

Christensen, Eric, and Samantha Geffin. "GATT Sets Its Net on Environmental Regulation: The GATT Panel Ruling on Mexican Yellowfin Tuna Imports and the Need for Reform of the International Trading System." *Interamerican Law Review*, vol. 23, no. 2, Winter 1991–92.

Clark, John, and Scott Barrett. *The Danish Bottles Case*. Washington, D.C.: Management Institute for Environment and Business, 1991.

Cline, William R. *The Economics of Global Warming*. Washington, D.C.: Institute for International Economics, 1992.

Cobb, Clifford W., and John B. Cobb, Jr. "The Cost of Free Trade." *Christian Century*, vol. 1081, no. 30, October 23, 1991.

Cobb, John B., Jr. "Against Free Trade." *Theology and Public Policy*, vol. 4, no. 2, Fall 1992.

———. *Sustainability: Economics, Ecology, and Justice*. Maryknoll, N.Y.: Orbis Books, 1992.

Commodity Research Bureau. *CRB Year Book*. New York: Commodity Research Bureau. Published annually.

Conroy, Donald B. "The Church Awakens to the Global Environmental Crisis." *America*, vol. 162, no. 6, February 17, 1990.

Cormie, Lee. "Vantage Points of the Historically Marginalized in North America: A Response to Gustavo Gutiérrez." In *Proceedings of the Forty-seventh Annual Convention*, vol. 47. Santa Clara, Calif.: Catholic Theological Society of America, 1992.

Crowell, George. "Free Trade: Canada's Morning After." *Christianity and Crisis*, vol. 29, no. 2, February 20, 1989.

Daly, Herman E. "From Empty-World Economics to Full-World Economics: Recognizing an Historical Turning Point in Economic Development." In *Population, Technology, and Life Style: The Transition to Sustainability*. Goodland, et al., eds., 1992.

———. "Problems with Free Trade: Neoclassical and Steady-State Perspectives." In *Trade and the Environment: Law, Economics, and Policy*. Zaelke, et al., eds., 1993.

———. "Toward a Measure of Sustainable Social Net National Product." In *Environmental Accounting for Sustainable Development*. Ahmad, et al., eds., 1989.

Daly, Herman E., ed. *Economics, Ecology, Ethics: Essays Toward a Steady-State Economy*. New York: W. H. Freeman & Company, 1980.

Daly, Herman E., and John B. Cobb, Jr. *For the Common Good: Redirecting the Economy Toward Community, the Environment, and a Sustainable Future*. Boston: Beacon Press, 1989.

Dean, Judith. "Trade and Environment: A Survey of the Literature." In *International Trade and the Environment*. Low, ed., 1992.

Deats, Paul, Jr., ed. *Toward a Discipline of Social Ethics: Essays in Honor of Walter George Muelder*. Boston: Boston University Press, 1972.

Durning, Alan Thien. *Saving the Forests: What Will It Take?* Worldwatch Paper 117, Washington, D.C.: Worldwatch Institute, December 1993.

Edwards, Douglas. "The Socio-Economic and Cultural Ethos of the Lower Galilee in the First Century: Implications for the Nascent Jesus Movement." In *The Galilee in Late Antiquity*. Levine, ed., 1992.

Elmeskov, Jürgen. "High and Persistent Unemployment: Assessment of the Problem and Its Causes." Economics Department Working Paper no. 132. Paris: OECD Publications, 1993.

El Serafy, Salah. "The Proper Calculation of Income from Depletable Natural Resources." In *Environmental Accounting For Sustainable Development*. Ahmad, et al., eds., 1989.

Esty, Daniel C. *Greening the GATT: Trade, Environment, and the Future*. Washington, D.C.: Institute for International Economics, 1994.

Faeth, Paul, Robert Repetto, Kim Kroll, Qi Dai, and Glenn Helmers. *Paying the Farm Bill: U.S. Agricultural Policy and the Transition to Sustainable Agriculture*. Washington, D.C.: World Resources Institute, 1991.

Finger, Michael J., and P. A. Messerlin. *The Effects of Industrial Countries' Policies on Developing Countries*. Washington, D.C.: World Bank, 1989.

Flavin, Christopher. "Harnessing the Sun and the Wind." In *State of the World 1995: A Worldwatch Institute Report on Progress Toward a Sustainable Society*. Brown, et al., 1995.

Flavin, Christopher, and Nicholas Lenssen. *Powering the Future: Blueprint for a Sustainable Electricity Industry*, Worldwatch Paper 119. Washington, D.C.: Worldwatch Institute, 1994.

Food and Agriculture Organization of the United Nations (FAO). *FAO Yearbook: Trade 1991*. Rome: Food and Agriculture Organization of the United Nations, 1992.

———. *FAO Yearbook: Forest Products 1992*. Rome: Food and Agriculture Organization of the United Nations, 1994.

French, Hilary. "Forging a New Global Partnership." In *State of the World 1995: A Worldwatch Institute Report on Progress Toward a Sustainable Society*. Brown, et al., 1995.

———. "Reconciling Trade and the Environment." In *State of the World 1993: A Worldwatch Institute Report on Progress Toward a Sustainable Society*. Brown, et al., 1993.

Godbout, Todd M. "Employment Change and Sectoral Distribution in Ten Countries, 1970–90." *Monthly Labor Review*, vol. 116, no. 10, October 1993.

Goklany, Indur M. "Richer Is Cleaner: Long-term Trends in Global Air Quality." In *The True State of the Planet*. Bailey, ed., 1995.

Goldin, Ian, and Odin Knudsen, eds. *Agricultural Trade Liberalization: Implications for Developing Countries*. Washington, D.C.: World Bank, 1990.

Goldschmidt, Walter R. *As You Sow: Three Studies in the Social Consequences of Agribusiness*. Montclair, N.J.: Allanheld Osmun Publishers, 1978.

Goodland, Robert, Herman E. Daly, and Salah El Serafy, eds. *Population, Technology, and Life Style: The Transition to Sustainability*, Washington, D.C.: Island Press, 1992.

Grinspun, Ricardo. "The Economics of Free Trade in Canada." In *The Political Economy of North American Free Trade*. Grinspun and Cameron, eds., 1993.

Grinspun, Ricardo, and Maxwell A. Cameron, eds. *The Political Economy of North American Free Trade*. New York: St. Martin's Press, 1993.

Grossman, Gene M., and Alan B. Krueger. "Environmental Impacts of a North American Free Trade Agreement." Discussion Papers in Economics, no. 158. Princeton, N.J.: Woodrow Wilson School, Princeton University Press, 1992.

Gustafson, James M. "An Analysis of Church and Society Social Ethics Writings." *The Ecumenical Review*, vol. 40, no. 2, April 1987.

Harris, Simon A., and Stefan Tangerman. "A Review of the EC Sugar Regime." In *The Economics and Politics of World Sugar Policies*. Marks and Maskus, eds., 1993.

Hausman, Daniel M. *The Inexact and Separate Science of Economics*. Cambridge: Cambridge University Press, 1992.

Hawken, Paul. *The Ecology of Commerce: A Declaration of Sustainability*. New York: HarperCollins Publishers, 1993.

Helleiner, Gerald. "Canada's Economic Relations with Developing Countries." In Cranford Pratt and Roger Hutchinson, eds., *Christian Faith and Economic Justice: Toward a Canadian Perspective*. Burlington, Ontario, Canada: Trinity Press, 1988.

Herrick, Bruce, and Charles P. Kindleberger. *Economic Development*. New York: McGraw Hill Book Company, 1983.

Hudson, Stewart. "Trade, Environment, and the Pursuit of Sustainable Development." In *The Greening of World Trade*. McAlpine and LeDonne, eds., 1993.

Hutchinson, Roger. "Study and Action in Politically Diverse Churches." In Cranford Pratt and Roger Hutchinson, eds., *Christian Faith and Economic Justice: Toward a Canadian Perspective*. Burlington, Ontario, Canada: Trinity Press, 1988.

International Trade Administration. "U.S. Foreign Trade Highlights: U.S. Trade in Goods, 1970–1993." U.S. Dept. of Commerce, Economics & Statistics Administration, *National Trade Databank*, Dec. 26, 1994, CD-ROM. January 1995.

Jacobson, Louis, Robert LaLonde, and Daniel Sullivan. *The Cost of Worker Dislocation*. Kalamazoo, Mich.: W. E. Upjohn Institute for Employment Research, 1993.

Jaffe, Adam B., Steven R. Peterson, Paul R. Portney, and Robert N. Stavins. "Environmental Regulation and the Competitiveness of U.S. Manufacturing: What Does the Evidence Tell Us?" *Journal of Economic Literature*, vol. 33, no. 1, March 1995.

Jones, Robert Leslie. *History of Agriculture in Ontario: 1613–1880*. Toronto: University of Toronto Press, 1946.

Kendrick, John W. "Service Sector Productivity." *Business Economics*, vol. 222, April 1987.

Kennedy, Paul. *Preparing for the Twenty-first Century*. New York: Random House, 1993.

———. *The Rise and Fall of the Great Powers: Economic Change and Military Conflict from 1500–2000*. New York: Random House, 1987.

———. "Too Serious a Business: A Reply to Professor Krugman." *Peace Economics, Peace Science, and Public Policy*, vol. 2, no. 4, Summer 1995.

Kohler, Heinz. *Intermediate Microeconomics: Theory and Applications*. Glenview, Ill.: Scott, Foresman and Company, 1982.

Krause, Florentin, Wilfrid Bach, and Jonathan Koomey. *Energy Policy in the Greenhouse*. New York: John Wiley & Sons, 1992.

Kromarek, Pascale. "Environmental Protection and the Free Movement of Goods: The Danish Bottles Case." *Journal of Environmental Law*, vol. 2, no. 1, 1990.

Krugman, Paul R. *The Age of Diminished Expectations: U.S. Economic Policies in the 1990s.* Cambridge, Mass.: MIT Press, 1992.

———. "Competitiveness: A Dangerous Obsession." *Foreign Affairs,* vol. 73, no. 2, March-April 1994.

———. "Does Third World Growth Hurt First World Prosperity?" *Harvard Business Review,* vol. 72, no. 4, July-August 1994.

———. "Europe Jobless, America Penniless?" *Foreign Policy,* no. 95, Summer 1994.

———. "The Illusion of Conflict in International Trade." *Peace Economics, Peace Science and Public Policy,* vol. 2, no. 2, Winter 1995.

———. "The Narrow and Broad Arguments for Free Trade." *American Economic Review,* vol. 83, no. 2, May 1993.

———. "Proving My Point." *Foreign Affairs,* vol. 73, no. 4, July-August, 1994.

———. "A Reply." *Peace Economics, Peace Science, and Public Policy,* vol. 2, no. 4, Summer 1995.

———. "Technology's Revenge." *The Wilson Quarterly,* vol. 18, no. 4, Autumn 1994.

Krugman, Paul R., and Robert Z. Lawrence. "Trade, Jobs, and Wages." *Scientific American,* vol. 270, no. 4, April 1994.

Krupp, Sherman Roy, ed. *The Structure of Economic Science: Essays on Methodology.* Engelwood Cliffs, N.J.: Prentice-Hall Publishers, 1966.

Lawrence, Robert Z. "Comment by Robert Z. Lawrence." In *North American Free Trade.* Lustig, et al., eds., 1992.

Leacy, F. H., ed. *Historical Statistics of Canada, Second Edition.* Ottawa: Statistics Canada, 1993.

Leonard, Rodney E., and Eric Christensen. "Lax Enforcement of Environmental Laws in Mexico." In *Trading Freedom.* Cavanagh, et al., eds., 1992.

Levine, Lee I., ed. *The Galilee in Late Antiquity.* New York: Jewish Theological Seminary of America, 1992.

Lewis, Sanford J., Marco Kaltofen, and Gregory Ormsby. "Border Rivers in Peril." In *Trading Freedom: How Free Trade Affects Our Lives, Work, and Environment.* Cavanagh, et al., eds., 1992.

Little, David. "Economic Justice and the Grounds for a Theory of Progressive Taxation in Calvin's Thought." In *Reformed Faith And Economics.* Stivers, ed., 1989.

Low, Patrick. "Trade Measures and Environmental Quality: The Implications for Mexico's Exports." In *International Trade and the Environment.* Low, ed., 1992.

Low, Patrick, ed. *International Trade and the Environment.* World Bank Discussion Paper No. 159. Washington, D.C.: World Bank, 1992.

Low, Patrick, and Alexander Yates. "Do 'Dirty' Industries Migrate?" In *International Trade and the Environment.* Low, ed., 1992.

Lustig, Nora, Barry P. Bosworth, and Robert Z. Lawrence, eds. *North American Free Trade.* Washington, D.C.: Brookings Institute, 1992.

Lutz, Ernst, ed. *Toward Improved Accounting for the Environment.* Washington, D.C.: World Bank, 1993.

McAlpine, Jan C., and Patricia LeDonne, eds. *The Greening of World Trade.* A Report to EPA from the Trade and Environment Committee of the National Advisory Council for Environmental Policy and Technology, EPA 100-R93-002. Washington, D.C.: U.S. Environmental Protection Agency, 1993.

McCulloch, Rachel. "The Optimality of Free Trade: Science or Religion?" *American Economic Review*, vol. 83, no. 2, May 1993.

Maddison, Angus. *Monitoring the World Economy: 1820–1992*. Paris: OECD, 1995.

Malabre, Alfred L., Jr., and Lindley H. Clark, Jr. "Dubious Figures: Productivity Statistics for the Service Sector May Understate Gains." *Wall Street Journal*, August 12, 1992.

Marks, Stephen V., and Keith E. Maskus, eds. *The Economics and Politics of World Sugar Policies*. Ann Arbor: University of Michigan Press, 1993.

Marquardt, Manfred. *John Wesley's Social Ethics: Praxis and Principles*. John E. Steely and W. Stephen Gunter, trans. Nashville: Abingdon Press, 1992.

Meadows, Donella H., Dennis L. Meadows, Jürgen Randers, and William W. Behrens. *The Limits to Growth: A Report for the Club of Rome's Project on the Predicament of Mankind*. New York: Universe Books, 1972.

Mendelowitz, Allan I. "International Trade: Reauthorization of the Generalized System of Preferences Program." Testimony before the House Sub-committee on Trade, Committee on Ways and Means, GAO/T-GGD-95-104. Washington, D.C.: United States General Accounting Office, 1995.

Mitchell, B. R. *European Historical Statistics 1750–1970*. New York: Columbia University Press, 1975.

Munasinghe, Mohan, and Walter Sherer, eds. *Defining and Measuring Sustainability: The Biogeophysical Foundations*. Washington, D.C.: World Bank, 1995.

Nash, James A. *Loving Nature: Ecological Integrity and Christian Responsibility*. Nashville: Abingdon Press, 1991.

Niebuhr, H. Richard. *Christ and Culture*. New York: Harper, 1975.

Nivola, Pietro S. *Regulating Unfair Trade*. Washington, D.C.: Brookings Institution, 1993.

Oldroyd, David. *The Arch of Knowledge*. New York: Methuen, 1986.

Olson, Macur. *The Logic of Collective Action: Public Goods and the Theory of Groups*. Cambridge: Harvard University Press, 1965.

Organisation for Economic Co-operation and Development (OECD). *Agricultural Policies, Markets, and Trade: Monitoring and Outlook*. Paris: OECD Publications. Published annually.

———. *The Costs of Cutting Carbon Emissions: Results from Global Models*. Paris: OECD Publications, 1993.

———. *Employment Outlook: July 1994*. Paris: OECD Publications, 1994.

———. *International Direct Investment Statistics Yearbook*. Paris: OECD Publications. Published annually.

———. *Labor Force Statistics 1962–1982*. Paris: OECD Publications, 1984.

———. *Labor Force Statistics 1972–1992*. Paris: OECD Publications, 1994.

———. *Life-Cycle Management and Trade*. Paris: OECD Publications, 1994.

———. *Main Economic Indicators: Historical Statistics: 1969–1988*. Paris: OECD Publications, 1990.

———. *Main Economic Indicators: Historical Statistics: Prices, Labour, and Wages*. Paris: OECD Publications, 1993.

———. *The OECD Jobs Study: Evidence and Explanations*. Part 1: Labour Market Trends and Underlying Forces of Change. Paris: OECD Publications, 1994.

———. *Project and Policy Appraisal: Integrating Economics and Environment*. Paris: OECD Publications, 1994.

—. *Services: Statistics on International Transactions, 1970–1992*. Paris: OECD, 1995.

Organisation for Economic Co-operation and Development (OECD)/International Energy Agency (IEA). *Energy Balances of OECD Countries: 1991–1992*. Paris: OECD/IEA, 1994.

—. *Energy Prices and Taxes*. Paris: OECD/IEA, 1993.

—. *World Energy Outlook: 1994 Edition*. Paris: OECD/IEA, 1994.

Outka, Gene. *Agape: An Ethical Analysis*. New Haven: Yale University Press, 1972.

Pearce, David W., and Jeremy J. Warford. *World Without End: Economics, Environment, and Sustainable Development*. Oxford: Oxford University Press, 1993.

Pearce, I. F. *International Trade*. New York: W. W. Norton and Company, 1970.

Pearson, Charles S., and Robert Repetto. "Reconciling Trade and Environment: The Next Steps," Appendix A: "Empirical Studies of Trade Effects and Industry Relocation Due to National Differences and Environmental Control Costs." In *The Greening of World Trade*. McAlpine and LeDonne, eds., 1993.

Peet, Gerard. "International Cooperation to Prevent Oil Spills at Sea: Not Quite the Success It Should Be." In *Green Globe Yearbook of International Cooperation on Environment and Development*. Bergesen and Parmann, eds., 1994.

Peterson, W. L. "International Farm Prices and the Social Cost of Cheap Food Policies." *American Journal of Agricultural Economics*, vol. 61, no. 1, February 1979.

Pope, Stephen J. *The Evolution of Altruism and the Ordering of Love*. Washington, D.C.: Georgetown University Press, 1994.

Potter, Ralph B. "The Logic of Moral Argument." In *Toward a Discipline of Social Ethics: Essays in Honor of Walter George Muelder*. Deats, ed., 1972.

Pratt, Cranford, and Roger Hutchinson, eds. *Christian Faith and Economic Justice: Toward a Canadian Perspective*. Burlington, Ontario, Canada: Trinity Press, 1988.

President of the United States. *Economic Report of the President*. Washington, D.C. Published annually.

Radetzki, Marian. "Economic Growth and Environment." In *International Trade and the Environment*. Low, ed., 1992.

Raloff, J. "Digging Up Cleaner-Burning Cooking Fuels." *Science News*, vol. 144, no. 20, November 13, 1993.

Rasmussen, Larry. "The Integrity of Creation: What Can It Mean for Christian Ethics?" In Harlan Beckley, ed., *Annual of the Society of Christian Ethics*, 1995.

Rawls, John. *A Theory of Justice*. Cambridge: Harvard University Press, 1971.

Repetto, Robert. "Note on Complimentarities Between Trade and Environment Policies." In *The Greening of World Trade*. McAlpine and LeDonne, eds., 1993.

Ricardo, David. *The Principles of Political Economy and Taxation*. 3rd edition, 1821. Reprint, London: J. M. Dent & Sons, 1911.

Ritchie, Mark. "Free Trade versus Sustainable Agriculture: The Implications of NAFTA." *The Ecologist*, vol. 22, no. 5., September-October 1992.

—. "Free Trade versus Sustainable Agriculture." In *Trading Freedom: How Free Trade Affects Our Lives, Work, and Environment*. Cavanagh, et al., eds., 1992.

—. "GATT, Agriculture, and the Environment: The U.S. Double Zero Plan." *The Ecologist*, vol. 20, no. 6, November-December 1990, p. 214.

Rockwell, Llewellyn H., Jr. " 'Free Trade' as Interventionism." *The Free Market* (Newsletter of the Ludwig von Mises Institute) vol. 9, no. 8, August 1991.

Rogin, Leo. *The Introduction of Farm Machinery in Its Relations to the Productivity of Labor in the Agriculture of the United States During the Nineteenth Century.* Berkeley, Calif.: University of California Press, 1931.

Roningen, Vernon O., and Praveen M. Dixit. "Economic Implications of Agricultural Policy Reforms in Industrial Market Economies." U.S. Department of Agriculture, Economic Research Service. Staff Report No. AGES 89-36, 1989.

Rothstein, Richard. "Free Trade Scam." In *Trading Freedom: How Free Trade Affects Our Lives, Work, and Environment.* Cavanagh, et al., eds., 1992.

Rubin, Seymour J., and Thomas R. Graham, eds. *Environment and Trade: The Relation of International Trade and Environmental Policy.* Totowa, N.J.: Allanheld, Osmun & Co., 1982.

Ryan, John C. *Life Support: Conserving Biological Diversity.* Worldwatch Paper 108. Washington, D.C.: Worldwatch Institute, April 1992.

Salvatore, Dominick, ed. *National Trade Policies.* New York: Greenwood Press, 1992.

Samhaber, Ernest. *Merchants Make History: How Trade Has Influenced the Course of History Throughout the West.* New York: Day, 1964.

Sassen, Saskia. "Economic Globalization: A New Geography, Composition, and Institutional Framework." In *Global Visions: Beyond the New World Order.* Jeremy Brecher, John Brown Childs, and Jill Cutler, eds. Boston: South End Press, 1993.

Saxon, E., K. Anderson, and R. Tyers. "Historical Trends in Grain, Livestock Products, and Sugar Markets: The Price Data." Annex B to "Distortions in World Food Markets: A Quantitative Assessment." R. Tyers and K. Anderson, background paper prepared for the World Bank's *World Development Report 1986.* Washington, D.C.: January 1986.

Schmitz, Andrew, and Douglas Christian. "The Economics and Politics of U.S. Sugar Policy." In *The Economics and Politics of World Sugar Policies.* Marks and Maskus, eds., 1993.

Schott, Jeffrey. *The Uruguay Round: An Assessment.* Washington, D.C.: Institute for International Economics, 1994.

Schwarz, Frederic D. "O Pioneers." *Invention and Technology,* vol. 10, no. 1, Summer 1994.

Scurlock, J. M. O., and D. O. Hall. "The Contributions of Biomass to Global Energy Use." *Biomass,* vol. 21, no. 1, 1989.

Serageldin, Ismail, and Andrew Steer, eds. *Making Development Sustainable: From Concepts to Action.* Environmentally Sustainable Development Occasional Paper Series, no. 2. Washington, D.C.: World Bank, 1994.

Shane, Mathew D., and Harald von Witzke, eds. *The Environment, Government Policies, and International Trade: A Proceedings.* Agriculture and Trade Analysis Division, Economic Research Service, U.S. Department of Agriculture, Staff Report No. AGES 93-14, September 1993.

Sherwood, Mark K. "Difficulties in the Measurement of Service Output." *Monthly Labor Review,* vol. 117, no. 3, March 1994.

Shrybman, Stephen. "Selling the Environment Short." In *Trading Freedom.* Cavanagh, et al., eds., 1992.

Silver, Morris. *Prophets and Markets: The Political Economy of Ancient Israel.* Boston: Kluwer-Nijhoff Publishing, 1983.

Skully, David W. "The Governance of Agricultural Trade: Perspectives from the 1940s." In *The Environment, Government Policies, and International Trade: A Proceedings.* Shane and von Witzke, eds., September 1993.

297

Smith, Adam. *An Inquiry into the Nature and Causes of the Wealth of Nations*. London: W. Strahan and T. Cadell, 1776. Reprint, Edwin Cannan, ed. New York: Modern Library, 1937.

Solow, Robert. "The Economics of Resources or the Resources of Economics." *American Economic Review*, vol. 64, no. 2, May 1974.

Sorensen, Sandra. "Developing Healthy Economies: An Interview with Sandra Sorensen." In *Trading Freedom: How Free Trade Affects Our Lives, Work, and Environment*. Cavanagh, et al., eds., 1992.

Statistics Canada. *Agricultural Profile of Canada*. Part 2, num. 93-351, Ottawa: Industry, Science and Technology Canada, Agriculture Division, 1992.

———. *Canada Year Book 1990*, Ottawa: Communications Division, 1989.

———. *Canada Year Book 1994*. Ottawa: Communications Division, 1993.

Steer, Andrew, and Ernst Lutz. "Measuring Environmentally Sustainable Development." In *Making Development Sustainable: From Concepts to Action*. Serageldin and Steer, eds., 1994.

Stivers, Robert L., ed. *Reformed Faith and Economics*, Lanham, Md.: University Press of America, 1989.

Stolper, Wolfgang F., and Paul A. Samuelson. "Protection and Real Wages." *Review of Economic Studies*, vol. 9, no. 1, November 1941.

Summers, Lawrence. "Internal Memo." *The Economist*, vol. 322, no. 7745, February 8, 1992.

Thurow, Lester C. "Microchips, Not Potato Chips." *Foreign Affairs*, vol. 73, no. 4, July-August 1994.

Tierney, John. "Betting the Planet." *New York Times Magazine*, December 2, 1990.

Troeltsch, Ernst. *The Social Teaching of the Christian Churches*. 2 vols. Olive Wyon, trans. Chicago: University of Chicago Press, 1981.

Turnham, David. *Employment and Development: A New Review of the Evidence*. Paris: OECD Publications, 1993.

Tyers, Rod, and Kym Anderson. *Disarray in World Food Markets: A Quantitative Assessment*. Cambridge/New York: Cambridge University Press, 1992.

———. "Distortions in World Food Markets: A Quantitative Assessment." Background paper prepared for the World Bank's *World Development Report 1986*. Washington, D.C., January 1986.

———. *Liberalizing OECD Policies in the Uruguay Round: Effects on Trade and Welfare*. Australian National University, Working Papers in Trade and Development No. 87/10, 1987.

United Nations. *International Trade Statistics Yearbook*, vol. 1. New York: United Nations Publication. Various years.

———. *UN Statistical Yearbook*. New York: United Nations Publication. Various years.

United Nations Development Programme (UNDP), United Nations Environment Programme (UNEP), and The World Bank. *Global Environmental Facility: Independent Evaluation of the Pilot Phase*. Washington, D.C.: World Bank, 1994.

Urquhart, M. C., ed. *Historical Statistics of Canada*. Toronto: Macmillan Company of Canada Ltd., 1965.

U.S. Bureau of the Census. *Historical Statistics of the United States: Colonial Times to 1970*. Bicentennial Edition, Part 1. Washington, D.C., 1975.

———. *Statistical Abstract of the United States*. Washington, D.C. Published annually.

U.S. Department of Commerce. National Income and Product Accounts (NIPA) Database. Downloaded from INFORUM online database. Department of Economics, University of Maryland, College Park, Md., 1993.

U.S. Department of Labor. *Labor Composition and U.S. Productivity Growth: 1948–90.* Bulletin 2426. Washington, D.C., December 1993.

———. *Trends in Manufacturing: A Chartbook.* Bulletin 2219. Washington, D.C., April 1985.

U.S. Environmental Protection Agency. *Environmental Investments: The Cost of a Clean Environment.* Office of Planning and Evaluation, EPA 230-12-90-084. Washington, D.C., December 1990.

van Tongeren, Jan, et al. "Integrated Environmental and Economic Accounting: A Case Study for Mexico." In *Toward Improved Accounting for the Environment.* Lutz, ed., 1993.

Walter, Ingo. "Environmentally Induced Industrial Relocation to Developing Countries." In *Environment and Trade: The Relation of International Trade and Environmental Policy.* Rubin and Graham, eds., 1982.

Walzer, Michael. *Spheres of Justice: A Defense of Pluralism and Equality.* New York: Basic Books, 1983.

Ward, Tony. "The Origins of the Canadian Wheat Boom, 1880–1910." *Canadian Journal of Economics,* vol. 27, no. 4, November 1994.

Wesley, John. *The Works of John Wesley.* 3rd ed. T. Jackson, ed. 14 vols. London, 1872. Reprint, Grand Rapids: Zondervan Publishing House, 1958.

Whalley, John, and Randall Wigle. "Terms of Trade Effects, Agricultural Trade Liberalization and Developing Countries." In *Agricultural Trade Liberalization: Implications for Developing Countries.* Goldin and Knudsen, eds., 1990.

White, Lynn, Jr. "The Historical Roots of Our Ecologic Crisis." *Science,* vol. 155, no. 3767, March 10, 1967.

Wilkinson, Bruce W. "Trade Liberalization, the Market Ideology, and Morality: Have We a Sustainable System?" In *The Political Economy of North American Free Trade.* Grinspun and Cameron, eds., 1993.

World Bank, The. *World Development Report 1990.* Oxford: Oxford University Press, 1990.

———. *World Development Report 1994: Infrastructure for Development.* Oxford: Oxford University Press, 1994.

World Resources Institute. *World Resources: 1992–93. A Guide to the Global Environment: Toward Sustainable Development.* In collaboration with the United Nations. New York: Oxford University Press, 1992.

———. *World Resources: 1994–95. A Guide to the Global Environment: People and the Environment.* In collaboration with the United Nations. New York: Oxford University Press, 1994.

World Resources Institute, The World Conservation Union, and United Nations Environment Programme. *Global Biodiversity Strategy: Guideline for Action to Save, Study, and Use Earth's Biotic Wealth Sustainably and Equitably.* Washington, D.C.: World Resources Institute, 1992.

Zaelke, Durwood, Paul Orbuch, and Robert F. Housman, eds. *Trade and the Environment: Law, Economics, and Policy.* Washington, D.C.: Island Press, 1993.

299

Zeitz, Joachim, and Alberto Valdés. "The Potential Benefit to LDCs of Trade Liberalization in Beef and Sugar by Industrialized Countries." *Weltwirtschaftliches Archiv*, vol. 122, no. 1, 1986.

Zinser, Adolfo Aguilar. "Authoritarianism and North American Free Trade: The Debate in Mexico." In *The Political Economy of North American Free Trade*. Grinspun and Cameron, eds., 1993.